IRELAND FOR EVERYMAN
éiRe do cáċ

IRELAND
FOR EVERYMAN

éire do cách

BY

H. A. PIEHLER

WITH AN ATLAS OF 20 COLOURED MAPS
EDITED BY JOHN BARTHOLOMEW, F.R.G.S.

Allons! Whoever you are, come travel with me!
Travelling with me you find what never tires.

WALT WHITMAN

London: J. M. DENT & SONS LTD
New York: W. W. NORTON & CO. INC

TO

D. M. P.

COMPANION, COUNSELLOR, COOK

He made you all fair,
  You in purple and gold,
You in silver and green,
  Till no eye that has seen
  Without love can behold.

DORA SIGERSON

FOREWORD

IRELAND has hitherto been strangely neglected as a holiday ground, in spite of its manifold attractions. It is a small country, but not too small, offering even the tourist with only a fortnight to spare a wonderful variety of beautiful scenery. No part of the interior, with its fine rivers and extraordinary number of lakes, is more than sixty miles from the coast. And the Irish Atlantic coast, with mountains and fiords of the utmost subtlety of colouring and fascinating variations of light, is one of the finest in Europe, with nothing between it and America, 2,400 miles away.

Add to natural beauty a wealth of prehistoric and medieval antiquities; a climate that is warm and equable, free from bitter east winds and, though rainy in the winter in the west, for the most part as dry as England's; clear roads for the motorist, the cyclist, and the hiker; unsurpassed sporting facilities; a placid Victorian atmosphere and a general absence of hustle; and contact with a witty, courteous folk of ready speech and delightful brogue, possessing an ancient and fascinating culture of their own. No better holiday can be recommended for all except those who are unhappy when away from congested motor traffic, noisy aircraft, crowded beaches, bungalow colonies, super-cinemas, and the rest.

The present guide is a companion volume to the same author's *England for Everyman, Scotland for Everyman*, and *Wales for Everyman*, which have established themselves in the favour of the touring public as practical compendia of all the information required by the average traveller.

The description of the scenic beauties and principal antiquities of Ireland is here divided into eleven tours, and is adapted equally for the needs of the motorist, the traveller by motor-bus or railway, the cyclist, and the walker, and especially of those who prefer to combine several of the available means of transport. Each tour, starting where the last left off, covers from 200 to 400 miles, and can be comfortably accomplished in three or four days by the motorist, and in some cases almost as speedily by those who depend on public conveyances. Motorists who conscientiously followed out the whole series of tours would, in the course of about 3,500 miles' travelling, occupying six or more weeks, see a very large proportion of the best mountain and marine scenery of Ireland, together with its Celtic antiquities, its cathedrals, ruined abbeys and castles, and its historic sites.

It would, of course, be futile to attempt a description of all the touristic attractions of Ireland within such a brief compass without adopting a concise style of writing and abandoning any idea of comprehensiveness. Throughout the volume nothing is mentioned unless it is considered to be well worth seeing and, as a general rule, the description follows the main routes of tourist traffic, i.e. the coastal roads. The interior, however, with its less dramatic scenery, is not entirely neglected. One whole tour is devoted to central Ireland, and at suitable points diversions are made to points of special interest.

Introductory sections deal with the questions of How to Travel and Where to Stay, Sports and Games, Irish History, Irish Place Names, the Irish Language, an Irish Calendar, and a Bibliography of Books about Ireland. The full Index makes the volume equally useful as a reference book for the library shelf.

At the beginning of the book will be found Bartholomew's layered and coloured Map of Ireland, on a scale of twelve miles to an inch and in the form of a twenty-page atlas. On it the various classes of roads are clearly distinguished, and the road mileages from point to point are given. In the text of the volume the official road-numbers, the condition of the surfaces, the steepness of the gradients, etc., are mentioned.

There are no abbreviations of any kind in the book, except self-explanatory ones.

Free literature, and advice and assistance on any question of interest to the traveller to the Republic of Ireland, can be obtained from the Irish Tourist Offices in

London (150 New Bond Street, W.1), Manchester (16 Mount Street), Birmingham (11 Bennett's Hill), Glasgow (35 St. Enoch Square), Paris, Frankfurt, New York, Chicago, San Francisco, Montreal, and Toronto. Similarly, intending travellers to Northern Ireland may consult the Northern Ireland Tourist Board (6 Royal Avenue, Belfast, and 13 Lower Regent Street, London, S.W.1).

Sincere thanks are due to the Irish Tourist Board and the Northern Ireland Tourist Board for valuable assistance and advice; also to Mr. Stephen Gwynn, Canon Hannay, Mr. R. M. Lockley, Miss Kate O'Brien, Dr. E. Œ. Somerville, and Mr. L. A. G. Strong for information concerning, and permission to quote from, their writings. Practically the whole text of the volume is based on first-hand and up-to-date information obtained in the course of an almost complete tour of Ireland carried out by the author. Absolute accuracy, however, is difficult of achievement, and corrections, criticisms, and suggestions will be received by the author with gratitude, promptly acknowledged, and incorporated in the book at the earliest opportunity.

H. A. P.

1938.

THIS fourth edition of my little book, once again reprinted with corrections, incorporates the many emendations contributed by my readers and has in other respects been brought up to date in readiness for the holiday season of 1966. The assistance of Mr. J. C. Coleman, of Bord Fáilte Éireann, in the work of revision, has once again been particularly valuable.

H. A. P.

1966.

IRELAND'S WELCOME FOR YOU

'I FEEL more at home here,' said a visitor, 'than I ever did at home.' These words represent fairly well, not the reaction of every visitor—for some people do not take to Ireland so quickly—but of a very large and, we think, discerning, group. The people who like Ireland instinctively are, on the whole, the people who feel that the industrialized modern world is becoming impersonal and inhuman. If you are one of these you will readily respond in Ireland to people who have never become units or cogs, but have remained themselves.

In making yourself at home in Ireland you will be helped also by the feeling—a little deceptive perhaps but not unpleasantly so—that here is a country you can easily get to know. Ireland is a small country. You can 'see everything' within a few weeks, and if you still feel after that that you don't know all that there is to know about the country, you can always come back. But in any case you will have made friends. You will know that you have not been simply an anonymous figure in the 'tourist traffic.'

We mention first this sense of feeling at home because, if you are susceptible to this feeling, it is the greatest attraction of Ireland. But even apart from that Ireland happens to be a particularly pleasant place to spend a holiday. We shall mention briefly a few of the reasons that make it so.

The first is the natural beauty of the country: the green hills in the extraordinarily soft and subtle Atlantic light, and the ubiquitous sea.

The coast-line is so winding that no part of the interior is more than sixty miles from the sea. From most of the towns a man can run down in his car to spend an afternoon on the Atlantic coast, where the sea stretches westward for 2,400 miles to America. Robert Flaherty—who made the films *Nanook, Moana,* and *Man of Aran*—said that nowhere except at Cape Horn has the sea a greater majesty and, in storm, greater spectacle and might than on the coast of Ireland.

And this is quite near London and the crowded cities of Europe. An overnight journey by rail and sea from London, or by air from America, takes you from crowded streets and workshops to the finest ocean coast in Europe, with glorious sandy beaches, narrow green fiords running for miles between mountains, and outside, when the wind rises, a panther sea that can leap hundreds of feet upon the cliffs.

Add to this the eight hundred lakes and rivers of inner Ireland. You might, indeed, make your way through the heart of the island from Dublin to Sligo, 140 miles, without ever losing touch with them. The alternation of land and water gives Irish journeys their charm and variety for the traveller, who may discover at any moment at the corner of a road the waters of an unsuspected lake.

Here is a country which has never been over-industrialized. The sky is not dark with screens of smoke from batteries of chimneys such as befoul whole regions in lands enriched by the age of coal and iron. Here rivers do not run rancid with the waste of mills. There are no small mountains of slag like ogres on the horizon. The salmon still come up from the sea through bright waters that remain unsullied.

In Ireland the people still know how to talk, and they like meeting strangers. Their speech is seldom a series of counters, a game of question and answer, or a succession of cold courtesies. Here, if you hail a man on the road, as likely as not he will hold you far beyond the point of information you are seeking. It is not impertinence; it is simply a friendly interest in one's neighbour, a genuine refinement of communal feeling. *Sympathie* is a word of great meaning among the French. The Irish desire to talk to the stranger is full of that French quality.

It is pleasant to walk through some of the newer towns with old castles and abbeys out of remote times standing without incongruity by the factories and shops of the twentieth century. The Round Towers, many of them as graceful and almost as sound as when they were first built, still mark the sites of universities and foundations that flourished a thousand years ago.   Monuments, impressive in antiquity and in design—such, for example, as the royal burial-mounds of Newgrange and Dowth and the medieval 'Acropolis' of the Rock of Cashel—everywhere remind the visitor that he stands on historic ground.

It is natural enough, then, that Ireland is a country which strangers like to visit.   It is true that unlike some other countries Ireland has not great and long traditions of catering for foreign visitors as a highly specialized industry, as a science—indeed almost as an art.   She does not boast palatial hotels, fashionable spas and casinos, or elaborately equipped resorts.   Yet the great beauty of her country-side, the friendliness of her people, her many sports—including excellent hunting and fishing—and international events such as the Dublin Horse Show, draw hundreds of thousands of visitors to her shores each year.   Indeed it is probably true to say that nowhere in the world, in peace time, has the individual citizen been the host of such a multitude.

*(By kind permission of the Department
of External Affairs, Dublin.)*

CONTENTS

MAPS

N.B. Some of the railways shown on these maps have been closed to passenger traffic.

NOTE TO MAP SECTIONS

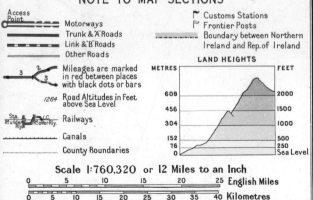

Access Point

— Motorways

— Trunk & "A" Roads

— Link & "B" Roads

— Other Roads

3 2
3   Mileages are marked in red between places with black dots or bars

1264 Road Altitudes in Feet above Sea Level

Sta. Rly.
R.under R.over Rly. Railways

— Canals

...... County Boundaries

⌐ Customs Stations

⌐ Frontier Posts

Boundary between Northern Ireland and Rep.of Ireland

LAND HEIGHTS

METRES		FEET
609		2000
456		1500
304		1000
152		500
76		250
0		Sea Level

Scale 1:760,320 or 12 Miles to an Inch

0   5   10   15   20   25 English Miles

0 5 10 15 20 25 30 35 40 Kilometres

771

© —John Bartholomew & Son. Ltd. Edinburgh

Continu

Lᵗ Hoᵒ Tory
Island

Tory Sound

Horn Hᵈ
833

Sheep Haven

Ross

Inishbofin
Dunfanagh

Carricka

Cres

Bloody Foreland
754

Falcarragh

Muckish
Mⁿ 2197

Barnes
Gap

36

Bedlam

170

Gola I.

1554

345

Derrybeg

Errigal
Mⁿ 2466

Cas.
Beagh

638

Gweedore

Nacung

Derryveagh Mⁿˢ

Lᵗ Hoᵒ Rosses
B.

The
Rosses

L Anure

Slieve
Snaght
2240

800

Gartan

300

Aran
Island Burtonport

200

378

1771

1430

1112

Crohy Hᵈ

Dunglow
1301

230

Doocharry

780

1134

805

876

1252

DONEG

Gweebarra
Bay

Flintown

Cark Mⁿ
1205

1193

Portnoo

Gweebarra
Bᵉ 1100

L. Finn

Cloghan

Nairn
or Maas

Aghla Mⁿ
1961

600

200 R.Fi

2961

Rossbeg

Gausin
1863 Mⁿ

Loughros More B.

Glenties

Owenea R.

Ballybo

Slieve
Tooey
1458

206

809

1979

1035

605

1291

900

Ardara

Croaghgorm or
Blue Stack Mⁿˢ
2219

Mou

Glen B. Glencolumbkille

1157

1724

592

Rossan Pᵗ

1652

Ouvr

Eske

Barnesmore
gap

500

Malin
More

Crownstad
1621

Inver

1323

Rathlin
O'Birne I. Lᵗ Hoᵒ Slieve
League 1972

Carrick

Donegal

1442

Killybegs

10

Kilcar

Muckros Hᵈ

Mc Swynes B.

Dunkineely

Laghy

Lough
Derg

St John's Pᵗ

Ballintra

16

Black
Gap

Fettigo

Coolmore Rossnowlagh

Cavangarden

Letter

Donegal Bay

Ballyshannon

Lower
Lou

Bundoran

Cloghore
Belleek

24

Mullaghmore

Kinlough

Sᵗᵈˢ
Caldwell

166

Inishmurray

128

Cliffony

Lough
Melvin

Garrison

Derrygannell

22

1712

Truskmore
2113

Rossinver

1233

Grange
Benbulbin
1722

Glenade

Killyclogher
1511

Drumcliff

Glencar

Dartry

Sligo Bay

Rosses
Point

16

Macnean
Upper

F

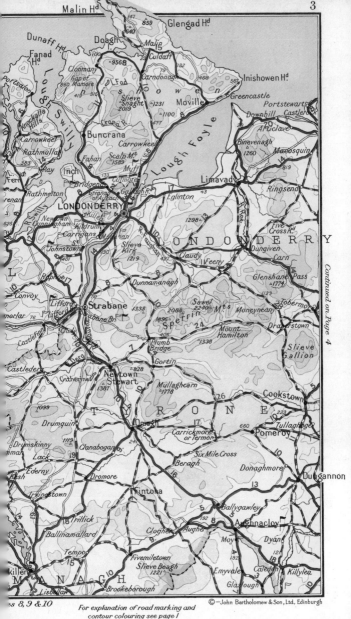

Continued on Page 4

Malin Hd
Glengad Hd
Dunaff Hd
Doagh
Fanad Hd
147 859
640
Malin
Culdaff
Clonmany
Gap of 419 Mamore 956 I. Fad
860 818
Carndonagh
132
468
56½
Inishowen Hd
Greencastle
Portstewart
Downhill Castle
Slieve 1231 Snaght 2019
Moville
1100
477
Articlave
Buncrana
Carrowkeel
Crana R.
Binevenagh
1260
Macosquin
Portsalon
Knockalla Hills
Carrowkeel
Rathmullan
333
Scalp Mt
1589
56
Fahan
Muff
Lough Foyle
819
4
Ray
Inch
133
Bridgend
Culmore
Limavady
Ringsend
Rathmelton
Galliagh R.
Eglinton
43
Londonderry
Grange of Doagh
L
Newton Cunningham
625
Carrigans
St.
Johnstown
Kildrum
Nixon
Slieve Kirk 1219
R. Faughan
1298
Five Cross Rd
LONDONDERRY
Claudy
Feeny
Dungiven
Carn
Convoy
Raphoe 17
Dunnamanagh
Glenshane Pass
1774
1123
Tobermore
Lifford
Lifford
Strabane
1333
Sawel 2240
Spelin Mts
Moneyneany
morlar 76
Castlefin
Strabane Br.
2088
1696
24
Draperstown
Slieve Gallion
Castlederg
Dooo
Plumb Bridge
Mount Hamilton 1338
828
Crithemie
Newtown Stewart
1387
Gortin
Cookstown
Mullaghcarn 1778
26
1099
Drumquin
T Y R O N E
Omagh
17
660
223
Tullaghoge
Drumskinny
1119
Carrickmore or Termon
Pomeroy
10
Clanabogan
Six Mile Cross
Lack
19
Ederny
Beragh
Donaghmore
13
Dungannon
Irvinestown
Dromore
18
Fintona
Aughnacloy
Trillick
Ballinamallard
5
Ballygawley
192
8
Moy
Dyan
Tempo
Clogher
Aughe
121
18
15
killen
Fivemiletown
Slieve Beagh 1221
Emyvale
Caledon
Killylea
M A N A G H
Lisbellaw
Brookeborough
Glaslough

© —John Bartholomew & Son, Ltd., Edinburgh

es 8, 9 & 10

For explanation of road marking and
contour colouring see page 1

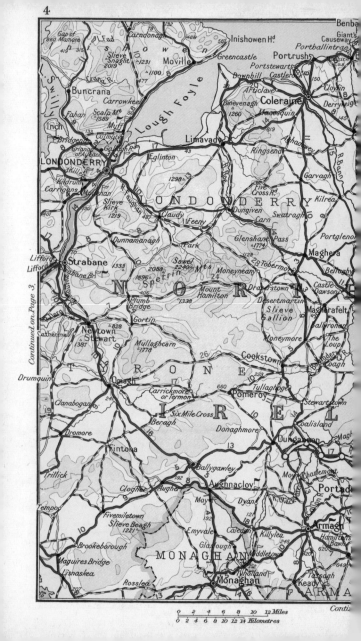

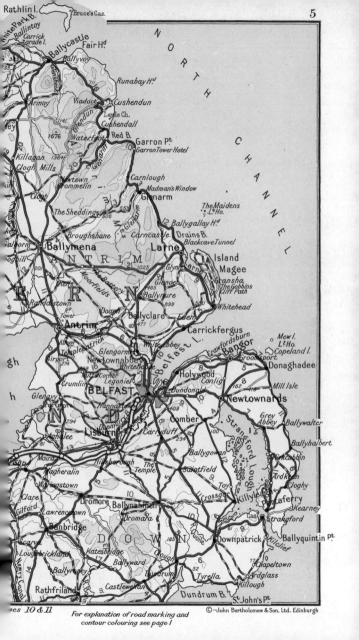

For explanation of road marking and
contour colouring see page 1

©—John Bartholomew & Son, Ltd., Edinburgh

Stags of
Broadhaven
Benwee Hᵈ
Kid I.
Erris Hᵈ
Porturlin
Belderg Harb.
Broad
Eagle I.
Lᵗ. Ho.
Haven
Belders
Ballycast
The Mullet
Corclogh
130
138
126
260
Belmullet
Pollatomish
126
232
Inishglora
27
55
Glenamoy R.
Cross
80
Carrowmore
Lough
233
Inishkea
39
Bangor
Glenmore R. 276
Dahybaun
Cro
L Ho.
Owenmore R.
233
Blacksod
Roy
Slieve Car
220
Bay
10⁺
2369
Duvillaun
Owenduff
Bunaveela
More
Fahy
Nephin
220
Beg
Ballycroy
2065
Slievemore
Bitrteen
2204
Doogort
Corrsloughaphuill L.
2295
Achill
Croaghaun
Annagh
Cushcamcarragh
Belt
Head
2192
2343
Lough
Achill
Achill
Feeagh
Island
Curraun
Mallaranny
Furnace
M
Curraun
Peninsula
Newport 12
Achillbeg
Curraun
Castle
Clew
Islandeady
14
163
Clare
06
Westpor
Bay
Croagh Patrick
Louisburgh
2510
Roonah
1245
M s Nacorra
Moher
Caher I.
334
Inishturk
M
Benbury
Doo Tawnyard
2610
Partry Mᵗⁿ
Inishbofin
Bengorm
Benwee
Inishark
Mweelrea
2305
2239
Ballynakill
2688
Harb
Killary
Harbour
Devils Mother
Renvyle
L.Fee
2131
Hotel
770
157
Aughavalmore
Omey
Kylemore
186
Leenane Maumtrasna
Castles
2395
Cruagh
Letterfrack
Maumturk Mᵗⁿ
Maam Br.
Turbot I.
The Twelve Pins 2336
nagh
Hotel
Clifden
2395
Henr
Con em ara
Mannin Bay
Derryclare
Recess
202
Glendollagh
Maam
153
Cross
82
Slyne Hᵈ
Cashel
Curreel
Bofin
Lᵗ Ho.
86
Roundstone
Letterfrack
Screeb
Bertraghboy Bay
Bola
Iar C
Carna
Croaghnakeela I.
37
Contin

0 2 4 6 8 10 12 Miles
0 2 4 6 8 10 12 14 Kilometres

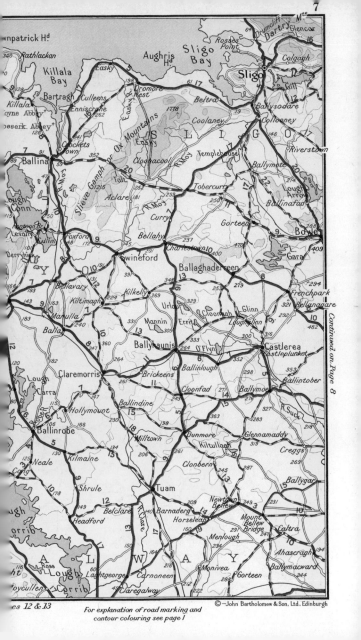

For explanation of road marking and
contour colouring see page 1

©—John Bartholomew & Son, Ltd. Edinburgh

Continued on Page 8

es 12 & 13

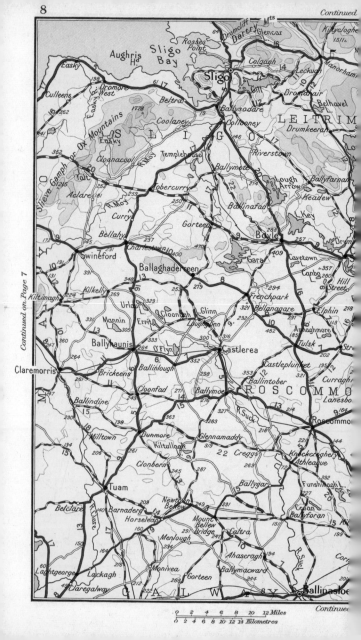

Continued on Page 10

For explanation of road marking and
contour colouring see page 1

© —John Bartholomew & Son, Ltd., Edinburgh

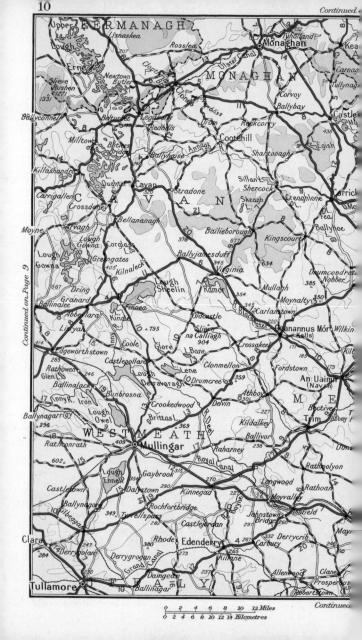

Continued

Upper FERMANAGH
Lough
Erne
Lisnaskea
Rosslea
207
Monaghan
Tyholland
Kea
MONAGHAN
Slieve
Rushen
1331
Newtown
Butler
Clones
bliss
Corvoy
Ballybay
Castle
Ballyconnell
Betturbet
Legakilly
Redhills
Union
Rockcorry
Egish
436
Milltown
Butlers
Bridge
Annagh
Cootehill
Shantonagh
Killashandra
Ballyhaise
Oughter
Cavan
320
Stradone
Sillans
Shercock
Skeagh
Creaghlone
Carrick
Mc
Carrigallen
Crossdoney
21
Ballieborough
Kingscourt
Ballyhoe
Moyne
Arvagh
Bellananagh
378
634
Drumcondra
Nobber
Lough
Gowna
Corglass
Greengates
Kilnaleck
Ballyjamesduff
345
Virginia
Mullagh
385
350
Dring
405
Lough
Sheelin
Ramor
354
Moynalty
567
Granard
Fianea
Blackwater
345
Carlanstown
220
Ballinalee
Abbeylara
Kinale
795
Oldcastle
Slieve
na Calliagh
904
Crossakeel
Cananus Mor
Kells
Wilkin
Lisryan
414
Coole
Glore
L Bane
Clonmellon
Fordstown
185
Kilt
Edgeworthstown
289
Castlepollard
Lene
Drumcree
359
An Uaimh
(Navan)
173
Rathowen
246
Glen
Ballinalack
Bunbrosna
Lough
Derravaragh
Athboy
304
ME
Bective
Abbey
Trim
Inny R. Iron
Crookedwood
Delvin
Ballynagarrigy
296
Lough
Owel
Brittas
13
Kildalkey
Ballivor
Duns
WESTMEATH
409
Mullingar
Raharney
238
Rathmolyon
Rathconrath
602
15
Royal Canal
Rathcon
Lough
Ennell
Gaybrook
313
270
Longwood
Castletown
354
Dalystown
290
Kinnegad
221
Moyvalley
Ballynagore
Rochfortbridge
282
Castlejordan
Johnstown
Bridge 260
Clonbeggan
349
Turrellspass
297
Enfield
Mayr
Clara
Rhode
Edenderry
267
Carbury
Derrycri
246
284
Derrygolan
390
273
265
20
Derrygrogan
Daingean
Killane
237
Allenwood
Clane
Tullamore
Grand Canal
Ballinagar
Robertstown
Prosperous

Continued on Page 9

Continued

0 2 4 6 8 10 12 Miles
0 2 4 6 8 10 12 14 Kilometres

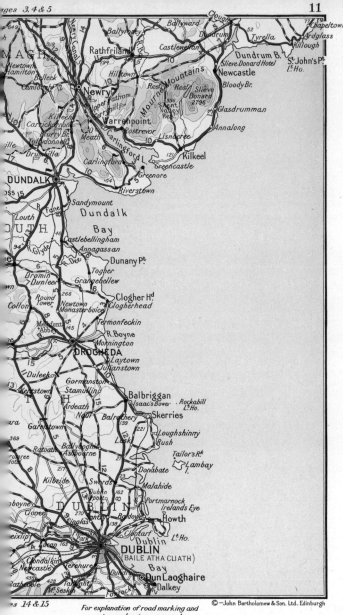

For explanation of road marking and
contour colouring see page 1

Continued

Continued

0 2 4 6 8 10 12 Miles
0 2 4 6 8 10 12 14 Kilometres

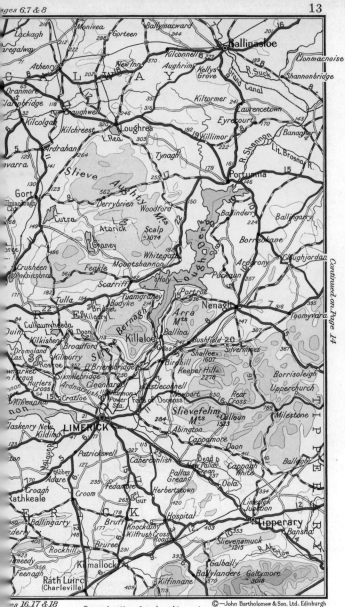

Continued on Page 14

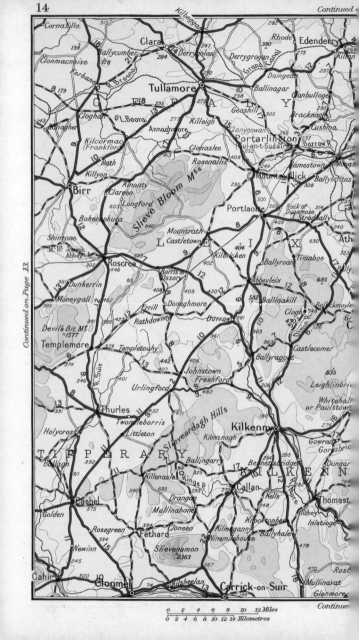

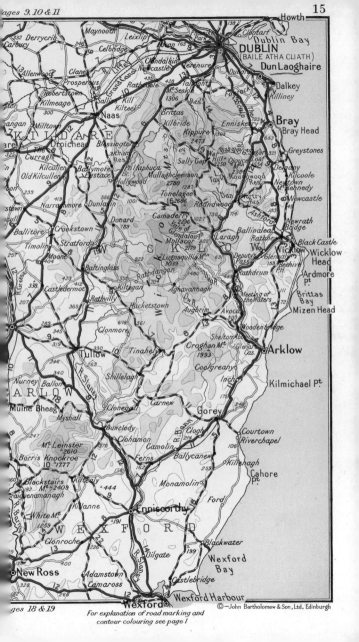

Derrycrib
Carbury
Maynooth
Leixlip
Clondalkin
Newcastle
Terenure
DUBLIN
(BAILE ATHA CLIATH)
Dun Laoghaire
Dublin Bay
Clontarf
Park

Allenwood
Clane
Celbridge
Rathcoole
Tallaght
M. Seskin
Dalkey
Killiney

Prosperous
Robertstown
Kilmeage
Sallins
Kill
Kilteel
Brittas
Kilbride
BRAY
Bray Head

KILDARE
Naas
Kippure
2473
Enniskerry
Greystones

The
Curragh
Droichead
Blessington
Sally Gap
Delgany
Kilcoole
Newtown

Kilcullen
Old Kilcullen
Ballymore
Eustace
Hollywood
Mullaghcleevaun
2788
Tonelagee
2686
Roundwood
Res.
Ashford
Newcastle
Newrath
Bridge

Narraghmore
Dunlavin
Donard
789
Camaderry
2296
Vale of
Glendalough
Laragh
Deputy's
Pass
WICKLOW
Wicklow
Head

Ballitore
Crookstown
Stratford
Baltinglass
Mullacor
Lugnaquillia Mt.
3039
Rathdrum
Beehive
P.H.
Ardmore
Pt.

Timolin
Moone
Rathdangan
Kiltegan
Aghavannagh
Aughrim
Meeting of
the Waters
Avoca
Brittas
Bay
Mizen Head

Castledermot
Rathvilly
Hacketstown
WICKLOW
Woodenbridge
Arklow

Clonmore
Tullow
Tinahely
Croghan Mt.
1993
Kilmichael Pt.

CARLOW
Shillelagh
Coolgreany
Inch

Muine Bheag
Myshall
Clonegal
Carnew
Gorey
Courtown
Riverchapel

Mt. Leinster
2610
Bunclody
Clohamon
Camolin
Killenagh
Cahore
Pt.

Borris
Knockroe
1777
Ferns
Ballycanew
Monamolin
Ford

Blackstairs
Mt. 2409
Killanne
White Mt.
1259
Enniscorthy
WEXFORD

Clonroche
Oilgate
Blackwater
Wexford
Bay

New Ross
Adamstown
Camaross
Wexford
Castlebridge
Wexford Harbour

©—John Bartholomew & Son, Ltd., Edinburgh

For explanation of road marking and
contour colouring see page 1

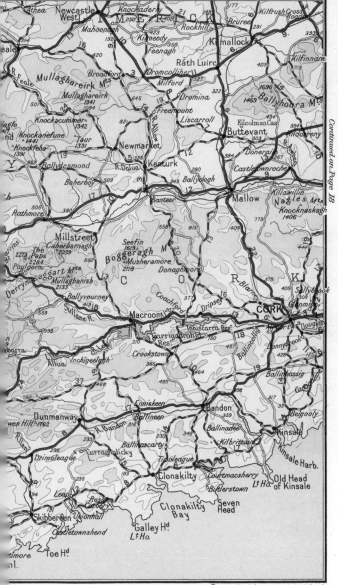

Continued on Page 18

Newport 650 Rear Cross
Upperchurch
Thurles 452
Slievefelim Callaun Milestone 788 13 391 Twomileborris 471
M.ts 1533 Holycross Littleton Slieveardagh H.
Abington Kilmanagh
Cappamore TIPPERARY 332 Ballingar
Daon 411 Ballagh Killenaule Kings R. 325
New Pallas R. Cappagh 311 293
Pallas Grean 37 White 635 Drangan
Grean 25 Oola 334 540 Mullinahone
Limerick CASHEL Cloneen
Junction 12 575 Rosegreen 394 Fethard
Hospital TIPPERARY Golden 15 Slievenamon
12 403 353 Bansha Newinn 334 2363 567
Slievenamuck 245
1215 R. Ahe How 300 10 Kilsheelan 13
Galbally Galtymore Caher Abbey 74 Carrick
Ballylanders M.ts Ardfinnan 229 Clonmel
570 Gaitee 3018 18 364 9 R. Suir Comeragh
Caves 251 Knockanaffrin
Mitchelstown Ballyporeen Clogheen R. Tar Ballymacarbry 2478 M.ts
305 Monavullagh
Mildorrery Kilworth M.ts Knockmealdown M.ts Seefin 2387
Glanworth 249 Welleray M.ts
218 Kilworth Monastery Cappoquin
19 145 Ballyduff 9 Lismore
FERMOY R. Bride 11 Dungarvan
19 202 Conna Tallow Dungarvan
Rathcormack 13 Strancall English Helvic
R. Bride 185 Ballynoe 609 Drum Ringville
383 431 558 Hills
Watergrasshill 383 Cashmore 403
323 C O R K Dungourney 332 19 Mine Hd
Sallybrook Killeagh Ardmore Ardmore B.
Glanmire 10 Carrigtohill 54 Youghal
12 Midleton Castlemartyr Youghal
Passage Cobh 39 Ballymacoda Bay
West (Queenstown) Cloyne 107
Ballycotton Ballycotton
Whitegate Bay
Crosshaven 169
Carrigaline

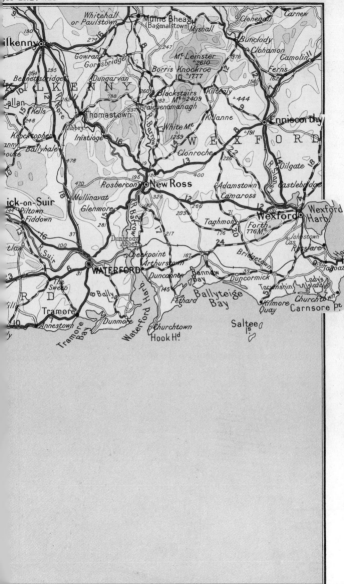

For explanation of road marking and
contour colouring see page 1

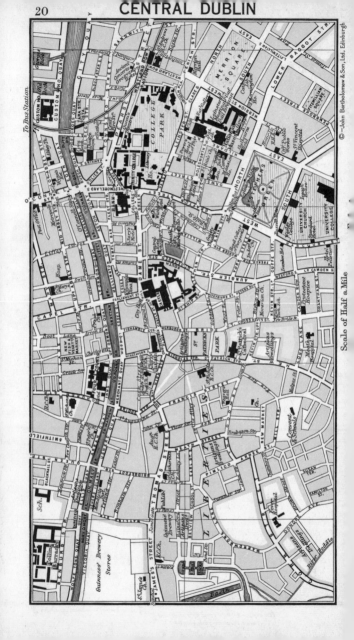

© —John Bartholomew & Son, Ltd. Edinburgh

Scale of Half a. Mile

HOW TO TRAVEL

MOTORING. Motorists wishing to take their cars with them to Ireland usually do so through the Automobile Association (A.A.) or the Royal Automobile Club (R.A.C.), either of which will relieve them of most of the formalities involved in a sea passage. Motoring visitors may drive in Ireland on their own national driving licences. Visitors from Great Britain may drive their cars in Ireland on their current tax discs and registration books, but they should take their log-book with them, carry a G.B. rear plate, and obtain in advance from their insurance company a 'green card' covering third-party claims. The motorists' associations issue handbooks and road books containing lists of recommended hotels and other information useful to the motorist, plan itineraries, and even provide free legal defence when their members come into conflict with the police. The latest information regarding road conditions, etc., is obtainable at their offices. The A.A. maintains offices at Dublin (23 Suffolk Street), Cork (5 South Mall), and Belfast (5 Oxford Street), while the R.A.C. has an office at Belfast (65 Chichester Street) and there is a reciprocal association between the R.A.C. and the Royal Irish Automobile Club (R.I.A.C.), with offices at Dublin (33–34 Dawson Street) and Cork (55 South Mall), whereby members of the R.A.C., when touring in Eire, receive all the services to which their R.A.C. membership would entitle them in their own country.

The laziest and most care-free way of getting about the country is to hire a car and the services of a chauffeur. There are several firms of good repute ready to accommodate the tourist in this way. Alternatively, reliable cars can be hired on much lower 'drive yourself' terms.

One of the jolliest ways of touring in Ireland is by motor caravan or by car and trailer-caravan (speed limit for the latter 25 m.p.h. in the Republic, 30 m.p.h. in Northern Ireland); the charges for taking a trailer-caravan across the water are about the same as for taking a car. The Caravan Club (46 Brook Street, London, W.1) provides its members with a list of camping sites, etc. A list of sites is also available at the Irish Tourist Board offices. Farmers generally allow the use of a site free of charge or for a small fee, and in return caravanners should buy their milk, butter, eggs, etc., from them, keep farm gates shut, and leave no litter.

The cheapest method of carrying out a motor tour is to have front seats in your car that let down to form a bed at night. Breakfast, luncheon, and tea can be taken in picnic fashion, with the help of a spirit stove, and a good evening meal (too often 'meat tea') and a bath obtained at an hotel.

Ireland is the motorist's paradise, in view of the absence of traffic congestion and the comparative freedom from restrictions. Except in the large towns, cars may be parked almost anywhere, and no parking lights are necessary. In spite of the hilly nature of much of the surface the main roads are well adapted for motoring and remarkably free from severe gradients. Many of them are in process of widening or reconstruction. The road surface, usually tar-macadam or concrete, varies from county to county, but on the whole is not up to the English standard. In the mountain districts some of the roads are stony or loose-surfaced, narrow, and tortuous, sometimes with breakneck gradients, providing the adventurous driver with the maximum of thrills. Owing to the number of cows, sheep, donkeys, goats, and poultry grazing by the roadside throughout the country, to say nothing of motor-phobe sheep-dogs, high speeds are extremely inadvisable, especially as the country folk occasionally prefer to drive their donkey-carts on the wrong side of the road. Garages and filling-stations are often closed on Sundays. The chief roads are lettered and numbered—T for trunk roads, L for link, or second-class, roads (in Northern Ireland A and B).

Bartholomew's road map of Ireland, on a scale of twelve miles to an inch, is supplied with this volume, and will be found adequate for most motoring purposes. Those requiring more detail are recommended to acquire a set of Ordnance or Bartholomew's quarter-inch maps in five sheets.

The tourist who does not bring a car with him to Ireland can get from anywhere to practically anywhere else by railway or by MOTOR-BUS, or by a combination of the two. Motor-buses are slower than trains and more liable to change of times and routes, and they do not carry heavy luggage. Another drawback is that in summer, when the buses are often full, a passenger cannot be sure of obtaining a seat, and thus runs a risk of being stranded in some remote spot. Apart from the regular services from point to point, a variety of whole-day and half-day trips by motor-coach is available at every tourist resort. During the summer, circular tours by motor-coach, embracing the leading beauty-spots and other points of interest, are arranged, particulars of which can be obtained from any tourist agent. 'C.I.E.' (page 24), for instance, have a nine-day tour from Dublin to Glendalough, Cashel, Cork, Glengarriff, Killarney, Limerick, Galway, Connemara, Sligo, and back to Dublin, fare including hotel accommodation, meals, and gratuities, and a six-day tour from Dublin through Northern Ireland and Donegal. The Ulster Transport Authority has a similar ten-day tour from Belfast.

There is no complete time-table for motor-buses in Ireland, and those who intend to make constant use of them should lose no time in providing themselves with the omnibus time-tables of 'C.I.E.' and the Ulster Transport Authority, which cover most of the country.

CYCLING. One of the cheapest, freest, and most delightful methods of travelling is a combination of cycle, rail, and walking, varied according to the weather and one's fancy. Owing to the comparative absence of motor traffic, Ireland is a splendid touring country for the cyclist who does not mind a great deal of hill-climbing, and bicycles can be taken over many mountain routes that are inaccessible to cars. Membership of the Cyclists' Touring Club (C.T.C.), 3 Craven Hill, Paddington, London, W.2, offers many advantages. Its *Handbook and Guide* contains a list of recommended hotels, boarding-houses, and farm-houses, besides much other valuable information. The most useful scale for cycling maps is half-inch to a mile (Ordnance Survey).

WALKING is undoubtedly the best way of seeing Ireland, and, owing to the absence of heavy motor traffic, Ireland is a glorious country for walking tours, but there are certain disadvantages. Good accommodation is hard to find in the remoter districts (the *C.T.C. Handbook* and the Irish Tourist Board offices provide lists of farm lodgings), and days' marches of excessive length are sometimes necessary. The climate is uncertain, and rain and mists are prevalent on the west coast. It is almost essential to possess an Ordnance map (one inch to a mile), on which the farm tracks ('boreens') and the comparatively rare footpaths are marked. A desirable outfit for hill-walking includes also nailed boots, a rucksack with webbing straps, and a compass. 'Trespassers will be Prosecuted' notices are extremely rare, and one can walk almost anywhere, except, of course, through growing crops and hayfields. Be careful not to damage fences and walls. Beware of the ubiquitous bogs, the presence of which is often indicated by light green patches or by cotton-grass.

RAILWAYS. The railways are worked mostly by the traffic merger known as Córas Iompair Éireann or C.I.E. (in Eire) and by the Ulster Transport Authority (for Northern Ireland). Diesel trains with buffet cars run on most of the C.I.E. main lines. Tourist tickets, excursion tickets, period tickets, tickets for circular tours and combined rail and motor-coach tours, etc., are available in great variety at reduced rates. Through direct tickets, and tourist, excursion, and circular tour tickets, starting from London and other places in Great Britain, are also issued by British Railways. On Sundays the services are for the most part the same as on week-days, but in Northern Ireland they are reduced. Many of the railway lines shown on our maps have recently been closed for passenger traffic.

A generous allowance of personal luggage is carried free on the railways, but special tickets must be obtained for cycles. Each article must bear the owner's name and address and destination, and must be labelled and placed in the luggage van by a porter. The passenger receives no baggage check, and should claim his property immediately on arrival at his destination. If he has to change *en route*, he should keep his eye on his luggage and see that it is put into the proper train. This means 'tips' everywhere (from 1s. according to the quantity of luggage). The *Irish Red Guide* covers all the Irish services; *Baird's Rail and Bus Guide* is restricted to Northern Ireland; and the railway organizations, of course, all publish their own time-tables.

ROUTES TO IRELAND. Sailing tickets are required at busy periods, and these are issued without extra charge when the steamer tickets are purchased. It is advisable to book both passenger and motor-car accommodation well in advance (also the return journey). The fares given below are those prevailing in 1965, and are liable to increase.

The most frequented crossing of the Irish Sea is the Royal Mail route from Holyhead to Dun Laoghaire (Kingstown) by the large and comfortable steamers of British Railways, which cover the 66 miles in 3¼ hours every night and, in summer, every afternoon except Sundays. Fares: first class 48s., second class 25s. 6d. From London (Euston) to Dublin: first class 131s., second class rail and first class steamer 103s., second class throughout 82s. Motor-cycles (40s.) and cars (from 155s. according to length) are conveyed by these steamers, and there is also a car-ferry service two to six times a week in summer, besides a car-carrier train from London. Dun Laoghaire is 15 minutes by train to Westland Row Station at Dublin.

The total cost of taking an average-sized car to Dublin and back by the Holyhead route, including the necessary documents, car transport on the steamer, customs clearances, and two passenger tickets (first class), but excluding the R.A.C. or A.A. subscription and gratuities, is about £40.

For southern Ireland a favourite route is by the British Railways steamers from Fishguard to Rosslare, which cover the 54-mile crossing of St. George's Channel in $3\frac{1}{4}$ hours daily and nightly in summer (except on Sunday-Monday night) and three nights a week in winter. Fares: first class 55s., second class 27s. 6d., return tickets 91s. and 55s. From London (Paddington) to Rosslare: first class 136s., second class rail and first class steamer 108s. 2d., second class throughout 83s. Car from 135s. according to length; motor-cycle 35s. 9d. Cars are put on railway trucks to be conveyed along Rosslare Pier.

The Liverpool–Dublin route of the British & Irish Steam Packet Co., nightly except Sundays, is a long crossing ($9\frac{1}{2}$ hours); your car travels with you and you can drive it off the quay. There is also a car-ferry service three times a week in summer. Fares: first class 62s. 6d., second class 36s. From London (Euston) to Dublin: first class 131s., second class rail and first class steamer 108s., second class throughout 82s. Car from 155s. according to length, motor-cycle 45s. Passengers and cars embark at Princes Dock East, Liverpool, and are landed at North Wall, Dublin.

There are two nightly Royal Mail routes (not Sundays) to Belfast: (a) Via Liverpool, by the steamers of the Belfast Steamship Co. in 10 hours. Fares: first class 62s. 6d., second class 35s. From London (Euston) to Belfast: first class 131s., second class rail and first class steamer 108s., second class throughout 81s. Car from 145s. according to length; motor-cycle 35s. (b) Via Heysham, by British Railways steamer in $7\frac{1}{4}$ hours. Fares: first class 57s., second class 29s. 6d. From London (Euston) to Belfast: first class 131s., second class rail and first class steamer 107s. 6d., second class throughout 80s. Car from 145s., according to length; motor-cycle 35s.

The Royal Mail route of the British Railways steamers via Stranraer and Larne, once or twice daily (not Sundays), is the shortest sea passage ($2\frac{1}{4}$ hours; open sea 70 minutes) and is quite convenient for rail passengers from London and the south (London to Belfast in 15 hours). Fares: first class 32s. 6d., second class 16s. 6d. From London (Euston) to Belfast: first class 172s., second class rail and first class steamer 126*s.*, second class throughout 111*s.* Car from 80*s.* according to length; motor-cycle 16*s.* (return ticket 20*s.*).

Other steamer services to Ireland by which cars are conveyed are from Fishguard to Cork (thrice weekly in summer in 9¼ hours), from Liverpool to Cork (once weekly in 10 hours), from Ardrossan to Belfast on weekdays in summer in 4¾ hours), from Glasgow to Belfast (nightly except Sunday, in 9½ hours), from Glasgow to Dublin (two or three times weekly in 13½ hours), and from Preston to Larne or Belfast (daily except Sunday).

AIR SERVICES. 'Aer Lingus' and associated companies operate services between Dublin and London (fare £12 4*s.*, flying time 85 minutes), Isle of Man (£4 6*s.*, 35 minutes), Liverpool (£7, 40 minutes), Manchester (£7 14*s.*, 45 minutes), Birmingham (£9 3*s.*, 60 minutes), Bristol (£8 6*s.*, 70 minutes), Glasgow (£8 12*s.*, 60 minutes), Paris (£21 15*s.*, 2½ hours), etc. The Dublin Airport is at Collinstown, 5½ miles from the city air terminus at the Central Bus station (Busaras). There are also air services between Cork and Cardiff, Bristol and London.

From the Belfast Airport at Aldergrove, 9 miles from the city air terminus in Great Victoria Street, there are B.E.A. services to and from London (£5 to £10, 75 minutes), Isle of Man (£2 6*s.* to £3 2*s.*, 30 minutes), Liverpool (£4 13*s.* to £5 14*s.*, 85 minutes), Manchester (£5 1*s.* to £6 2*s.*, 50 minutes), Birmingham (£5 17*s.* to £7 1*s.*, 65 minutes), etc. The fares vary according to the time of year and the length of stay. The times given are those from city centre to city centre. B.K.S. operate services from Belfast to Leeds and to Edinburgh, and from Dublin and Belfast to Newcastle.

Shannon Airport is a port of call for the transatlantic air liners (see page 141).

CROSS-CHANNEL AIR FERRIES. Aer Lingus operate car-ferry services between Liverpool and Dublin, Bristol and Dublin, Bristol and Cork, and Cherbourg and Dublin.

CUSTOMS REGULATIONS. All journeys between Great

Britain or Northern Ireland and Eire (Republic of Ireland) involve an examination of luggage by the customs officials. A reasonable quantity of cigarettes and tobacco, spirits, perfumes, sweets, etc., required by the traveller for his personal use, is not necessarily charged with duty, if duly declared. Certain books and periodicals are banned in Eire, and their importation is prohibited.

When passing between Eire and Northern Ireland (by railway or by one of the approved roads—no others may be used), or on the return to Great Britain, the traveller is usually asked to produce all articles purchased 'abroad'; those not required for personal use (e.g. presents) may be charged with duty. Additions or alterations to the car (but not running repairs) are also liable to duty.

On the first occasion of crossing the Eire–Northern Ireland border, the motorist must report at the customs examination station on a week-day between 9 a.m. and 5 p.m. Otherwise he may cross at any time of day or night; the customs stations are closed at night and on Sundays, but motor-cars are liable to be held up and inspected by the mobile police. If merchandise is being carried, severe penalties can be inflicted.

There is no customs barrier between Great Britain and Northern Ireland.

PASSPORTS. Nationals, subjects, or citizens of the member states of the British Commonwealth do not require any travel documents in Ireland. United States subjects do not require Irish visas on their passports.

WHERE TO STAY

HOTELS. Late years have witnessed a remarkable improvement in Irish hotels. All hotels and guest-houses are registered by the Bord Fáilte Éireann (Irish Board of Welcome) and the Northern Ireland Tourist Board, which publish comprehensive lists (free) with details of accommodation and charges. Large, first-class hotels (often managed by the railways), with corresponding charges, will be found in Dublin and Belfast, in the more fashionable tourist resorts, and in some isolated places, where they usually offer fishing, shooting, and golf. Otherwise, Irish hotels are mostly small and simple, providing, instead of dinner in the evening, a 'meat tea' at any time between 5 and 11 p.m. Bath-rooms (baths are sometimes an extra) are all too few. On the other hand, the beds are clean and comfortable, the bedrooms are nearly always equipped with hot and cold running water, and home-produced food (bread, butter, bacon, etc.) is of excellent quality. The staffs are almost always extremely obliging, and do their best to make up for any inadequacies. The traveller receives a warmer welcome than in England, and there is a refreshing absence of rules and regulations. Good small second-class hotels and decent village inns are rare, and it is somewhat risky to try any place outside the Bord Fáilte Éireann or A.A. lists of hotels, guest houses, lodgings, and farmhouse accommodation.

Alcoholic drinks in Eire are much cheaper than in the United Kingdom. Hotel residents, of course, are served at any time. Licensed houses—bars at the back of grocers' shops are a peculiarity in Eire—are open throughout Ireland on week-days from 10.30 a.m. to 11 p.m. (in summer to 11.30 p.m.; till 9 p.m. nightly in Northern Ireland towns with a population of under 5,000). In Dublin, Cork, Limerick, and Waterford they close from 2.30 to 3.30 p.m. On Sundays and St. Patrick's Day they are open 12.30 to 2 p.m. and 4 to 10 p.m., and on Good Friday and Christmas Day they are closed altogether. In

Northern Ireland the only place to get a drink on Sundays is at a club.

A 10 per cent service charge is added to the bill at some hotels. Otherwise, a fairly satisfactory solution of the vexed question of 'tips' is to distribute among the staff a sum equal to at least 10 per cent of the total bill (rather more for one-night visitors, or if an unusual amount of trouble has been given), or to hand in a similar amount to the cashier for distribution.

YOUTH HOSTELS. Hikers should enrol themselves as members of a Youth Hostels Association—for England and Wales, Trevelyan House, St Albans, Herts.; for Scotland, 9 Bruntsfield Crescent, Edinburgh 10; for Eire, 'An Oige,' 39 Mountjoy Square, Dublin; for Northern Ireland, 28 Bedford Street, Belfast—and thus become entitled to use without formality any of the hostels that have so far been opened in Ireland (38 in Eire, 24 in Northern Ireland). The charge for accommodation is 4s. per night. In districts where there is no hostel, cheap accommodation can be found at affiliated hotels.

Luncheons, afternoon teas, and evening meals are obtainable at hotels, at fixed charges, and there is an ever-increasing number of wayside cafés and snack bars on the main road routes.

	Great Britain and Ireland	Commonwealth	Foreign
REPUBLIC OF IRELAND:			
Letters	5d. for 2 oz., then 1d. per oz.		8d. for 1 oz., then 5d. per oz.
Postcards	3d.		5d.
Printed papers	3d. for 4 oz., then 1½d. per 2 oz.		3d. for 2 oz., then 1½d. per 2 oz.
Telegrams	6s. for 12 words, then 5d. per word. Inland: 5s. and 5d.		
NORTHERN IRELAND:			
Letters	4d. for 2 oz., then 2d. per 2 oz.	4d. for 1 oz., then 1½d. per oz.	6d. for 1 oz., then 4d. per oz.
Postcards	3d.	3d.	4d.
Printed papers	3d. for 2 oz. 5d. for 4 oz. then 1d. per 2 oz.	2½d. for 2 oz., then 1½d. per 2 oz.	2½d. for 2 oz., then 1½d. per 2 oz.
Telegrams	5s. for 12 words, then 5d. per word		

Registration fee: Eire 1s., Northern Ireland 1s. 9d.

Eire has its own postage stamps; Northern Ireland uses United Kingdom stamps.

The larger offices are open on Sunday morning from 9 to 10.30. The smaller offices are closed at one o'clock on the local early closing day.

Picture postcards may be sent anywhere in the world at printed paper rates, provided that the words 'Post Card' be altered to 'Printed Paper,' and that they bear no writing except the date, addresses, and a formula of courtesy not exceeding five words.

Letter-boxes are painted green in Eire and red in Northern Ireland.

SPORTS AND GAMES

(See the various folders issued by the Irish Tourist Board and the Northern Ireland Tourist Board.)

FISHING starts on 1st January and lasts, except for close periods, until 31st October. The countless loughs and rivers of Ireland abound in salmon, sea trout, and brown trout. The best salmon and sea trout fisheries are preserved, of course, but there are plenty of waters which are entirely free or free to the guests of certain hotels. Salmon fishing is at its best from March to July, and sea trout fishing from July to the end of August. The great speciality of Ireland, however, is brown trout fishing, which is free nearly everywhere and requires no licence; nowhere else in Europe is such free trout fishing to be obtained. Irish coarse fishing (pike, perch, bream, rudd, etc.) is second to none.

HUNTING. Ireland's fame as a hunting and racing country is world-wide, and buyers from all over the world come to the Dublin Horse Show to buy hunters and racehorses. There are eighty-five recognized packs of hounds: thirty-two of foxhounds, forty-one of harriers, two of staghounds, and ten of beagles. In addition, there are many other packs followed on foot. Hiring charges and 'caps' are lower than elsewhere, and there is less need to worry about smartness of turn-out.

SHOOTING. Rough shooting is available all over the west and centre of Ireland, either free or free to the guests of certain hotels. Much of the best shooting is in the hands of the Irish Land Commission, Merrion Street, Dublin, to which application should be made. The snipe, woodcock, and waterfowl shooting of the Shannon lakes is especially famous. Fire-arms and ammunition cannot be taken into Eire except under licence, to be obtained from the Department of Justice, Merrion Street, Dublin. Application forms are obtainable from the Irish Embassy.

HURLING, GAELIC FOOTBALL, and HANDBALL are the Irish national games. Hurling is played by teams of fifteen a side, somewhat on the lines of hockey and Scottish shinty, but with variations that make it a much more strenuous and spectacular game. The stick, or hurley, has a narrow shaft widening out to a flat end, $3\frac{1}{2}$ inches wide at the base. The ball is small and not so solid as a hockey ball. The goal-posts resemble those used for Rugby, with a cross-bar 7 feet high. If the ball is sent under the cross-bar, a goal (three points) is scores; if over, one point. Women's hurling is known as 'Camogie.'

Gaelic Football is played by teams of fifteen a side, with a ball smaller than a 'Soccer' ball. It differs from 'Soccer' in certain respects. Any player may catch the ball while it is off the ground and run with it three paces before kicking. Any player may strike the ball once with his hand to make it rebound from the ground, in order to evade an opponent or secure a better kick. Substitutes are allowed to take the place of injured players. Goals and points are scored as in hurling. The inter-provincial finals at hurling and Gaelic Football are held at Croke Park, Dublin, in March, and the All-Ireland finals in September.

Handball is played especially in rural districts, and tournaments are held at various provincial centres. It is a kind of fives, played by two or four players. The game is started by one player 'tossing' the ball against the front wall, either after he has made it rebound from the ground, or has released it from his hand and hit it while in the air. The ball is in play as long as it is hit against the front wall without allowing it to touch the ground more than once each time it rebounds. The game is 21 aces.

MISCELLANEA

MONEY. Eire has its own currency (with some of the world's most graceful designs) and bank-notes (issued by the Central Bank), identical in denominations and values with those of Great Britain. But British coins and notes are current everywhere. The banks are open from 10 a.m. to 12.30 p.m. and from 1.30 to 3 p.m., on Fridays till 5 p.m.; closed on Saturdays and Sundays.

NEWSPAPERS. English newspapers are obtainable on the day of publication almost anywhere in Ireland, and some of them have special Irish editions. The chief Eire papers are the *Irish Times*, the *Irish Independent*, and the *Irish Press*. The *Cork Examiner* is the best-known provincial paper. In Northern Ireland the leading newspapers are the *Belfast Telegraph*, the *Northern Whig*, and the *Belfast News Letter*.

TOBACCO. In Eire cigarettes and tobacco, whether imported or locally manufactured, are much cheaper than in the United Kingdom. In Northern Ireland prices are the same as in England.

POLICE. In Eire police duties are carried out by the Civic Guards (Gardai Siothchana), in blue uniforms, unarmed but trained in the use of arms. In Northern Ireland the old R.I.C. has survived under the name of Royal Ulster Constabulary, in dark green uniforms.

A BRIEF OUTLINE OF IRISH HISTORY

In the Bronze Age the inhabitants of Ireland were Picts, a short, dark Mediterranean race. That they themselves were immigrants is probable from such legends as that of the victory of the Tuatha Dé Danaan ('People of the Goddess Danu') over the Firbolg on the plains of Moytura.

The first Celtic invasion occurred about 400–350 B.C., when the tall, fair-haired Gaels, or Milesians, a people in the La Tène stage of civilization, with a knowledge of iron, began to arrive from Central Europe, probably by way of Spain.

The characteristic settlement site of the early inhabitants of Ireland was the circular earth wall, or 'rath' (of which some 28,000 examples survive), or the lake dwelling ('crannog'), or, where stone was plentiful, the 'dun,' 'lis,' or 'cahir.' The last were sometimes magnificent structures of dry, unmortared stone, such as Staigue Fort and Dun Aengus (Aonghusa). 'Clochans,' or beehive huts, served as dwelling-places. No country is richer than Ireland in megaliths: dolmens (sepulchral monuments of the neolithic people)—at Carrowmore, Co. Sligo, there is a group of sixty-five—tumuli (notably the royal mausolea of Newgrange and Dowth), cairns, stone circles, and standing stones, or 'gallans.' The wealth of Ireland in Bronze Age antiquities is astonishing. Apart from the superb collection in the Dublin Museum, gold ornaments of Irish provenance—Co. Wicklow must have been a veritable Eldorado—have been found all over the Continent, particularly in Scandinavia.

Gaelic Ireland, which escaped the Roman conquest, was a pentarchy of five major kingdoms, or groups of states, the 'Five Fifths,' of which the modern provinces are survivals—Ulster, North and South Leinster, Munster, Connaught. The people were governed according to the Brehon code of laws, and lived largely under the influence of the Druids, an association of wise men, learned in religion and astronomy.

In the third century of the Christian era the kings of Connacht occupied Tara and acquired the high-kingship of all Ireland. From about this period till the middle of the fifth century the Irish were persistent raiders of Britain, under the name of Scots (i.e. plunderers), and their settlement of Dalriada in Argyll ultimately developed into the Scottish monarchy. A small standing army, the Fianna, or companions of Finn, came into being.

The first historical figure to emerge from the mists of legend was Cormac MacArt, who flourished as high-king from about 250 to 300. The Tara kingship reached the height of its power towards the beginning of the fifth century, under Niall of the Nine Hostages, ancestor of the Neill princes of Ulster.

In 432 Christianity was introduced by St. Patrick, the Apostle of Ireland and the national saint (though not the first missionary to Ireland), who chose Armagh as his metropolitan see.

The period from the sixth to the ninth century saw an extraordinary outburst of intellectual activity, due to the introduction of Latin learning and the monastic system, probably by way of South Wales. The abbey of Clonard was founded by St. Finian, and thence Derry and Kells (by St. Columba, or Columcille), Clonmacnoise and Bangor, and many others were colonized. Starting with Columba's foundation of Iona in 563, Ireland sent Christian missionaries all over western Europe and was a chief instrument in the revival of Latin culture in Britain, France, and Germany. Latin characters took the place of the heathen Ogham inscriptions, and in the seventh century an Irish literature came into being. The monastic schools attracted students from all parts of Europe. Marvellous works of art were produced in the form of illuminated manuscripts and ecclesiastical metalwork. Architecture flourished, and Ireland can boast an unrivalled collection of early Christian monuments. Some seventy round towers, characteristic features of the primitive Irish monasteries, survive, besides 250 high crosses, which were erected to commemorate eminent persons or notable events, or to mark the boundaries of sacred precincts. From 734 till 1022 the high-kingship was held alternately by the kings of Ailech (Derry) and Midhe (Meath).

In the year 807 came the first inroads of the vikings (Danes and Norsemen), who began by plundering the coasts and the abbeys but soon established permanent settlements and founded the trading cities of Dublin, Wexford, Waterford, Cork, and Limerick. (The Irish were no city builders, such towns as they had being for the most part religious centres.) Finally the Danish power was broken for good and all by Brian Boru at Clontarf on Good Friday, 1014. Brian and his sons, however, fell in the battle, and after him there were no more kings of all Ireland, but only high-kings 'with opposition.' In the midst of these troubled times Ireland produced some of the finest and most individual Romanesque churches in Europe (Cashel, Clonfert).

The fateful Norman invasion of Ireland originated—in a manner reminiscent of the Trojan War—in the rape of Dervorgilla by Dermot MacMurrogh, King of Leinster. Expelled from Ireland by Roderic O'Conor, the high-king, Dermot sought help from Henry II of England. The latter, to whom Pope Adrian IV (an Englishman) had secretly granted the feudal lordship of Ireland in 1155, supplied Dermot with troops and enabled him to recover his kingdom in 1169. In the following year Dermot brought over 'Strongbow' (Richard de Clare, Earl of Pembroke) and gave him his daughter in marriage. After Dermot's death Strongbow claimed the lordship of Leinster and was supported by Henry II, who landed at Waterford in 1172 with an overpowering force. The Irish kings submitted, and Henry granted Leinster to Strongbow, Ulster to John de Courcy, Meath to Hugh de Lacy, and Dublin to the citizens of Bristol. The Geraldines, Norman-Welsh barons in Strongbow's service, established themselves at Maynooth and Kildare, while another branch of the family settled in Munster. Everywhere the Normans consolidated their power by the erection of great stone castles, and the Irish chieftains were gradually driven into the mountains or into the western bogs. In Ulster, however, the O'Neills and the O'Donnells drove off the Norman invaders with the aid of 'galloglasses' from the Hebrides, and the O'Conors maintained their power in Connacht, the O'Briens in Thomond, and the MacCarthys in south-west Munster. The power of the English Crown was confined to a fluctuating area around Dublin known as the Pale, and as yet there was no general colonization by English settlers. On the other hand, the Norman adventurers intermarried with the Irish and their descendants became Irish chiefs. Prince John, appointed Lord of Ireland in 1177, paid an unpopular visit to his fief in 1185.

In May 1315 Edward Bruce, brother of the more famous Robert, King of Scotland, accepted an invitation from the O'Neills and landed at Larne, captured Carrickfergus, and was crowned King of Ireland at Dundalk, 1st May 1316. Joined by his brother, he pushed on to Limerick, but when left alone he was defeated by Roger Mortimer, Edward II's lieutenant in Ireland, and slain by John de Bermingham at Faughart, near Dundalk, October 1318.

Between 1316 and 1329 the Geraldine earldoms of Leinster and Munster, and the Butler earldom of Ormonde, were created. Thereafter Irish history was dominated by the Fitzgeralds until the time of Elizabeth ('aristocratic home rule'), the Butlers, politicians rather than soldiers, succeeding them under the Stuarts. The Statutes of Kilkenny (1367) vainly sought to prevent the rise of a new class, 'Irish to the English and English to the Irish.'

In 1394, and again in 1399, Richard II landed at Waterford with a large army, in an unsuccessful effort to put a stop to the raids of Art MacMurrogh, King of Leinster.

In 1494, under the Lord-Deputy, Sir Edmund Poynings, the Irish Parliament passed several Acts restricting Irish independence, notably one ('Poynings' Law') providing that no Act should be valid unless previously approved by the Privy Council of England.

Henry VIII was the first sovereign to take the title of King of Ireland, a country which was becoming of increasing importance owing to his European entanglements and the discovery of America. In 1536 the Reformation was introduced by Lord Leonard Grey, but was received unwillingly both by the Irish and the 'Old English,' the dissolution of the monasteries not being completed till 1607. 'Silken Thomas,' the ninth Earl of Kildare, was tricked into rebellion and executed, together with his five uncles, at Tyburn, 1537.

Mary I adopted a policy of confiscation and plantation, and in her reign King's and Queen's Counties were colonized. An age of English adventurers and land speculators—Carew, Sidney, Raleigh, Gilbert, Cork—ensued in the reigns of Elizabeth and James I. Risings against Elizabeth were fomented by Spain, but a landing at Smerwick was crushed, and the Earl of Desmond, chief of the Munster Geraldines, was slain in 1583. In 1591, Trinity College, Dublin ('the college of the heretics'), was founded.

In 1594 came the rising of Hugh O'Neill, Earl of Tyrone, and Hugh Roe O'Donnell, lord of Tyrconnell, in Ulster, aided by the 'Sugan' (straw rope) Earl of Desmond. Victorious over Bagnal and Essex, they marched south to the aid of a Spanish force which had landed at Kinsale under Don Juan del Aguila, but were defeated by Mountjoy and Carew (1601). The 'Flight of the Earls' (Tyrone and Tyrconnell) from Rathmullen in 1607, with a hundred northern chieftains, was a fatal blow to the Catholic and Gaelic cause. The Plantation of Ulster followed, the forfeited estates being divided among Scottish Protestants, and Derry and its county being handed over to the City of London. Ulster, formerly the most Irish, became the most British of the provinces.

The years 1641–9 were a time of confused warfare—on one side, the dispossessed Ulsterites under Owen Roe O'Neill, the Catholic Confederation of Kilkenny under Thomas Preston, and Protestant Royalists led by the Marquis of Ormonde, with the papal nuncio Rinuccini complicating matters by his unwise interference; on the other, the Ulster Scots under General Monro, the Earl of Inchiquin at the head of the Munster army, and Michael Jones holding Dublin for Parliament. In 1649 Cromwell landed in Dublin with the army of the New Model and broke the back of the Irish resistance, storming Drogheda and Wexford and massacring their garrisons. The measures of repression and proscription that ensued reached the extreme of barbarity. Men, women, and children were sold as slaves to the plantations in America. Ten more counties were planted with Puritan soldiers and adventurers, the Irish landowners being driven 'to hell or Connaught.' Even after the restoration of Charles II, who dared not upset the Cromwellian settlement, only a barren third of the country was held by the 'Old Irish.'

Under James II the pendulum swung the other way, and many Protestants were driven to take refuge in Ulster. The king's last fight for his throne was made in 1689, when he landed at Kinsale with officers, arms, and money supplied by Louis XIV and put himself at the head of his loyal Irish subjects. The siege of Londonderry and its relief from the sea were followed by the landing of Schomberg and William III with an army partly of mercenaries. The death-knell of the Stuart dynasty was sounded at the battle of the Boyne, 1st July 1690. The last fight of Catholic Ireland as a nation in arms was behind the walls of Limerick, where Patrick Sarsfield held out against William but surrendered in the following year on honourable terms (religious liberty and retention of estates) that were subsequently dishonoured. Seven thousand Irishmen who refused to take the oath of allegiance sailed for France—the 'Flight of the Wild Geese.' Henceforth the Continent was crowded with Irish exiles, who took military or other service in France, Spain, Germany, Poland, and Russia.

The Penal Laws of 1691–1715 reduced Ireland to a condition of utter despair and agrarian decay. Catholics were excluded from corporations and professions, forbidden to vote or hold the smallest office, teach, carry arms, or even own a horse. Only one-ninth of the soil was left in the hands of the old landowning families. The export trade in Irish woollens was deliberately ruined in the English interest. In 1719 the English Parliament formulated a claim to legislate for Ireland, and the Dublin Parliament became a mere dependency. On the other hand, the Ulster linen trade was fostered, Dublin was beautified, and manufactures introduced.

The patriotic movement of Flood and Grattan, initiated in 1760, extorted concessions from England, under the influence of the American War of Independence. The Constitution of 1782 removed the worst abuses and freed the Irish Parliament from complete subjection to London. In 1793 Catholics were admitted to the franchise, though parliamentary reform was refused. A long overdue period of national prosperity was initiated. But disaffection and French revolutionary ideas led to the foundation of the Society of United Irishmen under Wolfe Tone and Lord Edward Fitzgerald—the Orange Society was its counter-blast—to the abortive French expedition to Bantry Bay under Hoche in 1797, and to the peasant rising in Wexford in 1798, mercilessly crushed. Both Wolfe Tone and Lord Edward died under arrest in 1798—the former committing suicide, the latter succumbing to wounds.

The Act of Union was passed in May 1800, despite Grattan's eloquence.

Robert Emmet's rising (a mere street riot) and execution in 1803, after a romantic love-affair with Sarah Curran, made him a national hero. In 1805 the Catholic Association was founded, which, under Daniel O'Connell, the Liberator (according to Gladstone, 'the greatest popular leader the world has ever seen'), resulted in the Catholic emancipation of 1829. Though industries prospered (especially brewing, distilling, and the linen trade), the condition of the land workers was appalling, owing to the absenteeism of the landlords, the exactions of tithes for the upkeep of a State Church on behalf of a small minority, but most of all from over-population. The population rose from 1¼ millions in 1700 to 4½ millions in 1800 and over 8 millions in 1841 (it is now about 4¼ millions). There were half a million small holdings of less than five acres.

In 1846 and 1847 Ireland was visited by one of the greatest calamities that have ever overwhelmed a nation—the potato blight, which destroyed the staple crop of the country. Over 21,000 people starved to death, and the total mortality between 1846 and 1851 was nearly a million. Between 1846 and 1857 more than a million and a half Irish emigrated. Abortive rebellions (such as the Young Ireland rising of 1848 in Tipperary) multiplied, and secret societies sprang up. Reforms were slow in coming, but they came. Tithes were commuted in 1838, the

Church disestablished in 1868. The Land Act of 1881 granted 'the three F's'—fair rent, free sale, and fixity of tenure; the Labourers' Act of 1883 enabled 50,000 cottages to be built; in 1885 the first Land Purchase Act was passed, which tackled the problem of congestion and enabled the government to finance the acquisition of land by tenants; and the Irish Agricultural Organization Society (founded in 1889) and the Congested Districts Board (1891) did much to put agriculture on a proper footing. By 1921 two-thirds of Irish soil had been transferred to the tenants, and the rest has since been compulsorily acquired.

The Home Rule movement, founded by Isaac Butt in 1870, was a constitutional one, but there were numerous parallel secret societies working for the establishment of an Irish Republic, notably the Irish Republican Brotherhood (1855) and the Fenian Society, founded in the United States in 1863. Outrages were frequent; there was a Fenian rising in Dublin and Kerry in 1867, and the whole world was shocked by the Phoenix Park murders of 1882. The Land League, founded by Michael Davitt in 1879, strove under Parnell's leadership both for land reform and for national independence. By a system of boycott and blackmail it came to dominate the whole countryside. In 1893, the Gaelic League started the movement for an 'Irish Ireland.'

Gladstone's first Home Rule Bill of 1886 was rejected; his second passed the Commons but was thrown out by the Lords; and the same fate befell Asquith's Bill of 1913. As the last would have automatically become law if passed in three successive sessions, Ulster made preparations for armed resistance. Sir Edward Carson enrolled the Ulster Volunteers, and the Irish Volunteers were formed as a counter-measure. At the same time a Citizen Army of Dublin workers was created by James Larkin and James Connolly, as a result of clashes with the police during the six months' strike of 1913. The deadlock thus created was relieved by the outbreak of the First World War, a Home Rule Bill being passed in September 1914, with a proviso suspending its operation till after the war.

The Irish Nationalist leaders (Redmond, Dillon, etc.) supported England in the First World War, and 134,000

Irishmen joined the British forces. But Sinn Fein ('Ourselves'), a movement founded by Arthur Griffith in 1900, with full control of taxation, a tariff system, and the revival of Gaelic as its objects, was an ever-growing force.

The Easter Rebellion of 1916, though aided by the Citizen Army, was mainly the work of the Volunteers. A thousand rebels seized the General Post Office, and it took five days' shelling and street fighting to dislodge them. Fifteen leaders, including Patrick Pearse and James Connolly, were executed; thousands were deported.

At the general election of 1918 the seventy-three Sinn Feiners who were elected formed themselves into a National Assembly (Dáil Éirann), which chose a ministry, set up courts of justice, and collected taxes.

Martial law was declared, and guerrilla warfare lasted from January 1919 till June 1921. The Volunteers ambushed the regular troops and the police (the latter including 1,500 'Auxiliaries' and 6,000 'Black and Tans'), shot policemen, civilians in the British service, and informers, and burnt or blew up roads, bridges, and other property, both public and private. Terrorism was met by ruthless reprisals—executions, deportations, burning of suspects' houses and creameries, etc. The Home Rule Act of 1920, dividing Ireland between the twenty-six southern counties and six of the nine Ulster counties, each to have self-government but with Westminster still holding the purse-strings, was rejected by Sinn Fein.

At length, in June 1921, a truce was arranged, and as a result of negotiations initiated by the Prime Minister, Lloyd George, and De Valera, President of the Dáil, the Anglo-Irish Treaty was signed in December. The Irish Free State, with a status similar to that of the Dominion of Canada, thereby came into being. The six Ulster counties opted out of the measure and were given partial autonomy while retaining their representation at Westminster.

Civil war then broke out between the Free State government under President Cosgrave and the anti-treaty Republicans, who were not crushed until 1923. In the course of these 'troubles' the Customs House and the Four Courts were badly damaged, and the national records destroyed. A new Constitution, with a President of Eire instead of a governor-general, and a Prime Minister instead of a President of the Dáil, came into force on 28th December 1937. The name 'Irish Free State' disappeared in favour of *Eire* (pronounced 'air-ă'). The remaining constitutional links between Eire and the United Kingdom were severed, one by one, by the Dáil, and Eire remained neutral in the Second World War. In 1948 the Republic of Ireland (Poblacht na Éireann) was proclaimed as a sovereign, independent, democratic state.

The National Parliament (Oireachtas) consists of the President (Uachtaran), elected by direct vote for seven years, and of two houses: a Senate (Seanad Éireann) of 60 members and a House of Representatives (Dáil Éireann) of 144 members. The Prime Minister (Taoiseach) is the head of the Government, with a Deputy (Tánaiste).

Irish Gaelic (p. 49) is the first, English the second, official language. The national flag is green, white, and orange, in vertical stripes; the national anthem is *A Soldier's Song*.

Northern Ireland, faithful to the United Kingdom, comprises the six counties of Antrim, Armagh, Down, Fermanagh, Londonderry, and Tyrone. It has a Governor and a Parliament, consisting of a Senate (26 members) and a House of Commons (52 members), which legislates for its own area, except for matters of imperial concern and for certain reserved subjects such as the post office. It returns 12 members to the House of Commons at Westminster.

POPULATION. The reduction of the population of Ireland by one-half during the last hundred years, through emigration and late marriage, is a social phenomenon of revolutionary significance. From a maximum of 8,175,124 in 1841 the population sank to 6,552,392 in 1851, to 5,174,836 in 1881, to 4,390,219 in 1911, to 4,204,476 in 1946–7. In 1961 it was 4,243,803. Of these Eire claimed 2,818,341, of whom about 94 per cent were Roman Catholics, while Northern Ireland had 1,425,462, of whom about 62 per cent were Protestants. It is estimated that the Irish communities abroad number at least sixteen millions, one-half of whom are in the United States and one-eighth in Great Britain.

GLOSSARY

THE following list, mostly of common elements in Irish place-names, will be found useful by the traveller who likes to know the meaning of Irish terms he is almost certain to come across and of the sometimes rather strange-looking names of the places through which he is passing.

Aeridheacht, open-air 'feis' (q.v.)
Alt, height
Ard, height
As, waterfall
Ath, ford
Augh, field
Ay, island

Balla, wall
Bally, township
Ban, white
Bawn, enclosure
Beg, small
Bel, mouth
Ben, beinn, mountain
Bord, board
Boy, yellow
Brack, speckled
Bray, hill
Bullan, cup-marked stone
Bun, end

Cahir, stone fort
Cam, crooked
Carn, heap of stones
Carrig, rock

Carry, weir
Cashel, stone fort
Cathair, stone fort
Cavan, cave
Ceilidhe, a gathering for Gaelic song and dance
Claddagh, beach
Clar, flat
Cloch, stone
Clochan, a beehive-shaped stone hut
Clon, meadow
Cool, corner
Crannog, lake dwelling
Crock, hill
Cros, cross-roads
Curragh, corragh, plain. Also a keelless coracle with a wooden frame and wicker sides, over which tarred canvas is stretched

Dáil (pronounced 'Doil'), Chamber of Deputies
Dare, derry, oak
Derg, red
Donagh, church
Doo, black

46

Drim, drom, drum, ridge

Dun, hill-top stone fort

Eighter, lower

Eireann, Irish

Ennis, island, river meadow

Esker, morainic ridge of gravel left behind by glacier

Ess, waterfall

Fáilte, welcome

Feis, assembly, Gaelic festival (singing, drama, dancing, music, etc.), on lines of Welsh 'eisteddfod' and Scottish 'mod'; *feis ceoil,* music festival

Fert, grave

Fianna Fail (pronounced 'Fee-anna Faw-il'), 'Sons of Destiny,' the De Valera Party

Fin, fair

Fine Gael (pronounced 'Fineh Gale'), 'Race of the Irish,' a political party

Ford, fiord

Gal, river, bright, foreigner

Gallan, pillar-stone, menhir

Gariff, garve, rough

Glas, grey-green

Gorm, blue

Gort, ploughland

Grianan, palace

High Crosses, dedicated to saints, or commemorating famous men, or marking boundaries. The circle around the intersection represents a halo

Inch, innis, island, river meadow

Inver, mouth of a river

I.R.A., Irish Republican Army, a secret military organization

Keel, narrow

Ken, head

Kil, church

Kin, head

Knock, hill

Lee, grey

Lis, stone fort

Low, beacon

Mac, son

Maghera, plain

Mam, pass

Monaster, monastery

Mor, great

Moy, plain

Muck, pig

Mullagh, summit

Multy, mills

Mweel, bare

Na, of the

Og, young

Ogam, Ogham, a mysterious alphabet based on Latin, with letters made up of from one to five notches, cut on the edge of a stone

Oireachtas, National Parliament, i.e. Dáil and Seanad (Senate)

Oughter, upper

Owen, river

Pattern, festival of the local patron saint

Port, port, fort

Pool, hole

Rath, circular earthen rampart

Roe, red

Ros, promontory, wood

Round Towers, of which about seventy survive, dating from the 8–12th centuries, were campaniles, or bell-towers (handbells only being used), which could be used as treasuries, watch-towers, and refuges in time of trouble, the doorway being unusually high above the ground. Each of the wooden floors, which were reached by ladders, has a small window, each direction being commanded by one window. The usual four windows in the ringing loft at the top command the points of the compass. The conical cap is domed on the underside

Scoil, school

Seanad, Senate

Shiela-na-gigs, nude figures of the pagan goddess of fertility, built into the walls of churches and castles (A.D. 900–1300)

Silla, willow

Sinn Fein (pronounced 'Shin Fane'), see page 44

Skerry, rock

Slieve, mountain

Stran, pasture

Tanist, chief's heir-apparent, chosen from his family by election. *Tánaiste* is the present-day name for the Deputy Prime Minister

Taoiseach, Prime Minister

T.D., *Teachta Dala*, member of Parliament

Teampull, church

Tholsel, town hall

Ti, *tagh*, house

Tober, well

Tra, *traw*, beach

Tully, hillock

Tyr, land

Uachtaran, President of the Irish Republic

NOTES ON THE IRISH LANGUAGE

OWING to its escape from Roman occupation, Ireland is the only self-governing state in Europe that has preserved its Celtic language. It was not until the nineteenth century that Gaelic yielded to English as the vernacular, its disappearance being due to the creation of a network of purely English primary schools. As a result, Gaelic became confined to a few districts on the western seaboard. The revival began with the foundation of the Gaelic League in 1893, and soon became associated with the physical force movement for national independence. One of the main objects of the new Government is the restoration of Irish as the national language, which is now an essential part of the curriculum in both primary and secondary schools. Nevertheless, only some 9,000 children speak Irish at home. A knowledge of Irish is either essential or very advantageous for all public services, Government or local.

Irish Gaelic is akin to the Gaelic, or Erse, of the Highlands of Scotland and belongs to the Goidelic group of the Celtic languages, as opposed to the Brythonic group (Welsh, Breton). It contains a rich vocabulary with a wealth of inflections and is capable of expressing the subtlest shades of meaning; it is said that if you can master Gaelic, any other European language is child's play.

ALPHABET. The Irish alphabet of eighteen letters is not of Celtic origin, but was introduced from the Continent by the Christian missionaries of the fifth and sixth centuries, being the alphabet in general use at that period for writing Latin, with some Greek characters. There is no *j, k, q, v, w, x, y,* or *z* in Irish. The characters used in printed Irish (written Irish is practically the same) differ but slightly from those used in English and are all easily recognizable, with the exception of:

ᴀ = *a*		ι = *l*	
ᴅ = *d*		ɲ = *r*	
ꜰ = *f*		ꞃ = *s*	
ᵹ = *g*		ꞇ = *t*	

Capital letters are simply larger versions of small letters, except that ᴦ and ꞇ are used for capital ɲ and capital ꞃ. The ι is not dotted.

PRONUNCIATION, difficult enough in any case, is complicated by the local peculiarities that distinguish the Irish of Munster, Connaught, and Ulster, that of the south being more conservative and purer than the north. c and ᵹ (*g*) are always hard.

Each of the five vowels has a short sound and a long sound, the latter indicated by an accent:

ᴀ	is pronounced like	*o* in *not*
á	,,	*au* ,, *taut*
e	,,	*e* ,, *net*
é	,,	*ay* ,, *day*
ι	,,	*i* ,, *fit*
í	,,	*ee* ,, *fee*
o	,,	*o* ,, *done*
ó	,,	*o* ,, *vote*
u	,,	*u* ,, *put*
ú	,,	*u* ,, *rule*

ᴀ, o, and u are broad vowels, e and ι are slender vowels. When next to a broad vowel, ᴅ is pronounced like *th* in *the* (a sound sometimes represented by *dh*), and ꞇ like *th* in *think*. ꞃ next to a slender vowel is pronounced *sh*, next to a broad vowel *ss* (there is no *z* sound in Irish). The pronunciation of ɲ slender and of some of the ι and ɲ sounds cannot easily be learnt except from a Gaelic speaker.

All consonants when slender have a slight *y* sound after them.

Diphthongs.

$$\left.\begin{array}{l} \text{ᴀe} \\ \text{ᴀo} \end{array}\right\} \text{ are pronounced like } ay \text{ in } day$$

$$\left.\begin{array}{l} \text{ᴀɪ} \\ \text{eᴀ} \end{array}\right\} \qquad\text{,,}\qquad a \text{ ,, } bat$$

$$\left.\begin{array}{l} \text{eɪ} \\ \text{oɪ} \end{array}\right\} \qquad\text{,,}\qquad e \text{ ,, } net$$

$$\left.\begin{array}{l} \text{ɪo} \\ \text{uɪ} \end{array}\right\} \qquad\text{,,}\qquad i \text{ ,, } fit$$

Diphthongs with one of the two vowels accented are pronounced like the accented vowel.

In words of two syllables, the stress is usually on the first syllable.

Final e is never mute.

Nine of the consonants (b, c, ᴅ, ꝼ, ᵹ, m, p, ꞃ, and ꞇ) can be 'aspirated,' or softened; this is denoted by placing a dot above the consonant or inserting an *h* after it.

$$\begin{array}{lll} \dot{ꝼ} & \text{is silent} & \\ \dot{p} & \text{is pronounced like } f & \\ \dot{ꞃ} & \text{,,} & h \\ \dot{ꞇ} & \text{,,} & h \end{array}$$

Syntax. Initial consonants are in certain circumstances 'eclipsed' by their kindred consonants, e.g. bó, 'cow'; ᴀ mbó, 'their cow.'

$$\begin{array}{lll} \text{b} & \text{is eclipsed by} & \text{m} \\ \text{c} & \text{,,} & \text{ᵹ} \\ \text{ᴅ} & \text{,,} & \text{n} \\ \text{ꝼ} & \text{,,} & \dot{b} \\ \text{ᵹ} & \text{,,} & \text{nᵹ} \\ \text{p} & \text{,,} & \text{b} \\ \text{ꞇ} & \text{,,} & \text{ᴅ} \end{array}$$

n-, ꞇ-, and h- are prefixed to words according to another set of rules (h- to prevent elision).

-óᵹ, -ín, and -ᴀn are diminutive terminations.

The definite article is ᴀn (plural and feminine genitive singular nᴀ).   There is no indefinite article.

All forms of the verb 'to be' are ᴀτᴀ (in the negative nîτ).   There is no verb 'to have,' such sentences as 'I have a horse' being expressed by 'is horse to me.'

Adjectives are usually placed after the noun, and the subject after the verb.

The complexity of Irish syntax will be seen from the fact that there are two genders (the neuter has disappeared), five declensions of nouns, four declensions of adjectives, a dual number, and two conjugations of verbs, each with three forms (synthetic, analytic, and autonomous) and two sets of terminations (broad and slender).

AN IRISH CALENDAR

(See also 'Calendar of Events in Ireland,' a booklet published by the Irish Tourist Board, and 'Coming Events,' published by the Northern Ireland Tourist Board.)

January.	1 January: New Year's Day. Salmon fishing season opens in some districts. Coursing meetings.
February.	1 February: Brown-trout fishing season opens. Feast of St. Brigid.
	Last week (Wed. and Thurs.): Spring Show at Cork. National coursing meeting at Powerstown Park, Clonmel, Co. Tipperary.
March.	17 March: St. Patrick's Day, the national festival, observed throughout Ireland. Wearing of shamrock (any kind of small-leaved clover or trefoil). Dog show of the Irish Kennel Club at Ballsbridge, Dublin.
	Easter Monday: Irish Grand National at Fairyhouse, near Dublin.
April.	Summer time begins (day after 3rd Saturday, or if that be Easter Sunday, day after 2nd Saturday).
	Matthew Feis at Cork.
	Punchestown Races.
May.	Eve of May Day: Maypole celebrations at Holyrood, Co. Down.
	First week: Royal Dublin Society's Spring Show and Industries Fair at Ballsbridge, Dublin.
	Second week: Feis Ceoil at Dublin.
	Irish Two Thousand Guineas and One Thousand Guineas at the Curragh.

May.	Last week: Royal Ulster Society's show at Balmoral, Belfast.
June.	1 June to 15 August: Pilgrimages to St. Patrick's Purgatory, Lough Derg.
	Curragh Races at Galway.
	Last week: Irish Derby at the Curragh; Cork Summer Show.
July.	First week: Pilgrimage to St. Brigid's Shrine at Faughart, Co. Louth.
	12 July: Anniversary of the Battle of the Boyne on 1 July (O.S.) 1690 (Orangemen's processions and demonstrations in Northern Ireland).
	Irish Oaks at the Curragh.
	Regattas at many centres.
	Killarney Races.
	Last Sunday ('Garland Sunday'): Pilgrimage to Croagh Patrick.
August.	First Monday: Bank Holiday.
	First week: Dublin Horse Show at Ballsbridge.
	Second week: Muintir na Tire Rural Week; Puck Fair at Killorglin (3 days).
	12 August: Celebration of the Relief of Derry (in Northern Ireland).
	15 August: Pilgrimage to Our Lady's Island, Wexford.
	Galway Races.
	Third week: Tramore Races.
	Connemara Pony Show at some centre in West Galway.
September.	1 September: Grouse, duck, snipe, and woodcock shooting begins.
	First Sunday: All-Ireland Final Hurling at Dublin.
	9 September: Pattern (p. 48) at Clonmacnoise.
	Oyster Festival at Galway.
	Dublin Theatre Festival.
	Waterford Festival (light opera).
	Cork Festival (films).

September.	Third week: Irish St. Leger at the Curragh.
	Fourth Sunday: All-Ireland Final Gaelic Football at Dublin.
October.	Coursing and Rugby football seasons open.
	Wexford Festival (music and the arts).
	Irish Cambridgeshire at the Curragh.
	Feile an Oireachtais, Dublin.
	Day after 1st Saturday: Summer time ends.
November.	Hunting season opens.
	11 November: Armistice Day, celebrated in Northern Ireland, and by some sections of the community in Eire.
	Irish Cesarewitch at the Curragh.
December.	12 December: Celebration at Derry of the Shutting of the Gates by the Apprentices in 1688.
	26 December: Boxing Day (St. Stephen's Day). Dog Show at Ballsbridge.
	31 December: New Year's Eve celebrations.

BIBLIOGRAPHY

Out of the large field of literature dealing with various aspects of Irish life, the following works, mostly published in recent years, have been selected as most suitable for the general reader.

The classic descriptions of travelling in Ireland are the *Topographia Hibernica* of Giraldus Cambrensis, who visited Ireland in 1184, Richard Stanyhurst's *Description of Ireland*, contributed to Holinshed's *Chronicles* (1577), the *Tour in Ireland* of Arthur Young, who was agent to Lord Kingsborough in Co. Cork in 1777–9, and Thackeray's amusing *Irish Sketch-Book*, the result of his 1842 tour.

A History of Ireland, by Edmund Curtis (Methuen, 1950); *Ireland under the Normans, 1169–1333*, by G. H. Orpen (4 vols., London, 1911–20); *A History of Ireland under the Union, 1801–1922*, by P. S. O'Hegarty (Methuen, 1951); *Ireland from the Flight of the Earls to Grattan's Parliament, 1607–1782*, *Ireland from Grattan's Parliament to the Great Famine, 1783–1850*, and *Ireland from the Great Famine to the Treaty, 1851–1921*, a documentary record edited by James Carty (C. J. Fallon, Dublin, 1949); *Essays in British and Irish History*, edited by H. A. Cronne, etc. (Muller, 1949); *A Short History of Ireland*, by J. C. Beckett (Hutchinson, 1951); *County and Town in Ireland under the Georges*, by Constantia Maxwell (Dundalgan Press, Dundalk, 1950); *The History of Partition, 1912–1925*, by D. Gwynn (Browne & Nolan, Dublin, 1950); *The Irish*, by S. O'Faolain (Penguin, 1948); *Facts about Ireland* (Department of External Affairs, Dublin, 1963); *The Stranger in Ireland*, by Constantia Maxwell (Cape, 1954).

The Irish Tangle, by Shane Leslie (Macdonald, 1946); *Anglo-Irish Relations*, by Hugh Shearman (Faber, 1948); *Ireland Her Own*, by T. A. Jackson (Cobbett Press, 1949); *Irish Nationalism and British Democracy* (Methuen, 1951); *Peace by Ordeal*, by Frank Pakenham (Mercier Press, 1951);

The Irish Republic, by Dorothy Macardle (Irish Press, 1951).

The Economic History of Ireland, by G. O'Brien (3 vols., 1919–21); *History of the Church of Ireland*, by W. A. Philips (3 vols., London, 1933–4); *Public Administration of Ireland*, edited by F. C. King (2 vols., Alec Thom, Dublin, 1949).

The Archaeology of Ireland, by R. A. S. Macalister (Methuen, 1949); *Prehistoric Man in Ireland*, by Cecil P. Martin (Macmillan, 1935); *Irish Stone Age*, by H. L. Movius (Cambridge, 1942); *Antiquities of the Irish Countryside*, by S. P. O'Riordan (Methuen, 1953); *Irish Castles and Castellated Houses*, by H. G. Leask (Dundalgan Press, Dundalk, 1942); *Irish Churches and Monastic Buildings*, in two volumes (Dundalgan Press, Dundalk, 1955); *The Cathedrals of the Church of Ireland*, by J. G. F. Day and H. E. Patton (S.P.C.K., 1932).

Ireland: Its Physical, Historical, Social, and Economic Geography, by T. W. Freeman (Methuen, 1965); *Introduction to the Geology of Ireland*, by J. Kaye Charlesworth (Oliver & Boyd, 1951); *The Mountains of Ireland*, by D. D. C. Pechin Mould (Batsford, 1955).

Natural History of Ireland: Its Flora and Fauna, by R. Lloyd Praeger (Collins, 1950); *Some Irish Naturalists*, by R. Lloyd Praeger (Dundalgan Press, Dundalk, 1950); *The Botanist in Ireland*, by R. Lloyd Praeger (Hodges, Figgis & Co., Dublin, 1935); *An Irish Flora*, by D. A. Webb (Dundalgan Press, Dundalk, 1943); *The Birds of Ireland* (Oliver & Boyd, 1954).

Irish Art in the Early-Christian Period, by Françoise Henry (Methuen, 1947); *Early Irish Literature: An Introduction to the Songs and Legends of Ancient Ireland*, by M. Dillon (Cambridge, 1949); *A Thousand Years of Irish Poetry*, edited by K. Hoagland (Falcon Press, 1947); *The Course of Irish Verse*, by R. Farren (Sheed & Ward, 1947); *Irish Poets of the XIXth Century*, edited by G. Taylor (Routledge, 1951); *The Irish Theatre*, by P. Kavanagh (Kerryman, Tralee, 1946); *The Irish Dramatic Movement*, by V. E. Fermor (Methuen, 1946).

An Irish Panorama, by Kees van Hoek (Longmans,

1946); *The Irish Tradition*, by Robin Flower (Oxford, 1947); *The Face of Ireland*, by Michael Floyd (Batsford, 1948); *The Face and Mind of Ireland*, by A. Ussher (Gollancz, 1949); *Irish Heritage: The Landscape, the People, and their Work*, by E. Estyn Evans (Dundalgan Press, Dundalk, 1942); *The Charm of Ireland*, by Stephen Gwynn (Harrap, 1951); *My Ireland*, by Lord Dunsany (Jarrolds, 1950); *This is Ireland*, 5 volumes by Richard Hayward (Barker, 1949–66).

Leinster, Munster, and Connaught, by Frank O'Connor (Hale's County Books, 1950); *Lovely is the Lee*, by Robert Gibbings (Dent, 1949); *Sweet Cork of Thee*, by Robert Gibbings (Dent, 1951); *Where the River Shannon Flows*, by Richard Hayward (Barker, 1950); *Green and Silver* (Irish canals), by L. T. C. Rolt (Allen & Unwin, 1949); *The Islands of Ireland*, by Thomas H. Mason (Batsford, 1950); *Journeys into Muskerry*, by J. C. Coleman (Dundalgan Press, Dundalk, 1950); *In the Kingdom of Kerry*, by Richard Hayward (Dundalgan Press, Dundalk, 1946); *Killarney: Land and Lake*, by D. O'Cahill (Kerryman, Tralee, 1948); *The Corrib Country*, by Richard Hayward (Dundalgan Press, Dundalk, 1943).

The Way that I Went: An Irishman in Ireland, by R. Lloyd Praeger (Methuen, 1947); *Ireland Revisited*, by Charles Graves (Hutchinson, 1949); *Irish Miles*, by Frank O'Connor (Macmillan, 1947); *In Search of Ireland*, by H. V. Morton (Methuen, 24th edition, 1930); *I Follow St. Patrick*, by Oliver St. John Gogarty (Constable, 1950); *An Irish Journey*, by S. O'Faolain (Longmans, 1951).

The Story of Dublin, by D. A. Chart (Dent's Mediæval Towns, 1932); *Dublin under the Georges*, by Constantia Maxwell (Harrap, 1936); *As I Was Going Down Sackville Street*, by Oliver St. John Gogarty (Rich & Cowan, 1939); *The Book of Dublin*, by Eric Whelpton (Rockliff, 1948); *Dublin: A Study in Environment*, by John Harvey (Batsford, 1949).

A History of Northern Ireland, by D. A. Chart (Belfast, 1928); *Rural Life in Northern Ireland*, by John M. Mogey (Oxford, 1947); *In Praise of Ulster*, by Richard Hayward (Mullan, Belfast, 1947); *Ulster and the City of Belfast*, by Richard Hayward (Barker, 1950); *The Land of Ulster,* vol. 1 of the Report of the Land Utilization Survey (Belfast, 1948); *The Official Year Book of Northern Ireland* (H.M.S.O., 1950); *Ulster*, by Hugh Shearman (Hale's County Books, 1950); *The Face of Ulster*, by Denis O'D. Hanna (Batsford, 1951); *Ulster Folklore*, by Jeanne Cooper Foster (H. R. Carter, Belfast, 1951).

Coarse Fishing in Ireland, by C. E. R. Sinclair (Witherby, 1948).

The Blue Guide to Ireland, edited by L. Russell Muirhead (Benn, 1949); *The A.A. Road Book of Ireland*; *Shell Guide to Ireland*, by Lord Killanin and Michael V. Duignan (Ebury Press, 1962).

TOUR I: DUBLIN

HOWTH—MALAHIDE—SWORDS—DUBLIN HILLS—
POWERSCOURT

Map of central Dublin on page 20

Dublin, the capital of the Republic of Ireland, is a city of over 537,000 inhabitants, excluding the suburbs. As Stanyhurst, the sixteenth-century chronicler, wrote:

> The seat of this citie is of all sides pleasant, comfortable, and wholesome. If you would traverse hills, they are not far off. If champaign ground, it lieth of all parts. If you be delited with fresh water, the famous river called the Liffie . . . runneth fast by. If you will take a view of the sea, it is at hand.

In fact, Dublin's site is one of the finest which any of the world's capital cities can boast. It is situated near the mouth of the fast-flowing River Liffey, which divides it into two roughly equal parts, its centre being less than a couple of miles from the sea and the exquisite landscapes of Dublin Bay. The pastures of the Liffey plain provide splendid grazing for cattle and, incidentally, enjoy the lowest rainfall in Ireland. In close proximity on the south rises a great range of rounded hills, and it is said that within six miles of the centre of the city you can hunt the fox, shoot grouse, and catch trout.

Dubh Linn, the 'black pool'—its Gaelic name is Baile Atha Cliath, 'town of the ford of the hurdle'—was founded by the vikings in the ninth century and was never a Gaelic city. The Danes were ousted by the Anglo-Normans under Strongbow in the year 1170. Henry II granted Dublin the 'rights of Bristol,' i.e. free trade within his empire, and thereafter, for seven and a half centuries, it was the seat of the English government of Ireland and the centre of the castle-guarded 'English Pale.' The three burning castles in the city arms refer to acts of retaliation against the marauding hill tribes.

From an architectural standpoint Dublin is an Anglo-

Irish creation of the eighteenth century, the period of its greatest prosperity, when it was one of the leading cities of Europe. Its wonderful series of distinguished public buildings in the classical style earned for it the title of 'the Western Athens,' its claim to which was reinforced by fame as a centre of literature, science, and art. From the Georgian period, too, date many of central Dublin's residential squares and streets (now mostly, alas! abandoned to commerce), with their mansions and rows of private houses in grimy red brick, adorned with elegant doorways and fanlights, wrought-iron lamp supports and balconies, carved mahogany doors and staircases, marble mantelpieces, and ornate plaster ceilings. On the other hand, though it escaped the Industrial Revolution of the nineteenth century and has very few factories, 'dear, dirty Dublin'—'a splendour built on squalor'— was until recent years notorious for its slums and its obtrusive signs of destitution. Drastic clearances of condemned areas, however, have already brought about a great improvement in this respect.

There is a certain Victorian air about Dublin that is very agreeable. Draught horses are still in common use in spite of the ever-growing volume of motor traffic and consequent introduction of traffic lights, one-way-street systems, and the rest. The first signs of the new regime that strike the newcomer are the use of Gaelic for street names and for public and other notices (the English version being mostly added), the green colour of the pillar-boxes, the grey-green army uniforms, the prevalence of betting offices, and the universal procurability of sweepstake tickets.

From the sightseer's point of view, Dublin is a city of simple plan. From O'Connell Bridge the bus services will take you anywhere. Of the two equal parts into which the city is divided by the Liffey, the south side is the more important. College Green, which may be taken as the centre of the city, is bounded on the east by Trinity College and on the north by the Bank of Ireland, with the head offices of the other Irish banks opposite. The Bank is a singularly noble building with a curved portico, erected in 1729–39 to house the Irish Parliament and occupied by

* C

it during the short period (1782–1800) in which it enjoyed, under Grattan's leadership (though a purely Protestant body), a certain measure of independence. This lovely building was designed by Sir Edward Lovet Pearce, a member of the Irish Parliament, and completed by Arthur Dobbs, the Surveyor-General. The east front was added by Gandon (cf. page 72) in 1785, the north colonnade by Robert Parke, 1787–94. The building was bought by the Bank of Ireland (founded 1782) after the Irish Parliament had voted for Union with Great Britain and its own abolition. Francis Johnston adapted the buildings to fit their new role.

The statues of Grattan, in the middle of the Green, and of Burke and Goldsmith ('a perfect study of tender humorous meditation'), flanking the entrance to their old college, are excellent works by Thomas Foley, the Dublin sculptor. On the other hand, that of Thomas Moore, the poet, is a poor production.

Trinity College, Dublin, commonly known as T.C.D., is the University of Dublin, for which Queen Elizabeth granted a charter in 1591, at the instigation of Archdeacon (afterwards Archbishop) Ussher. Opened for the admission of students in 1593, it has always been Protestant in atmosphere and tradition (just as the National University is the Catholic stronghold), though distinguished for its liberalism—Catholics were admitted to degrees in 1793, all religious restrictions were done away with in 1873, and degrees were granted to women in 1904. The students now number about 21,750; in social prestige T.C.D. ranks almost with Oxford and Cambridge.

The quadrangles are freely open to the public. For admission to the interiors of the buildings (other than the library), apply at the porter's lodge. None of the university buildings is earlier than the eighteenth century. The College Green frontage is a Palladian design of 1752–9. The first part of the quad, a wide expanse of cobble-stones, is called Parliament Square, because the funds for the erection of the entrance block were voted by the Irish Parliament. The campanile in the centre was built in 1853. On the right is the theatre, or examination hall (by Sir William Chambers, 1787), with a war memorial in the form of a hall of honour beyond it (over the entrance, *NIKH*, i.e. victory). On the left is the chapel (1789), similar in design to the theatre, and beyond it, set back a little, is the dining hall (1765), designed by a German architect named Richard Cassels (Cassel or Castle) and containing portraits of famous alumni of the college.

On the right of Library Square, the turfed part of the quad, beyond the Campanile, is the library (1712–32), one of the six great libraries that are entitled to claim a free copy of every work published in the United Kingdom and now containing more than 800,000 volumes. The magnificent hall on the first floor (visitors should ring) is adorned with a series of marble busts of eminent students of the college or ancient philosophers, fifteen of which are by Roubiliac.

Here are exhibited the library's greatest treasures, first and foremost the famous Book of Kells, 'the most beautiful book in the world,' made at the monastery of Kells in the eighth or ninth century. This copy of the Gospels in half-uncial script has marvellously intricate illuminations decorated with scrolls, spirals, trumpets, zoomorphs, etc., in the utmost diversity of design and brilliant colouring. A different page is shown daily, and it is only privileged visitors that are allowed to inspect the whole book. There are 339 pages in all. Some of the work on the illuminated pages is so minute that 185 interlacings to the square inch have been counted.

The language of eulogy is powerless to do justice to this marvellous volume; to the patience of the artist, and to his absolute accuracy. Never a fault has been detected among the millions of crossings in the knot-work; never a broken or a spluttering line.—MACALISTER.

Note also the ancient Irish harp (*c.* 1400), with the O'Neill arms, and the collection of autographs.

Opposite the library are the Graduates' Memorial Buildings (1892), beyond which is a small building housing the University Press (by Cassels, 1734). Among the dignified nineteenth-century buildings in New Square, farther on, are the schools, on the right, by Woodward & Deane (1854–5), with well-executed stone carvings of flowers and foliage on the exterior stringcourses. Beyond this stretches the spacious College Park, with the students' playing fields, and the Science and Medical blocks. The series of views within the grounds is delightful.

Grafton Street, with some of Dublin's smartest shops (on the left, an entrance to Jammet's restaurant), runs south from the main entrance of T.C.D. to St. Stephen's Green, a pleasant little park, 27 acres in area, surrounded by stately houses of the eighteenth century (now mostly used as offices). Among the monuments in its central portion are busts of J. C. Mangan, poet of the Young Ireland movement, Countess Markievicz (Constance Gore-Booth), who was a major in the Irish Citizen Army, and Thomas M. Kettle (a fine work by A. G. Power), the most eloquent speaker and writer of his time, who fell in Flanders in 1916.

In Earlsfort Terrace, near the south-east corner of St. Stephen's Green, is University College, Dublin (3,200 students). Together with the University Colleges of Cork and Galway it constitutes the National University of Ireland, which was founded in 1909 as the successor of the Royal University (an examining body only). The college, housed in the exhibition building of 1865, skilfully adapted for the purpose, has absorbed the not very successful Catholic University of Dublin, founded in 1854 with Newman as its first rector. His beautiful little university church faces St. Stephen's Green. In Merrion Row, near the north-east corner of the Green, is a Huguenot cemetery, dating from 1693. If you turn right at the far end of Earlsfort Terrace, you come to a cross-street called Synge Street, No. 33 in which was Bernard Shaw's birthplace.

St. Stephen's Green and College Park are united by Dawson Street and Kildare Street. In the former, on the right-hand side, are the Mansion House, residence of the Lord Mayor of Dublin since 1715, the premises (No. 19) of the Royal Irish Academy, a society founded in 1786 for the encouragement of science and learning, and the Royal Hibernian Hotel. At the corner of Kildare Street is the Shelbourne, Dublin's premier hotel, and on the right, farther up, is a courtyard bounded on the right by the National Museum, on the left by the National Library—scholarly Italian designs by Sir Thomas Deane, 1884–90—and at the back by Leinster House. The last-named, at present the meeting-place of the Irish Parliament—Senate and Dáil (i.e. Chamber of Deputies)—was built about the year 1745 as a town house for the Duke of Leinster, from the plans of Cassels. From 1815 to 1922 it was occupied by the Royal Dublin Society, an institution to which Dublin and indeed all Ireland owes so much. Founded in 1731 for the improvement of husbandry, manufactures, and other useful arts and sciences, it now has its premises (where excellent concerts and lectures are given) at Ballsbridge, outside the city, by the ground on which the famous horse show is held under the society's auspices in the first week of August (Tuesday to Saturday).

A visit to the National Museum is essential for anybody at all interested in the history and antiquities of Ireland, for here are displayed, besides prehistoric (i.e. pre-Gaelic) antiquities, an unrivalled collection of objects showing the pitch of perfection attained by Irish art and culture in the Bronze Age and the early Christian period—gold ornaments, torques, lunulae or neck-plates, penannular rings, bracelets, jewelled shrines and crosiers, cups and vases, swords, axes, and other weapons, household utensils, etc. The most famous individual specimens are the Ardagh Chalice, composed of 354 pieces (ninth or tenth century), the shrine of St. Patrick's bell, with a swastika pattern on the back (c. 1100; the bell itself, which was buried with the saint, is the oldest Irish metal-work in existence), the Tara and Dalriada brooches (the former, of the late seventh century, the oldest of the great Irish works of art; the latter probably eleventh-century), the Cross of Cong, head of a processional cross (between 1123 and 1136), and the Glenisheen collar (700 B.C.), weighing three-quarters of a pound of virgin gold. Note also the series of casts of 'high crosses,' collected here for comparison, the 'curraghs,' or ancient canoes, the 'Ogham' stones, inscribed with a notch alphabet, and the finds from 'crannogs,' or lake dwellings. One room is devoted to mementoes of the 'troubles' of 1916–23. The zoological section of the museum is excellent also (entrance in Merrion Street).

Prominent among the monuments and statues on Leinster Lawn, at the back of Leinster House, adjoining

Merrion Square, is the cenotaph commemorating the heroes of the revolution, particularly Arthur Griffith, the first president of the Dáil, Michael Collins, and Kevin O'Higgins (the last two murdered by anti-treaty irregulars).

Merrion Square, like Fitzwilliam Square, is lined with houses of the late eighteenth century (largely occupied by doctors and lawyers). Oscar Wilde spent his early years at No. 1 (birthplace 21 Westland Row). On the south side of the lawn is a block of government offices, designed by Sir Aston Webb, opposite which is Mornington House (24 Upper Merrion Street), birthplace of the Duke of Wellington, now occupied by the Irish Land Commission. On the north side is the National Gallery of Ireland (entrance in Merrion Square, adjoining the Leinster Lawn), one of the best of the smaller art collections of Europe. It is strong in late Italian and Dutch masters, early English water-colours, and views of Old Dublin, and part of the building is devoted to a National Portrait Gallery. Among the artists represented here are Titian, Moroni, Fra Angelico, Michelangelo (Holy Family), and El Greco (St. Francis); Rembrandt (study of a girl), and Cuyp; Romney, Hoppner, Constable, and Gainsborough; eighty-four canvases of the Barbizon and other schools, presented by Sir Chester Beatty in 1950; Sargent (President Wilson), John (Kuno Meyer, the Gaelic scholar), Orpen (self-portrait), J. B. Yeats (George Moore), and J. E. Blanche (James Joyce).

From the north-west corner of Merrion Square, Clare Street and its continuations bring you back to College Green, whence you keep straight on up Dame Street, with its oyster saloons.

Palace Street, near the top, on the left, forms the entrance to Dublin Castle, which was built *c.* 1200–20 by order of King John, together with the city walls (long since demolished). It occupies the end of a ridge parallel with the river—the only high ground in the city. Formerly the official seat of the Lord Lieutenant and an emblem of the hated yoke (the Upper Castle Yard is the 'Devil's Half-Acre'), it is now occupied by various Government offices. Except for a part of the curtain wall and two round towers—the Bermingham Tower, which was partly rebuilt in 1777 and used to be the state prison, and the Record Tower (adjoining the chapel), where the records are kept—all the castle buildings, mostly grouped around two courts, date from the eighteenth or nineteenth century. The state apartments are shown by a guide at 10, 12, and 3. The throne room has a curved ceiling, a canopied throne, and medallions by Angelica Kaufmann. St. Patrick's Hall was formerly used for the investitures of the Knights of St. Patrick. The Chapel Royal, now renamed the Church of the Most Holy Trinity, was built by Francis Johnston in 1814 and is adorned on the outside with ninety heads of saints and famous Irishmen. The Genealogical Office, under the clock-tower (Bedford Tower) by the castle gate, is a handsome building of 1759, originally the deanery of the Chapel Royal. It has a small heraldic museum, open free.

The City Hall, at the top of Dame Street, on the left, beyond Palace Street, has occupied since 1852 the Royal Exchange, a handsome building of 1769-79, designed by Thomas Cooley, who started life as a carpenter. The circular hall in the interior should be glanced at. The municipal buildings opposite show another pleasing eighteenth-century design, by Thomas Ivory. Lord Edward Street (named after Lord Edward Fitzgerald, the Irish rebel, who died of wounds received at his arrest in 1798) goes on to Christ Church, the senior of the city's two Protestant cathedrals—Dublin is peculiar in possessing two cathedrals of the same denomination.

Founded *c.* 1038 by Sigtryg Silkbeard, Christ Church, the cathedral of the archbishopric of Dublin and Glendalough, is unique among British cathedrals in being of Danish origin. Of the original church the great crypt with its crude arches is a doubtful survival. Strongbow (Richard de Clare, Earl of Pembroke) rebuilt the church after 1172, and of his work the beautiful transepts, in the Transitional style, are relics. The interior of the cathedral is extraordinarily dark. The nave (*c.* 1230) is considered to be the finest specimen of Gothic architecture in Ireland; only the north side, which leans two feet out of the perpendicular, is original, the south side being a copy by George E. Street, R.A., who restored the whole cathedral in 1871-8 at the expense of Henry Roe, the distiller. Note the arrangement of the clerestory and the triforium in triplets within a single arch. The choir and its chapels, likewise rebuilt, are in the fourteenth-century style. Lambert Simnel, the pretender, was crowned here in 1487. On the south side of the nave is a tomb which passes for that of Strongbow, but though old it is not Strongbow's, for the arms on the shield are those of FitzOsbert; the truncated effigy by its side (really that of a woman) is supposed to represent Strongbow's son, whom his father is said to have cut in halves for showing cowardice in the field. Note also the fine monument of the nineteenth Earl of Kildare (Sir Henry Cheere sc., 1743) in the south transept, an ancient memorial tablet to the builder of the cathedral (1170–5) in the adjoining chapel, and, in the south-east chapel (St. Laud's), a metal case said, without evidence, to contain the heart of St. Laurence O'Toole (d. 1180), the first Irish archbishop of Dublin and the last Irishman to occupy the see until after the Reformation. Visitors to the east end of the cathedral are expected to put a donation in the box. For admission to the crypt, the services of the verger are necessary. Stored here are a set of stocks, statues of James II and Charles II from the old Tholsel (city hall), the tabernacle and candlesticks used when Mass was celebrated in the cathedral for the visit of James II, etc. A covered bridge connects Christ Church with the modern Synod House.

Now turn left down Nicholas Street, through a poor quarter, to see St. Patrick's Cathedral, the national cathedral of the Protestant Church of Ireland, with its canons chosen from all the dioceses. It boasts the finest collection of sepulchral monuments in the country—the Westminster Abbey of the Anglo-Protestant element. John Comyn and Henry de Londres, the first Anglo-Norman archbishops, raised it to the rank of cathedral as a counterblast to Christ Church, the Celto-Danish priory. The present building, which is the largest church in Ireland, noteworthy for symmetry and beautiful proportions, was dedicated in 1191 and mostly dates from the first half of the thirteenth century. Its Early English architecture resembles that of Salisbury Cathedral. The cathedral was drastically restored in 1864–9 by Sir Thomas Drew, at the expense of the Guinness family. The massive tower was built in 1381, and the spire (250 feet high) added in 1749. There is a fine peal of bells. The entrance to the cathedral is on the south side. The nave is hung with banners. At the west end is the Boyle family monument, accounted in its day a world's wonder. It is an enormous, brilliantly coloured erection with sixteen figures, and was set up by the 'Great' Earl of Cork, that remarkable adventurer who, as plain Richard Boyle, landed in Ireland in 1588 with £28 in his pocket and became the richest landowner in the country. Strafford, Lord Deputy of Ireland, had the monument moved in 1633 from its original position in the choir; Cork's implacable enmity, thereby incurred, was one of the causes of his eventual impeachment and execution.

Swift's tenure of the deanery of St. Patrick's from 1713 to 1745 is one of the most famous epochs in its history. Here he wrote the *Drapier's Letters*, denouncing English injustice to Ireland. A brass floor-plate at the base of the column next to the Boyle monument marks the graves of Swift and his beloved 'Stella' (Esther Johnson, to whom he was perhaps secretly married), and in the aisle behind it is a striking bust of the Dean by Cunningham, with his self-composed Latin epitaph ('He lies where savage indignation can rend his heart no more. Go, traveller, and imitate, if you can, one who did a man's part in the defence of liberty'). His epitaph for Stella is on the other side of the doorway.

In the north aisle note, at the west end, the bust of J. P. Curran, judge, orator, and patriot, and, at the east end, the mural memorial to the novelist Samuel Lover. In the south transept, leaning against a pillar, is an old door with a hole through which the Earls of Kildare and Ormonde shook hands in token of reconciliation (1492). A printed account of the picturesque incident is at the visitor's service.

The choir was the chapel of the Most Illustrious Order of St. Patrick, founded in 1783 (investitures now take place in Westminster Abbey), and above the stalls are the banners, helmets, and swords of the knights. Among the many wall tablets in the south choir aisle, note the four sixteenth-century brasses. The Lady Chapel at the east end dates from *c.* 1270 and is a very beautiful, though heavily restored, structure. In the north choir aisle is a wall tablet marking the grave of the Duke of Schomberg, William III's general, who fell at the Boyne in 1690. The Latin epitaph by Swift—'The fame of his valour was more effective with strangers than consanguinity with his kinsmen'—refers to his German relatives' reluctance to subscribe for a monument. In the north transept there is a Burma war memorial, showing in amusing fashion the storming of the Shwe Dagon in 1852.

To the south-east of the cathedral, in Patrick's Close, is Marsh's Library of 25,000 theological books, founded by Archbishop Marsh in 1707, with its fittings and internal arrangements utterly unchanged for over two centuries. Dean Swift used to read in this delightful survival of Old Dublin. Visitors are admitted from 11 to 2 and 3 to 4.30; on Thursdays and Saturdays, 10.30 to 12.30. The Deanery of St. Patrick's is a gloomy eighteenth-century house opposite the library, facing Upper Kevin Street.

To continue the survey of Dublin with a look at the northern half of the city you cross O'Connell Bridge (1794, rebuilt 1880), not far from College Green. This, the principal bridge over the Liffey, is wider than it is long. The view from the bridge is not unlike that along the quays of Paris. (Wellington Bridge, seen upstream, is a slim iron footbridge erected in 1816 and sometimes known as the 'Rialto.') O'Connell Bridge is continued by O'Connell Street (formerly Sackville Street), one of the finest and widest thoroughfares (150 feet) in Europe; the whole east side has been rebuilt since the 'troubles' in a sort of Regent Street style. Down the middle of the street, which is divided into Lower and Upper O'Connell Street, is a series of monuments: Daniel O'Connell himself, the Liberator, a fine monument by Foley, begun in 1864 and unveiled in 1882; Smith O'Brien (d. 1864), leader of the Young Ireland party, and Sir John Gray (d. 1875), founder of Dublin's modern water supply, both by Sir Thomas Farrell; Father Mathew (d. 1856), the apostle of total abstinence, by Mary Redmond (1892); and the Parnell obelisk, with a statue by Augustus Saint-Gaudens, the American sculptor (1911). The Nelson Pillar, 134 feet high, designed by William Wilkins (1808), was blown up in March 1966.

Half-way up on the left-hand side is the General Post Office, built in 1814–18 from the designs of Francis Johnston. It has been rebuilt since the Easter rising of 1916, when it served as the headquarters of the rebels under Patrick Pearse and James Connolly (both of whom were executed), and was set on fire by shells. On the right-hand side of Upper O'Connell Street is the Irish Tourist Office (No. 14), which, apart from the usual supply of free folders, has a good collection of books about Ireland for sale. Higher up is the smart Gresham Hotel, and at the top of the street is the Rotunda, a curious combination of maternity hospital (by Cassels, 1751–7) and assembly rooms (by Johnston, 1755)—it was hoped that the profits on the latter would cover the expenses of the former. The maternity hospital, founded in 1745, is claimed as the first of its kind in the British dominions. The assembly rooms now form the Gate Theatre. Behind the Rotunda lies Parnell Square, at the back of which is Charlemont House, built by Sir William Chambers in 1773 as the town house of the Earls of Charlemont and now forming a beautiful setting for the Municipal Gallery of Modern Art, an excellent collection of Irish, British, and French paintings, including portraits of Irish patriots. One room is devoted to works by Sir John Lavery. The thirty-nine pictures bequeathed to the gallery by Sir Hugh Lane (who perished in the *Lusitania*), but retained by the National Gallery in London owing to the invalidity of the codicil, are shown partly here and partly in London, with a change-over every five years. There is a sculpture gallery by the entrance. The King's Inns, in Henrietta Street, seven minutes' walk away (by way of Granby, Dorset, and Bolton Streets), are Dublin's inns of court and were built by Gandon (1795–9).

Returning down O'Connell Street, you pass, on the left, Cathedral Street, which leads to the pro-cathedral of the Catholic archbishopric of Dublin, an impressive structure in the Doric style (1816–25). It has a reputation for its Gregorian music. Lower Abbey Street (commemorating St. Mary's Abbey, founded by the Danes, *c.* 948), on the

same side of O'Connell Street, lower down, leads to the
Abbey Theatre, which was built by Lady Gregory in 1904
for the Irish National Players, and, with State aid, became
famous through the plays of W. B. Yeats, J. M. Synge,
Sean O'Casey, Lennox Robinson, etc. Burned down in
1951, it was reopened in 1966 (architect, Michael Scott).

On this side of O'Connell Bridge, turn left along Eden
Quay and pass under the railway bridge to see the Customs
House, which is generally considered Dublin's finest build-
ing, unsurpassed of its kind and period. It was built in
1781–91 by James Gandon, a pupil of Sir William Chambers.
It measures 375 feet in river frontage and 205 feet in depth.
Fired by the rebels in May 1921, it has been faithfully
reconstructed and now houses various Government offices.
Close by are some of Dublin's new buildings: Bus Terminal,
by Michael Scott, and the skyscraping Liberty Hall.

Return to O'Connell Bridge and keep straight on along
the quays to see the Four Courts (with a lantern dome),
which, though begun by Cooley in 1784, is Gandon's second
masterpiece (1796–1800), with a frontage of 450 feet. It
houses the High Court of Justice, the original four courts
being the Exchequer, Common Pleas, King's Bench, and
Chancery. Bombarded in June 1922, after being held for
over two months by the anti-treaty irregulars under Rory
O'Connor, it has likewise been restored. In Church Street,
behind it, is St. Michan's Church, the vaults of which are
visited by lovers of the macabre for the sake of the mum-
mified bodies they contain. Behind the church is Jame-
son's whisky distillery, and beyond this again a great open
space called Smithfield, an interesting sight on Tuesdays
and Fridays when the hay market is in progress.

Continuing along the quays, we pass Burke's birthplace,
12 Arran Quay, and reach the main entrance to Phoenix
Park, one of the finest city parks in Europe, 1,750 acres
in area. It has charming dells, but is mostly a flat
expanse, partly used as playing fields. Its name is
thought to be derived from 'fionn uisge,' clear water. The
main drive through the park is 2½ miles long. On the right
of the entrance are the police headquarters, formerly the
Military Infirmary, one of Gandon's works (1786–8), and
the People's Gardens, with brilliant flower beds. On the

left is the Wellington Memorial, a huge obelisk 205 feet high, designed by Sir Robert Smirke, 1817, and commonly known as the 'Big Milestone.' Farther on, to the right, is the Zoo, famous for its success in lion breeding. The Viceregal Lodge, an unpretentious building, is now the official residence of the President of the Irish Republic. There is a picturesque polo ground just beyond it; in the main drive, opposite, Lord Frederick Cavendish, the Chief Secretary, and Thomas Burke, Permanent Under-Secretary, were assassinated by the 'Invincibles' in 1882. Farther on, to the left, is the United States Embassy, formerly the Chief Secretary's Lodge. Opposite the entrance to this, in the centre of the park, is the Phoenix Column, which was erected by Lord Chesterfield during his term of office as viceroy, 1747. Herds of deer wander over the western half of the park.

If you leave the park by the Island Bridge Gate (not far from the Obelisk), turn left, and cross the Liffey by Island Bridge, you will find the entrance to the War Memorial Park about a hundred yards beyond it on the right. The National War Memorial for 1914–18, opened in 1938, consists of a great formal Garden of Remembrance on the bank of the river, with stone retaining walls, terraces, fountains, and a great stone cross, the whole designed by Sir Edwin Lutyens. The roll of honour comprises 52,000 names.

On regaining the main entrance to Phoenix Park, bear right and cross the Liffey by King's Bridge, passing the very decorative King's Bridge Station (1844), to see what you can of Steevens's Hospital (1733) and, to the right, at the corner of Bow Lane, St. Patrick's Hospital, the first lunatic asylum in Ireland, founded by Dean Swift in 1725.

> He gave the little wealth he had
> To build a house for fools and mad,
> And showed by one satiric touch,
> No nation wanted it so much.

Bow Lane leads to Kilmainham Royal Hospital for veteran soldiers, a companion institution to Chelsea Hospital in London and founded by the Duke of Ormonde. It was closed in 1927 and is disused at present. It is an outstandingly beautiful building, erected in 1680–4 from designs ascribed

to Sir Christopher Wren but in reality by Sir William
Robinson, the Surveyor-General. The Great Hall, 100
feet by 50 feet, contains portraits of sovereigns and states-
men, regimental flags, military tokens, weapons, and
armour. The Chapel has old stained glass, oak carvings
and a stucco ceiling. Kilmainham Jail, of unhappy
memory, is now in use as a museum. In James's Street,
on the way back to the city centre, is Guinness's brewery,
which was founded in 1759 and is said to be the largest in
Europe. Visitors are admitted on work-days, any time
between 11 and 3, and many of them find it the most
enjoyable of all Dublin's sights.

Dublin's Botanic Gardens, 40 acres in area and of
remarkable beauty and interest, are at Glasnevin, two
miles north, reached by bus from the G.P.O. (If motoring, start off from the Four Courts by Church Street
and bear left past Broadstone Station, then bear right.)
Most of the Irish patriots (Curran, O'Connell, Parnell,
Griffiths, Casement, Collins, etc.) are buried in Glasnevin
Cemetery, which is a mile away from the gardens.

Howth and Malahide are favoured seaside resorts,
situated to the north-east of Dublin and well served
by buses and trains. A visit to them is not, however,
of first-class importance for tourists in a hurry. The
main road to Howth (L 86, 9 miles), leaving Dublin by
way of the G.P.O., Earl Street North, Talbot Street, and
Amiens Street, runs inland. On the left is the suburb of
Marino, built on the Earl of Charlemont's estate, but
preserving the famous 'Casino' built by Sir William
Chambers in 1771, a miniature masterpiece of stately and
beautifully detailed architecture. The more interesting
shore road, with a view of Dublin Bay and its vast expanses
of mud at low tide, then diverges to the right via Clontarf,
where Brian Boru, the first real king of all Ireland, decisively
defeated the Danes on Good Friday, 1014, but at the cost
of his own life and those of his sons, Murrough and Turlough. At Dollymount are the first-class links of the
Royal Dublin Golf Club. New streets of bungalows and
villas now stretch nearly all the way to Howth.

Howth (pronounced 'Hoathe'), with a large harbour,
crowded with herring boats in July, is a residential suburb

of Dublin. It lies on the north shore of the Hill of Howth, a rocky peninsula (Howth is the Norse Hoved, 'head') forming a detached outcrop of the Dublin Hills. St. Mary's Church dates from 1235 and contains the fine altar-tomb of Christopher St. Lawrence, Lord of Howth (1430). Howth Castle, seat of the Earls of Howth until the title became extinct in 1909, has gardens that are noted for their rhododendrons and azaleas, while the park contains a dolmen and Corr Castle, a tall, square building of the sixteenth century. The demesne is open to the public on Sunday and bank holiday afternoons from May to August. The Howth Peninsula, covered with heather, gorse, and bracken, rises to a height of 560 feet, and a grand walk or drive may be taken round it, past the tiny oratory of St. Fintan. Building activity, however, is in full swing hereabouts. About a mile off the coast is Ireland's Eye (i.e. 'Eria's island'), a craggy grey rock, and farther off is the green Lambay ('Lamb Island'), a bird sanctuary, haunt of the peregrine falcon and breeding place of the Manx shearwater.

The coast between Howth and Malahide is fringed with sand dunes, and the road between the two places (10 miles) passes a side turning for Portmarnock, with the 'Velvet Strand' and perhaps the finest golf links in Ireland. *Malahide* is a quiet seaside place, with the castle of Lord Talbot de Malahide, which has been held by the family since 1174. Beside the castle are the remains of an 'abbey,' with the tomb of Maud Plunkett, 'maid, wife, and widow in one day.'

The direct road from Malahide back to Dublin passes the quaint St. Doulagh's Church (Protestant), a unique structure with detached cells and an overcroft, combining Gothic forms of the late thirteenth century with the high-pitched stone slab roofs (now mostly slate) of the primitive Irish churches. By the entrance is a roadside cross, and there is an octagonal well-house in the field on the right. The church is open only on Saturday afternoons. At other times the permission of the Rector of Malahide must to obtained in advance.

Or you may return to Dublin via *Swords*, 3 miles west of Malahide. This important foundation of St. Columba's gets its name from the holy well (sórd). Of the ancient abbey, over which St. Finian the Leper was the first to preside, the sole survivals are the Round Tower (74 feet high), of primitive type, with its conical cap restored, and the fourteenth-century tower of the Abbey Church, now standing near the parish church—the whole forming a most picturesque group. At the north end of the village street are the thirteenth-century ruins of the Archbishop's Palace, with crenellated walls strengthened by square towers, a great gateway, a chapel, and various halls.

Between Swords and Dublin, at Collinstown, is the Dublin Airport, 5½ miles from the centre of the city.

The following drive, a round of about 35 miles, will give some idea of the *Dublin Hills,* a great range of rounded granite summits, with wildly magnificent heather-clad moors and miles of melancholy peat-bog, but devoid of peaks or crags. The beauty of the wooded glens is justly famed. Starting from Christchurch Cathedral, the route runs due south through dismal suburbs, via Rathmines, Terenure, Rathfarnham, and Whitechurch (bus service thus far). No. 41 Brighton Square, in Rathgar, adjoining Rathmines, was the birthplace of James Joyce. St. Enda's College at Whitechurch was once 'The Hermitage,' home of J. P. Curran and scene of the courtship of Robert Emmet (executed for his share in the rising of 1803) and Sarah Curran.

She is far from the land where her young hero sleeps.

The Military Road, steep and narrow, constructed after the rebellion of 1798, then ascends into the hills, leaving Mount Venus and Killakee (1,761 feet) on the left, while farther on Kippure (2,473 feet), the highest mountain in Co. Dublin, rises on the right.

At Glencree Reformatory, 12½ miles from Dublin, we turn sharp left by the rather rough road down lovely Glencree, with a superb view of the Sugarloaf, to Enniskerry, which lies 6 miles farther on, in the midst of charming scenery. Turn right, then right again, for *Powerscourt* (named from the De la Poer family), formerly the castle of the O'Tooles and splendid seat of Viscount

Powerscourt. The demesne (1,400 acres), with its exotic conifers, araucarias, etc., is inexpressibly beautiful. (Admission 1s., car 5s., including passengers. If you object to the magnitude of the admission fee, you can leave your car at the Deer Park Gate and walk thence to the waterfall in fifteen minutes). The drive, 4 miles long, leads south past the front of the house, and eventually (signposts) through the Deer Park Glen, in view of Djouce Mountain (2,384 feet) and War Hill (2,250 feet). It ends at the filmy and exquisitely graceful Powerscourt Waterfall, where the River Dargle is precipitated obliquely over a cliff, 400 feet high.

On the way back, turn right on leaving the Deer Park Gate, and return towards Enniskerry by the public road, which crosses the Dargle at Tinnahinch Bridge, another beauty-spot. Beyond this, and just short of the main gates of Powerscourt, is a notice, 'Dargle West Gate.' Thence you should walk down the Dargle Glen, two miles long, visiting the Lovers' Leap and the View Rock. The main road from the Enniskerry back to Dublin, a bus route, 13 miles, passes through the wild rocky defile known as the Scalp. On the left rise Two Rock Mountain (1,699 feet) and Three Rock Mountain (1,479 feet), which command the best general view of Dublin.

A good starting point for the exploration of the beautiful Wicklow Mountains, of weathered granite and heather and attaining 2,500–3,000 feet above sea-level, is Blessington, a pretty village with an inn, 25 miles south-west of Dublin (keep right at Terenure). In the vicinity lies the Pollaphuca Reservoir, 83 square miles in area, created in 1938 by damming the valleys of the upper Liffey and its tributary, the King's River. It supplies Dublin with water and also provides water-power for two electricity generating stations. Below the 100-foot dam is the Waterfall, where the Liffey falls 150 feet in a succession of cataracts.

Other places of interest in the vicinity of Dublin are mentioned at the beginning of Tour II, at the end of Tour X, and at the beginning and end of Tour XI.

TOUR II: DUBLIN TO WATERFORD

DUN LAOGHAIRE—BRAY—GLENDALOUGH—VALE OF AVOCA—
ARKLOW — WICKLOW — FERNS — ENNISCORTHY — WEXFORD
—ROSSLARE—NEW ROSS—JERPOINT ABBEY—KILKENNY—
WATERFORD—TRAMORE.

Total distance by road: about 275 miles.

THE main road and railway from Dublin to Waterford run
a long way inland, via Carlow, but we choose a route
nearer the coast on account of its greater scenic and
historical interest. The whole of this tour may be
accomplished by bus or train, or by a judicious combination
of both.

There is a variety of roads to choose from. To see
something of Dublin's seaside resorts you should select
the coastal route (T 44). The main road (T 7) runs direct
to Kilmacanogue via Stillorgan and the outskirts of Bray.
More exciting is the old Military Road (L 94) through the
Wicklow Hills, via Glencree (cf. page 76) and Sally Gap
(1,631 feet), beyond which it deteriorates on the descent
past the Glenmacnass Waterfall to Laragh—29 miles in
all, with gradients up to 1 in 9.

The coastal route (T 44) leaves Dublin by Merrion
Square (north side) and Lower Mount Street, and passes
through Ballsbridge, with the Royal Dublin Society's
rooms and show ground (cf. page 65), Merrion Gates,
where the sea is reached, Booterstown, and Blackrock.
After 7 miles you reach *Dun Laoghaire*, or Dunleary, the
port of entry for most visitors to Ireland. The name of
Kingstown, given in honour of the embarkation of George
IV in 1821, was abolished in 1921. The harbour, covering
250 acres and planned by John Rennie, was begun in
1817 but not finished till 1859. As a seaside resort Dun
Laoghaire wears a somewhat old-fashioned, late-Victorian
air, but great efforts have been made to modernize it
and furbish it up, and anyhow it commands most lovely

views of Dublin Bay. It is also the chief yachting station in Eire, being the headquarters of the Royal Irish and Royal St. George Yacht Clubs. The chief hotel is the Royal Marine. The population is 47,000.

The famous view of the Irish coast as seen from the Holyhead steamer is admirably described in L. A. G. Strong's *The Garden*:

Huge, overshadowing, and vivid, so full of dark massed colour that they seemed closer than the coast beneath their feet, the Dublin Mountains slid swiftly over the satin waters to meet the mailboat. From one dominant peak, of an intense, clear blue, they humped off in rich, uncouth profusion, huddling over the city which lay under their shelter in a silver haze of smoke: guarding it from the wilder, more arrogant peaks of Wicklow to the South. Beneath them, all was dark and vague, till a shaft of sun, falling on the spires of Kingstown, pulled them forth brilliantly from their brooding background, like a cluster of stiff, spiky flowers, rising suddenly above the water. And all the time the land came nearer, nearer. Soon the wide arms of Dublin Bay would open to let in the mailboat: the shapeless hill to the north-east would reach out past her, and take on the remembered contours of the Hill of Howth. Already that dim, insignificant mound near the spires had grown its tiny obelisk. It was Killiney Hill, which, once located, gave a clue to the changed shapes around it. Soon one would see the woods and rocks of Dalkey—and there, marvel, the shaft of sun struck nearer, and caught a low-lying green strip, crowned with a short fat pepper-pot: Dalkey Island!

The road from Dun Laoghaire to Bray, 8 miles, passes Sandycove and Bullock Castle, the latter a modern residence incorporating an excellent example of an ancient peel tower. *Ulysses* begins at the Sandycove martello tower, where Joyce lived for a time with Oliver St. John Gogarty and S. C. Trench, and which is now a memorial museum in his honour. 'Granny's cottage' in *The Garden*, 37 Glasthule Road, still exists.

You then interesect the town of Dalkey (pronounced 'Dawky')—'Torca Cottage' here was Bernard Shaw's home at one period—and take the road to the headland, Sorrento Point, for the sake of the view of the crescent curve and splendid beach of Killiney Bay beyond it. At your feet is Dalkey Island ('Thorn Island'), with its ancient oratory of St. Becnat and its martello tower.

The pure line, the nobility, the ease and grace of that long curving prospect, has never been captured in paint or words. It is one of those which, once seen, remain for ever in the imagination: yet, since no effort of the memory can summon up the whole, but is reduced to a loving enumeration, at each return the view sweeps away, with one perfect gesture of its long curved arm, the piecemeal sketches of memory, and once more confronts the spirit with a panorama beyond its compass to build. Those whose houses look out upon it see it every morning anew. Those who see it for the first time are apt to be silent.

L. A. G. STRONG, *The Garden*.

Killiney itself is a better-class residential place, with a primitive little church, on a gentle rise inland from the station. At Shankill the main road (T 7) is joined.

Bray, Brí Chualann, is Dublin's Brighton. Endowed by nature with a magnificent situation and a hinterland of exceptional beauty, it is the largest seaside resort on the east coast of Ireland, catering for all classes of visitors and greatly smartened up of late years. Its mile-long esplanade, with one-way traffic in part, stretches from the little harbour to the foot of Bray Head, the great feature of the place, a massy hill (793 feet) fantastic of outline and commanding a splendid view from its summit. The favourite excursion from Bray is to the Dargle Glen and Powerscourt (pages 76-7); another is the 15-mile circular drive to Greystones, a select little seaside resort, then inland via Delgany and back by the deep and wooded Glen of the Downs and Kilmacanogue.

The railway from Bray to Wicklow hugs the sea's edge all the way, and the road runs parallel with the coast. For Glendalough, however, you take the inland road (T 61), to the right at Kilmacanogue, which mounts the Rocky Valley (1 in 10), amid fine scenery that is partly impaired by bungalows. You pass between Long Hill (1,073 feet) and the Great Sugarloaf (1,659 feet), which is the best view-point in the district and a simple climb from hereabouts. From its summit you obtain a splendid survey of the sea coast and of the heathery, granite Wicklow Hills, which form the largest area of high ground in Ireland. The Welsh mountains, even, are occasionally to be descried. The road then undulates through wild and lonely upland country, with Djouce Mountain (2,384 feet) rising to the west. Beyond two great reservoirs for Dublin, formed by damming the River Vartry, lies Round-wood, a pleasant spot, with accommodation available. Hence some attractive excursions may be made, e.g. to Lough Dan and Lough Tay, among the hills to the west, the latter of rare beauty, overhung by granite cliffs; while to the south-east the Vartry may be explored as far as the Devil's Glen, a wild defile debouching on an amphitheatre of wooded cliffs. At Annamoe, the next hamlet, the seven-year-old Laurence Sterne fell into the mill-race in 1720, 'whence the miller luckily fished him out alive—fished out little Larry, and along with him Mr. Shandy, Uncle Toby, Doctor Slop, and all that pleasant company, hid away curiously enough in that young heart and brain' (Standish O'Grady, *Flight of the Eagle*).

At Laragh you must bear right (L 107) for the vale of *Glendalough* ('valley of the two lakes'), which is connected with Bray and Dublin by a direct bus service. This deep, rocky glen, steep-sided and sparsely wooded, is one of Ireland's loveliest, apart from the fact that its strange little ruined city is perhaps the most sacred of all Ireland's holy places. As Thackeray wrote: 'Directly you see it, it smiles at you as innocent and friendly as a little child; and once seen, it becomes your friend for ever, and you are always happy when you think of it.'

Glendalough of the 'Seven' Churches was founded in the sixth century by St. Kevin (Coemhgen), the 'fair-born' prince of the house of Leinster, who lived here first as a hermit and afterwards founded an abbey that, in spite of frequent plundering by the Danes, flourished for six centuries and more. Like St. Francis of Assisi, Kevin was a lover of birds and beasts, and it is related that a black-bird once laid her eggs on his hand and that, rather than disturb the bird, he kept his arms extended and his hands open until the eggs were hatched.

The first ancient building you come to, below the road on the left, is the Trinity or Ivy Church, which dates from the early tenth century and has lost its roof and round tower. The most important of the abbey buildings are situated at the back of the Royal Hotel, in an enclosure

('caiseal') which has been used for centuries as a graveyard. Beyond the remains of the gatehouse is the
cathedral, the largest structure in the glen, erected early
in the seventh century, with a chancel of later date. (The
see of Glendalough was united to that of Dublin in the
twelfth century.) Some of the tombstones in the chancel
are very old. On the south side of the cathedral are
St. Kevin's Cross, a monolith of granite, 11 feet in height
(the circle left unpierced), and the so-called Priest's House
(a modern reconstruction), which was really a mortuary.
The Round Tower, 103 feet high by 48 feet in girth at the
base, has its entrance 10 feet from the ground, and at the
top are the usual four window slits facing the points of
the compass. The hole under (but not directly under) the
doorway may have been a spy-hole, or it may have been
used to thrust a pole through in order to upset the assailants'
ladder. The conical cap is a reconstruction, but rebuilt
with the original stones. The most interesting building of
all at Glendalough is 'St. Kevin's Kitchen,' an outstanding
example of the early Irish oratory, with a steeply pitched
slab roof and a round bell-tower added at some subsequent
date. The interior measures 23 feet by 15 feet, and now
contains sculptural fragments. It once had a large overcroft, but the floor has disappeared. The chancel has been
pulled down, but adjoining the nave is an ancient 'eard-
ham,' or sanctuary. St. Mary's Church, some distance
outside the enclosure, across the field to the west of the
Round Tower, is noteworthy for the lintelled door of its
nave, which is composed of admirably hewn and fitted
great stones. It is thought to have been built over the
grave of St. Kevin (d. 618).

Beyond the 'Kitchen,' outside the swing gate, are the
remains of St. Kieran's (?) Chapel, and on the other side
of the bridge over the stream is the Deerstone, of which
legend relates that the saint used to milk a deer into its
hollow to provide nourishment for a foundling child that
he had taken under his protection. Take the path to the
left here for St. Saviour's Church, a good ten minutes' walk
to the east, in a field by the river, in the middle of a group
of fir-trees within a walled enclosure. This is the latest
and one of the most beautiful buildings at Glendalough;

its chancel arch shows elaborate Romanesque work (*c.* 1100) and the east window is curiously carved.

Amid lovely scenery on the south bank of the majestic upper lake, a mile from the hotel and near a ruined farmhouse, is the Rhefeart Church (also spent Reefert, Rifearta, and Righ-fearta), the name of which expresses its use as the burial-place of kings, i.e. the Wicklow chieftains. Two Celtic crosses, and a tomb slab with incised ornament, should be noted. 'St. Kevin's Bed' is a rocky ledge in the cliffs on the same side of the lake, accessible with considerable difficulty from the base of the rocks, to which visitors are taken by boat. It was here that the saint, according to the famous story, pushed the enamoured Kathleen into the lake (or, as an earlier legend has it, whipped her with nettles).

> By that lake whose gloomy shore
> Skylark never warbles o'er,
> Where the cliff hangs high and steep,
> Young Saint Kevin stole to sleep.
> 'Here, at least,' he calmly said,
> 'Woman ne'er shall find my bed.'
> Ah! the good Saint little knew
> What that wily sex can do.
>
> THOMAS MOORE.

Still further west, and likewise accessible only by boat, are the remains of the Church of the Rock (Teampull-na-Skellig), the hillside above which commands the best view of the whole glen.

Taking the road again, you return to Laragh and, bound for Arklow (20 miles), bear right by a switchback road high above the well-wooded Vale of Clara, which is watered by the Avonmore (i.e. Great Avon) and contains plantations of larch, Scots pine, and oak. Clara Bridge, on a side-road to the left, is an admirable view-point: on the north rises Trooperstown Hill (1,419 feet); on the west, Kirikee (1,559 feet).

Rathdrum is a small town, and its station is the nearest to Glendalough (8½ miles). It is worth while digressing to the right here, over the hill to Greenan and then up Glenmalure, the remarkably straight-sided, glacier-carved valley of the Avonbeg (Little Avon), wildest of the

Wicklow glens and once the fastness of the O'Byrnes. Drumgoff (7 miles), in Glenmalure, is the best jumping-off place for the ascent of Lugnaquilla (3,039 feet), the highest mountain in the east of Ireland, with its flanks carved into hollows like Pyrenean cirques.

The main road (T 7) beyond Rathdrum passes on the left a two-storeyed, cemented house called Avondale, which was Parnell's birthplace and is now a school of forestry, and on the right the grandly sited Castle Howard. You are now descending the *Vale of Avoca* (or Ovoca), of far-famed but perhaps somewhat overrated loveliness. The Meeting of the Waters, where the Avonmore and Avonbeg flow together to form the Avoca, is a beauty-spot celebrated in Moore's poem.

> There is not in the wide world a valley so sweet
> As the vale in whose bosom the bright waters meet.
> Oh! the last rays of feeling and life must depart,
> Ere the bloom of that valley shall fade from my heart.

The charms of the ensuing section are impaired by sulphur and ochre workings. Between Avoca village and Woodenbridge the valley is exquisitely beautiful, particularly in spring and autumn, though it must be confessed that the presence of the railway does not improve matters. On the left is the ruined church of Castlemacadam. At Woodenbridge (which is now of stone) is another and more charming Meeting of the Waters. Unfortunately the railway is particularly obtrusive at this point. The Avoca is joined here by the Aughrim and the Gold Mines River. The latter comes down from the Gold Mines Valley, to which there was a gold rush in 1796, though the mines have never proved very profitable. Still, it was Co. Wicklow that produced most of the gold from which the wonderful prehistoric ornaments in the National Museum at Dublin were made.

On down the lovely Avoca valley, passing on the right Glenart Castle, seat of the late Earl of Carysfort, and on the left Shelton Abbey, the former seat of the Earl of Wicklow, now the Forestry School. The sea is reached at *Arklow* ('low' is Norse for beacon), a fishing port and sea-side resort with potteries (at the harbour), an old bridge of nineteen arches across the river mouth, the remains of a castle of the Butlers, 'slighted' by Cromwell in 1649 (opposite the Catholic church), and a very handsome Protestant church built by Sir Arthur Blomfield in 1900 at Lord Carysfort's expense. You will notice that in this part of the country the war memorials are for the 1798 rebellion. The fisherfolk live west of the harbour, in a picturesque quarter of white thatched cottages, known as 'The Fisheries.' There are splendid sands and coast walks in both directions from Arklow.

A visit to the quaint old county town of *Wicklow*, 16 miles north, may well be interposed at this juncture. Perhaps the best way is to go via Rathdrum, so as to see the Avoca scenery from a new angle, returning by the coast road. Wicklow lies at the mouth of the River Vartry, and its name means 'the vikings' beacon.' Black Castle, now in ruins, was built by Maurice Fitzgerald at the time of the Anglo-Norman invasion. The chief walk is to Wicklow Head and the Silver Strand. A popular regatta is held at Wicklow on August Bank Holiday.

The next section of the tour, still by T 7 and still in company with the railway, is from Arklow south-west to Enniscorthy, 37 miles. The scenery is tame, compared with what has gone before, though an unspoilt countryside is never dull in an English townsman's eyes. You pass through Inch and Gorey—the conical Slieveboy (1,385 feet) is prominent on the right and Tara Hill (831 feet; not the famous Tara) on the left—then Clogh and Camolin, the latter on the River Bann. *Ferns*, 'the place of alders,' now the tiniest of towns, was once a royal and episcopal city, the capital of Leinster. The cathedral, founded by St. Edan in the sixth century, was burnt by the O'Byrnes in 1575 and is now only half its original length; it was restored in 1901. The Bishop's Palace is an eighteenth-century building; the see is now absorbed in that of Ossory. The remains of the Augustinian priory, to the east of the cathedral, are kept locked, but can be examined with a little trouble. They are notable for exquisite stonework, a group of five lancets, and a fine cylindrical tower. The priory was founded in 1161 by Dermot

D

MacMurrogh, who brought the Normans over to Ireland. Ferns Castle, of the twelfth and thirteenth centuries, was built on the site of the fortress of the Leinster kings; its chief relic is a round tower containing a chapel. It is worth while climbing the high ground to the west of Ferns in order to enjoy the view of Mount Leinster (2,610 feet) and Blackstairs (2,409 feet).

Soon reaching the pretty valley of the Slaney, you descend it to the left to *Enniscorthy* ('rock island'), a largish town built on the steep hillside, at the limit of navigation on the river. The castle, originally thirteenth century, with a fine keep and cylindrical corner-towers, was repaired by Sir Henry Wallop to serve the poet Spenser as a residence and restored in the nineteenth century by the Earl of Portsmouth, head of the Wallop family. St. Aidan's Catholic Cathedral, severe and dignified, is one of Pugin's neo-Gothic churches. To the south of the town, on the right bank of the river, is Borodale, birthplace of Admiral Lord Beatty. Overlooking Enniscorthy on the east is Vinegar Hill (Fidh-na-giaer, 'hill of berries'), famous as the scene of the final stand of the 1798 rebels. The view thence of the rolling plains of Wexford is delightful.

The direct road (T 7) from Enniscorthy to New Ross (21 miles) and Waterford is by Clonroche, but it is well worth the extra 27 miles to go via Wexford. If you decide upon this, you take T 8 and descend the beautiful valley of the Slaney, via Oilgate and Ferrycarrig Bridge, where you cross the estuary, a noble sight at high water, and pass the keep of the first Anglo-Norman castle to be erected in Ireland.

Wexford, a highly picturesque county town and seaport, is situated on Wexford Harbour, a large and shallow estuary, 1,600 acres of which have been drained in modern times. The name Wexford is Norse—Vaesfjord. The ruthlessness of Cromwell's massacre of the garrison in 1649 was surpassed only at Drogheda. Wexford is notable for its immensely long quay, its narrow streets, and its fine new, six-span bridge. There is a memorial in the Bull Ring for the peasant rising of 1798. Of the city's ancient defences and monastic houses there is little to show, apart from the West Gate Tower, shorts sections of wall, and scant remains of Selskar Abbey, St. Mary's, and St. Patrick's.

Outside Wexford Harbour, 11 miles south-east of the town, is *Rosslare Harbour*, the terminus of the mail steamer route from Fishguard. The seaside resort of Rosslare, famous for its splendid sands, is some distance to the north. The chief excursions are to Carnsore Point, the south-eastern extremity of Ireland, to Our Lady's Island, in a sea inlet, with a ruined monastery and castle (both dating from 1237), and to Crossfarnoge or Forlorn Point, 14 miles to the west, with grand coast scenery and a view of the Saltee Islands, on which there is a bird sanctuary.

The normal route from Wexford to New Ross (T 12, 24 miles) is by Camaross, but a much more pleasant way, especially when the gorse is in bloom, is by L 159 (37 miles). This takes you over the Bannow estuary by Wellington Bridge and at Tintern Cross Roads passes within a mile of Tintern Abbey, which was founded in 1200 by William Marshal, Earl of Pembroke, and colonized with Cistercians from the famous Tintern Abbey in Monmouthshire. Arthurstown is a choice spot on Waterford Harbour. From Ballyhack, close by, a ferry plies across the estuary to Passage Point (the shortest way to Waterford, but no motors taken). The road then runs close to the Barrow estuary, passing the important remains of Dunbrody Abbey, another Cistercian house, built in 1182 by the monks of St. Mary's Abbey, Dublin, and dissolved in 1539. The stately church, fairly complete, is notable for its lancet windows and filigree work on the west door.

New Ross, at the head of the splendid estuary of the Barrow, is a little seaport. President Kennedy's forbears came from here, and in 1963 he visited his (alleged) great-great-grandfather's cottage at Dunganstown, 3½ miles north. An excursion (13 miles) may be made up the Barrow to the pretty village of St. Mullins and the highly paintable little town of Graiguenamanagh. South of the latter rises the graceful Mount Brandon (1,694 feet), the top of which affords views of the Barrow and Nore valleys and of Mount Leinster and Blackstairs. The Catholic church at Graiguenamanagh was formerly the

Cistercian abbey church of Duiske, built by William Marshal, Earl of Pembroke, in 1212.

The main road from New Ross to Waterford (T 7, 15 miles) follows the west side of the beautifully wooded estuary of the Barrow, with a fine mountain view northwards from the top of the hill beyond Glenmore. Motorists, however, should interpose Kilkenny between New Ross and Waterford; others should visit it by bus or train from Waterford.

The road from New Ross to Kilkenny (T 20, 27 miles) crosses the River Barrow, leaves the shapely Mount Brandon on the right, and presently, beyond a roadside waterfall, descends into the delightful vale of the Nore. Inistioge (pronounced 'Innisteeg') is an Arcadian townlet in a perfect setting, with a ten-arch bridge and the remains of an Augustinian priory. Thomastown is named after Thomas FitzAnthony, seneschal of Leinster in the early thirteenth century. Its points of interest are the old bridge towers and the ruins of a large thirteenth-century church, inside which a modern church has been erected, with noteworthy monuments. Just south of the town are the remains of Grianan Castle, and two miles south-west is Dysert Castle, at a cottage near which Bishop Berkeley, the great philosopher, was born in 1685.

Jerpoint Abbey, a mile and a half south-west of Thomastown, on the Waterford road, is one of the finest monastic ruins in all Ireland. The key is kept at the adjoining cottage on the north (Thomastown) side. Founded for Cistercians in 1158 by the Lord of Ossory, the abbey has choir and transepts in the Romanesque style, with delicately carved capitals, while the nave is of slightly later date. The fifteenth-century tower, which can be safely ascended, has strange, stepped, almost Italianate battlements. The choir retains its curious sedilia and piscina, and its barrel vaulting and roof of stone. The Decorated east window is a fourteenth-century insertion. There are several fine abbatial tombs. The cloisters, with a surviving fragment of arcading, were rebuilt in the fifteenth century.

Kilkenny wears a clean and prosperous air and is indubitably one of the most interesting old towns in

Ireland. The fine local limestone of which it is mostly built has earned for it the surprising sobriquet of 'The Marble City.' Apart from its public buildings, the chief of which are in the west of the two halves into which the River Nore divides the city, it contains an unusual number of dignified eighteenth-century houses (especially in the Mall, opposite the castle). Now a county town, it was once the capital of the kings of Ossory, whose territory is represented by Co. Kilkenny. The Statute of Kilkenny, enacted by the Parliament of 1366–7, forbade the Anglo-Normans to intermarry with the Irish, to talk Irish, to take an Irish name, to wear Irish costume, or to let the Irish enter the walled towns. In 1642–8 Kilkenny was the seat of the Confederates' Parliament, but Cromwell captured the city in 1650, allowing the garrison to withdraw on honourable terms. The reputation of Kilkenny cats as fighters is said to be due to the Roundheads' pleasant practice of tying two cats together by the tails and slinging them across a rope.

The castle in 'High Town' was until recently the seat of the Marquis of Ormonde, head of the Butler family, which had held it (with intervals) since 1400 and is descended from Theobald FitzWalter, appointed Chief Butler of Ireland by Henry II. William Marshal, Earl of Pembroke, built the castle in 1192, but it has been repeatedly altered and modernized. A good view of this, one of the most striking of feudal strongholds, is obtained from the bridge. The main entrance to the castle is by a beautiful gateway in the Mall, in the dignified classical style of the late seventeenth century. The famous Butler archives formerly kept at the castle are now in the National Library at Dublin.

The cathedral of the Protestant bishopric of Ossory is dedicated to St. Canice (Choinnigh), the sixth-century saint from whom Kilkenny derives its name. It is situated in 'Irishtown' and, though small, much damaged by Cromwell's soldiers, and drastically restored by Sir Thomas Deane, is the finest building in the town and one of the most beautiful cathedrals in Ireland. Founded by Felix O'Dullany, first Abbot of Jerpoint (d. 1202), it mostly displays the First Pointed style of the mid-thirteenth century, in weathered stone which internally is of a marvellously attractive dove-grey shade. The western parts show a transition to the Decorated style. The central tower was only partly rebuilt after its collapse in 1332. Noteworthy features of the church are the stepped battlements and the quatrefoil windows of the clerestory. The adjacent Round Tower is 100 feet high and 46½ feet round, and lacks its original cap; it has eleven windows in all (six at the top, instead of the usual four). Internally, the cathedral is famed for its splendid collection of monuments, including many of recumbent knights in armour and the Ormonde tombs in the south transept. Note also the twelfth-century font of black marble, St. Kieran's chair in the north transept, and the exquisite lierne vaulting (1465) over the crossing. The sanctuary, with its floor of coloured marbles and its reredos bas-relief by Gilbert Ledward, is a very effective modern composition by Sir Reginald Blomfield.

St. Mary's Catholic Cathedral, built in 1857, has a tower 200 feet in height, conspicuous in all views of the town. In or near the High Street are the charmingly quaint Tholsel, or town hall (1764), and the Black Friars Church (1225), now again Dominican, with Flamboyant windows, in Abbey Street. St. Mary's Church, in St. Kieran Street, behind the Tholsel, is thirteenth century and has interesting tombs (but is kept locked), and on the east bank of the Nore is St. John's Priory (c. 1220), the Lady Chapel of which, now a parish church, is called the 'Lantern of Ireland,' from its many windows.

There is not much of interest on the road from Kilkenny to Waterford (T 14, 30 miles). On entering *Waterford* (i.e. Vaderfjord, the fiord of Father Odin) you pass from Leinster into the south-western province of Munster. The fifth city of Eire, Waterford is a busy seaport with a population of 28,000. It lies about 15 miles from the open sea, on the south bank of the River Suir, which lower down joins the united waters of the Nore and Barrow to form the estuary of Waterford Harbour. Waterford is the premier port of south-eastern Ireland for the export of cattle and agricultural produce. Its bacon is

far-famed. This was the first landing-place of Strongbow,
of Henry II (18th October 1171), and of many subsequent
English sovereigns. What is now Co. Waterford formed
part of the ancient kingdom of Ormond, and the city
became the chief stronghold of the Anglo-Normans in the
south. Its proud motto, 'Urbs intacta manet Waterford,'
was granted by Henry VII in view of its unswerving
loyalty. Waterford glass of the eighteenth and early
nineteenth centuries—the industry has recently been
revived—is highly prized, the best period being from about
1780 to 1810.

In spite of its mostly narrow and crowded streets,
Waterford is a peculiarly attractive town of continental
appearance. At the corner of the mile-long quay and the
spacious Mall, the principal thoroughfares, stands Reginald's Tower, a circular structure 80 feet high and dating
from 1003, according to the tablet on it. It is named
from Rognald, son of the Danish king Sigtryg Silkbeard
(page 67), and can be inspected. Here, in 1170, Strongbow was married to Eva, the daughter of Dermot Mac-
Murrogh, King of Leinster, and it housed the Waterford
Mint until the reign of Edward IV. The City Hall, in
the Mall, is a good building of 1788. Close by is the
Protestant Cathedral of the Holy Trinity, or Christ
Church, founded by Rognald c. 1050 but entirely rebuilt
in 1773. The architect, John Roberts, was the great-
grandfather of Field-Marshal Earl Roberts of Kandahar
and Waterford, who, though born at Cawnpore, came of
a Waterford family and married Miss Nora Bews of Waterford in 1859. The church, which was altered again by
Sir Thomas Drew in 1891, to fit it for cathedral status,
contains the macabre Rice monument (1469), with toads
crawling about the decomposing body; also the monument
to Nicholas Fitzgerald (1770) in white marble. The case of
old books and relics is worth study. The Catholic Cathedral of the diocese of Waterford and Lismore, in Barron-
strand Street, near the clock-tower on the Quay, was
likewise designed by Roberts (1793). The concrete bridge
(1913), with a central swing span, commands a good view
of the shipping.

A bus service connects Waterford with its popular

suburb and seaside resort of *Tramore*, 8 miles distant, which is built partly on a wide and exposed bay and partly on a large lagoon called Back Strand. The sands are remarkably fine, and there are golf links, a racecourse, and a popular dance hall. Each of the two headlands that bound the bay, Great Newtown Head (west) and Brownstown Head (east), is crowned with an old tower.

TOUR III: WATERFORD TO CORK

CLONMEL — DUNGARVAN — ARDMORE — YOUGHAL — MOUNT
MELLERAY — LISMORE — MALLOW — CORK — BLARNEY —
COBH—CLOYNE.

Total distance by road: about 325 miles.

THE main road, with the bus service, from Waterford to
Cork (T 12, 78 miles) is by way of Dungarvan and Youghal;
the railway runs via Dungarvan, Lismore, and Mallow.
The route described below follows the railway, except that
a digression is made so as to see Clonmel and the Suir
valley.

Between Waterford and Clonmel there is a road on
either bank of the Suir, both (especially the south bank
road) giving a good idea of the manifold charms of the
valley of the Suir, which, incidentally, is a first-class
salmon river. The main road (T 3, 30 miles), which is
that taken by the buses, leaves Waterford by the bridge
and Newrath Road and passes through the pretty villages
of Fiddown and Piltown. One of the prettiest spots on
the river, here fringed with reedy marshes, is Fiddown
Bridge. For the south bank road, which is 3 miles longer,
you turn right from the Cork road at Kilmeadan Post
Office and, by keeping left farther on, pass through the
dilapidated village of Portlaw, adjoining which is Curragh-
more, seat of the Marquis of Waterford and birthplace
of Admiral Lord (Charles) Beresford. The demesne, 10
square miles in area and outstandingly beautiful, may be
visited by ticket from the Estate Office, Parnell Street,
Waterford.

Carrick-on-Suir (Carrick means 'rock'), a gaunt-looking
place from the river, has the remains of a castle, one of
the strongholds of the Butlers, founded in the thirteenth
century and enlarged in the Tudor period. You pass a
modern housing estate as you leave the town by the north
bank road.

The higher you ascend the Suir, the more beautiful it is. To the south rise the Comeragh Mountains (2,597 feet), and to the north the rounded bulk of Slievenamon (2,363 feet), the 'Mountain of the White Women.' Gurteen le Poer, on the south bank of the river, was formerly the residence of Richard Lalor Sheil, the politician (d. 1851). The road on the north bank of the river passes two ruined towers.

Clonmel ('meadow of honey'), the capital of Co. Tipperary, is one of the most prettily situated towns in Ireland and a great sporting centre (hunting, racing, fishing). The Suir is here a wide stream with several islands, and there are pleasant riverside walks. The West Gate, rebuilt in the nineteenth century, is the only survivor of the four town gates. St. Mary's Church (turn right at the West Gate) is noteworthy for its octagonal steeple and its east window. Laurence Sterne was a native of Clonmel. The Main Guard, or Tholsel, is an attractive building of the eighteenth century.

The fast wide road from Clonmel due south to Dungarvan (26 miles; T 27 to Knockaraha Bridge, then T 25), with buses available, is a lovely drive. It undulates through a wild countryside, with the Comeragh and Monavullagh Mountains on the left and the Knockmealdown Mountains on the right. Ballymacarbry, rather less than half-way, lies in the idyllic glen of the Nier, and it is well worth while to stop the car and take a stroll upstream here. *Dungarvan*, on a splendid natural harbour, had one of King John's castles (1185), of which the massive keep and the crenellated walls survive. The sturdy single-arch bridge over the Colligan River, 75 feet in span, was built by the Duke of Devonshire in 1815. The things to do at Dungarvan are to explore the pretty glen of the Colligan and to make the 8-mile excursion to Helvick Head, at the west end of Dungarvan Harbour. Near the latter is Ring, inhabited by Gaelic-speaking fishermen and possessing a college for the study of Gaelic.

The Youghal road (T 12, 19 miles) ascends with two hairpin bends to the top of the gorsy Drum Hills, which are of no great elevation but command a splendid panorama, especially looking back over Dungarvan Bay. Take the road on the left that descends with a hairpin to *Ardmore*, a perfectly delightful village seaside resort with a quaint quay and most interesting group of ecclesiastical ruins, for which the Round Tower acts as a guide-post. St. Declan established a monastery here in the sixth century, and a very primitive, thick-walled little oratory contains his empty grave. The cathedral (caretaker at Court House) has an eleventh-century nave of the Hiberno-Romanesque type (the north wall is considerably older) and a Gothic choir. Its west front has unique arcading with quaint weather-worn carvings of scriptural scenes (Adam and Eve, Judgment of Solomon, Dedication of the Temple) and one showing St. Declan converting a pagan prince. Inside, the pointed choir-arch is noteworthy; two Ogham stones (page 47) are preserved here. The inevitable Round Tower, 96 feet high, is one of the best-known, best-preserved, and (perhaps) latest in Ireland; its special feature is the stringcourses that mark off its five storeys. Farther east, on the side of a cliff near the headland, are St. Declan's Well, with ancient carvings of the Crucifixion (pilgrimage on 24th July), and the thirteenth-century Teampull Deisceart (Church of the South). Famous pony races used to be held on Ardmore strand.

To get to *Youghal* (meaning 'yew cliff' and pronounced 'Yawl'), in Co. Cork, you cross the estuary of the River Blackwater by a long bridge constructed in 1963. This commands a grand view of the estuary, which provides a splendid natural harbour for the town. Youghal is perhaps the most interesting of the old seaport towns on the south coast. A Fitzgerald stronghold, it was the landing-place of Roger Mortimer in 1317, when he came to fight the Bruce. In 1579 it was sacked by the Earl of Desmond, in circumstances of peculiar barbarity. One of those who helped to suppress his rebellion was Sir Walter Raleigh, who was rewarded with Desmond estates to the extent of 60,000 acres, which he sold in 1602 for £1,000 to the first Earl of Cork. Cromwell, after making Youghal his base for his campaign in southern Ireland, embarked here on his return to England in 1650.

The town's main street is over a mile long. The narrow Church Street, on the right not far from the entrance to the town, leads to St. Mary's Church, which, formerly collegiate and now Protestant, was rebuilt in 1464 by the Earl of Desmond. If the church is locked, apply at the sexton's lodge. The graveyard is bounded by the old town wall. The detached bell-tower has walls 8 feet thick. Noteworthy features of the great cruciform church are the west and south doors, the east window, the oak roof, pulpit, and font-cover, the elaborate font, the bishop's pew, the mayor's sword-rest, and the numerous monuments. Among the last are those of the eighth Earl of Esmond, who rebuilt the church and was beheaded at Drogheda in 1467, and the 'Great' Earl of Cork (Richard Boyle, Baron Youghal and Viscount Dungarvan; cf. page 69), whose imposing monument portrays the family history—the first wife who died in childbirth, the second wife, and a lengthy string of daughters, one of whom was drowned. The tomb of Sir Edward Villiers, Lord President of Munster (d. 1626), has a quaint epitaph:

> The time that Villers came
> To make us worse
> By leaving such a name
> Of noble parts
> As none can imitate
> But those whose harts
> Are married to the State.
> But if they press
> To imitate his fame
> Munster may bless
> The time that Villers came.

Adjoining the church on the north is Myrtle Grove, the famous residence of Sir Walter Raleigh. Dating from Elizabethan times, it may have been built for him, or it may have been the house of the warden of the adjacent college. In any case, he seems to have stayed here for only six weeks. Here he entertained the poet Spenser, who lived at Kilcolman Castle (near Doneraile) from 1588 to 1598, and whose *Faerie Queene* has many descriptions of local scenery. In front of the house is a yew-tree, in the shade of which Raleigh used to sit, smoking the tobacco he had brought from Virginia; and here, according to a still more dubious tradition, he planted the first potatoes in Europe.

The main street farther on passes under the quaint Clock Gate (1777) and is continued round the Point by the Strand, with its hotels and boarding-houses, miles of sandy beach, and other concomitants of a seaside resort. Convent-made point lace and art pottery are specialities of Youghal.

The Blackwater is celebrated for its enchanting beauty and for its salmon. Its total length is 100 miles, and its valley should be ascended as far as Mallow (58 miles), by car, bus, or railway. For both the beauty of its wooded and pastoral landscapes and the number of its castles, the Blackwater has been called, a little absurdly, the 'Irish Rhine.' The lower reaches, as far as Cappoquin (17 miles), should be seen from the water, or as far as possible from the river bank, as the road misses most of the scenery. On the way you pass the castles of Templemichael, Strancally, and Dromana, and, on an island opposite the first-named, Molana Abbey. The road, which is bumpy, hugs the estuary at first, then ascends a beautifully wooded glen and crosses gorsy uplands, finally returning to the Blackwater beyond a bridge over the River Bride.

At Cappoquin, a dusty grey town, the river describes a great right-angled bend. The main road to Lismore (T 30) here diverges to the left, but it is essential first of all to pay a visit to the Knockmealdown Mountains. Drive through Cappoquin and take the first turning on the left out of the town. Farther on you pass within a mile of *Mount Melleray*, the famous Trappist monastery, which is seen across the valley on the right. It was founded in 1833 when all foreign Trappists were expelled from France and is named after Melleray in Brittany. Vowed to perpetual silence, the monks devote themselves to gardening, agriculture, and forestry, and they have succeeded in converting 500 acres of wilderness into a flourishing estate. Visitors are shown over the monastery, and excellent free accommodation and meals are provided in the guesthouse (an alms-box for donations is available). Women are put up in a guest-house outside the enclosure.

The road, wide and well engineered, with good surface, ascends, with two hairpin bends, to the Gap (1,114 feet) in the mountains, where a magnificent surprise view welcomes

you. To the east rises Knockmealdown, which is the
highest peak in the range (2,609 feet). On the left is a
beautiful little tarn, and far below you is the continuation
of the meandering road. The view from the Gap covers,
in clear weather, a large part of central Ireland. On
the opposite side of the valley at your feet are the Galtee Mountains. If descending to Clogheen (16 miles
from Cappoquin), the motorist must be careful of the
hairpin bends, especially of the notorious 'Vee,' or
'Devil's Elbow.' On the way back, you should bear
right for Lismore and enjoy a long free-wheel downhill, finally passing through a most delectable wooded
glen, in which there is barely room for the road and the
stream.

Lismore ('great enclosure'), one of the most fascinating
little towns in Ireland, is situated on the south bank of
the Blackwater. From the eighteenth-century bridge you
obtain an excellent view of the stately castle, which is
built on a rock high above the river. Founded by King
John in 1185, i.e. before his accession, it is now mostly a
reconstruction of the eighteenth and nineteenth centuries.
Sir Walter Raleigh sold it in 1602 to the 'Great' Earl of
Cork, whose sons, Roger Boyle, Earl of Orrery, and Robert
Boyle, the physicist, were both born here. Since 1753 the
castle has been the property of the Dukes of Devonshire.
Congreve, the dramatist, spent his childhood at Lismore,
where his father was land steward, and went to school at
Kilkenny.

Beyond the bridge bear left for the cathedral, which,
though founded in the seventh century by St. Carthach
(Carthage)—legend says that King Alfred studied at the
abbey school here—was extensively rebuilt by the Earl of
Cork in 1633, while the spire was added in 1827. In the
west wall are many ancient tomb-slabs, and close by is
the elaborately carved altar-tomb of John Magrath (1548).
The Catholic cathedral is a regrettable building in an
imitation Lombardic-Romanesque style, of red sandstone
with limestone dressings.

The main road from Lismore to Fermoy and Mallow
(T 30, 36 miles), the usual approach to Killarney, runs on
the north side of the Blackwater valley. For most of the

way there is a subsidiary road on the south side of the
river. Between Lismore and Fermoy (17 miles) you pass
Ballyduff and then two more castle ruins: Macollop (a
Desmond stronghold) and Carrigabrick.

We are now in Co. Cork, the largest in Ireland. Fermoy,
founded in 1789 by an enterprising Scot named John
Anderson, was a large garrison town until 1922, but its
military establishments, covering 27 acres, were laid in
ruins during and since the 'troubles.' Between Fermoy
and Mallow the Blackwater flows along the base of the
Nagles Mountains, which culminate in Knocknaskagh
(1,406 feet). At Ballyhooly, by the bridge, is a ruined
castle of the Roches—you can climb the tower and enjoy
a charming view. Farther on there is a descent of 1 in 10
and an ascent of 1 in 7 through the untidy village of
Castletownroche, which lies away north of the Blackwater,
in the pretty glen of the Awbeg. Castle Widenham here
incorporates the keep of the castle defended so valiantly
by Lady Roche against Cromwell in 1649. Beside the
station (and seen by a slight detour) are the relics of
Bridgetown Abbey, which Fitzhugh Roche founded in the
days of King John.

Mallow is Magh Ealla, the plain of the Allo, as the
Blackwater was once called. It is an important railway
junction, and the river is spanned here by a great railway
viaduct. Many dignified houses of the eighteenth century,
with bow fronts and beautiful doorways, remind one of
Mallow's former reputation as a spa and social centre.
Salmon fishing and racing now attract visitors. The
castle, belonging to the Norreys family, is modern. A
pleasant walk of about a mile is to the Lovers' Leap.

The winding road southwards from Mallow to Cork
(T 11, 22 miles) traverses open country of no special
interest. Cork is entered by Dublin Street, Watercourse
Road, and the bridge over the River Lee.

Cork, Corcaigh ('a swampy place') in Gaelic, is the
second city of the Republic, with a population of 78,000.
Situated on

> The spreading Lee that, like an island fayre,
> Encloseth Corke with his divided flood,

at the point where that river enters Lough Mahon, an arm

of Cork Harbour, it has very delightful surroundings. A creation of the Danes and the Anglo-Normans, Cork is now a busy manufacturing place (Ford and Dunlop works, etc.), with a trade in agricultural produce. There is an airport, besides a thrice-weekly steamer service to Fishguard. Chief hotels: Imperial, Metropole, Victoria, Intercontinental.

Cork is devoid of antiquarian interest, for its walls and castle, its ancient churches and abbeys, have all vanished; it has few buildings of real distinction, yet many people consider it the most charming city in Ireland. During the 'troubles' of 1920 a large part of the city was burnt down; Lord Mayor MacCurtain was shot by the police, while his successor, Terence MacSwiney, died in Brixton Prison after a seventy-five-day hunger strike.

The spacious main streets of Cork contrast strongly with its narrow and congested by-streets and alleys. The best shopping street is Patrick (or St. Patrick's) Street, which, like Grand Parade, to which it leads, is built over an arm of the river. One side of Patrick Street was burnt down by the Black-and-Tans in 1920, and has been rebuilt in a 'Regent Street' style. By St. Patrick's Bridge is Foley's statue of Father Mathew, apostle of temperance, who was the superior of a Capuchin friary on Charlotte Quay. As a result of his efforts (1838–43) the annual sale of whisky fell from twelve million to five million gallons. Washington Street leads from Grand Parade to the Court House, which was built in 1835 from the plans of James Pain. Grand Parade leads to South Mall, and at the corner is the National Memorial to the Irish patriots from 1798 to 1867. Cross the South Channel and turn right along the quays to see the three-spired cathedral of the Protestant bishopric of Cork. Dedicated to St. Finnbarr, who founded a monastery here in the sixth or seventh century, it was rebuilt in 1734 and again, from the sumptuous 'early French' designs of William Burges, in 1865–79. It is very short (163 feet) in proportion to its height (central spire 240 feet). Gill Abbey Street and College Road go on to University College (entrance in Fernhurst Avenue), which was founded in 1845 and is now a constituent part of the National University. The buildings, in the Tudor style, enclose three sides of a quadrangle. The chapel has good glass. The Public Museum is in Fitzgerald Park, to the north.

Following the South Channel quays in the opposite direction, it is nearly a mile to the City Hall, an imposing building on classic lines, opened in 1936 to replace the building burnt as a reprisal in December 1920. In the southern suburb of Turner's Cross the new concrete church of Christ the King merits a visit.

Two things which every visitor to Cork is expected to do are to hear the bells of Shandon and to kiss the Blarney Stone. To reach St. Ann's Church, Shandon, follow North Main Street from Washington Street, cross North Gate Bridge, and turn right from Shandon Street by Church Street. The church, in a poor quarter, was built in 1722–6, and the steeple is unusual, for it is faced on two sides with red sandstone, and on the other two with grey limestone. The bells, eight in number, which were cast at Gloucester in 1750, chime every hour and play hymns in the evening before vespers (they are also rung at any time on request). 'Father Prout' (Francis Sylvester Mahony, the ex-Jesuit), whose jingle has immortalized the bells, lies at the foot of the tower.

> With deep affection
> And recollection
> I often think of
>   Those Shandon bells,
> Whose sounds so wild would,
> In the days of childhood,
> Fling round my cradle
>   Their magic spells—
> On this I ponder
> Where'er I wander,
> And thus grow fonder,
>   Sweet Cork, of thee;
> With thy bells of Shandon
> That sound so grand on
> The pleasant waters
>   Of the River Lee.

More repaying is a visit to *Blarney* ('the plain'), 5 miles by bus. The square keep of its fifteenth-century castle (admission 2s.), in a lovely site on the bank of a rushing

stream, was once regarded as the strongest place in
Munster, with walls 18 feet thick and 120 feet high.
From the roof you get a delightful view of the surrounding
countryside. The world-famous Blarney Stone is the sill
of one of the machicolated battlements on the south side,
and kissing it, in order to acquire irresistible powers of
persuasion, can be accomplished without difficulty if not
without loss of dignity, one's legs being held by the guide.

> There is a stone there
> That whoever kisses,
> Oh, he never misses
>   To grow eloquent.
> 'Tis he may clamber
> To a lady's chamber
> Or become a member
>   Of Parliament.

The term 'blarney,' which cannot be traced farther
back than 1819, is traditionally said to have been first used
by Queen Elizabeth in reference to the evasive answers of
the castle's owner, The McCarthy, Lord of Muskerry.

Cork Harbour, 17 miles long by about 2 miles wide,
with many ramifications, is a magnificent natural harbour
with 60 square miles of water, affording safe anchorage for
any number of vessels. It is under the jurisdiction of the
city of Cork, in token whereof the lord mayor used to go
down every third year by boat to the harbour mouth and
cast a dart into the sea. If you go to Cobh by steamer, you
pass (right) Dundanion Castle, whence William Penn
sailed for America, to found Pennsylvania. Motorists
cross the bridge and turn right by MacCurtain Street.

On Great Island, which is connected with the mainland
by a road bridge (defended by an old keep) and a railway
bridge, is *Cobh* (meaning and pronounced 'Cove'), a port
of call for transatlantic liners and also a very bright and
attractive summer resort and place of residence, noted for
the mildness of its climate. Before 1922 it was called
Queenstown, in honour of Queen Victoria's landing in
1849. The number of emigrants embarking here for
America was at one period 100,000 annually. The Royal
Cork Yacht Club, which has its headquarters here, is the
oldest in the British Isles (1720). In the square facing

the quay is a really beautiful *Lusitania* memorial, by Jerome Connor, given by the U.S.A.; most of the victims were buried in the Old Church cemetery, 2 miles from Cobh. St. Colman's Catholic Cathedral, on the cliff above, is the glory of the diocese of Cloyne; it is a neo-Gothic structure begun in 1868 and not consecrated till 1919. The spire is 300 feet in height, and the carillon of forty-two bells, which plays daily, is the largest in the British Isles. On Haulbowline Island and Spike Island, off Cobh, are naval dockyards, which, like the Cork Harbour forts—Spike Island, Camden, Carlisle, Templebreedy—were handed over to the Eire Government in 1938. Haulbowline Island is the headquarters of the Irish Naval Service.

On the way back to Cork, motorists may bear right, and turn right again at the neat little town of Midleton, to visit *Cloyne*, which is 19 miles from Cork and served by buses. For non-ecclesiologists, however, the excursion is perhaps hardly worth while, as the countryside is not particularly interesting. Cloyne means 'meadow.' Founded by St. Colman in the sixth century, the cathedral, of an old-world simplicity that is very refreshing, dates from the thirteenth century but has been greatly altered. The see of Cloyne is now amalgamated with that of Cork. In the churchyard are the ruins of the 'Fire House,' i.e. St. Colman's oratory. On the north door are the most interesting details in the building—crude carvings of 'pre-Christian emblems of Creation,' including, at the base, two tau crosses, one with a human head, the other with the Egyptian symbol of life. The north transept contains a modern marble monument (by A. Bruce Joy, 1890) to Bishop Berkeley, the philosopher, who was bishop from 1734 to 1752 and made the name of Cloyne famous throughout the world (Berkeley, California, with its university, is named after him). He is buried in the cathedral at Oxford. Otherwise there is not much of interest in the cathedral save eighteenth-century wall monuments and a pre-Norman font. On the other side of the road is the usual Round Tower, in this case a perfect cylinder, of seven storeys, 86 feet in height; the castellated top is modern. The tower is still in use as the cathedral belfry and may be ascended. There is a complex system of

limestone caves in the Cloyne neighbourhood. Ballycotton, 4 miles beyond the town, enjoys immense repute
among sea anglers.

To see the west side of Cork Harbour, take the road via
Douglas, Passage West, and Carrigaline. From Passage
West, now a residential district, the paddle steamer
Sirius sailed for America on 4th April 1838, the first ship
to cross the Atlantic under continuous steam power, the
passage to New York taking 18½ days. From Carrigaline,
which has a good Perpendicular church, a branch road
leads to Crosshaven, a seaside resort of growing popularity
and headquarters of the Royal Munster Yacht Club, with
excellent bathing at Church Bay and Myrtleville Bay.

TOUR IV: CORK TO KILLARNEY

Total distance by road: about 350 miles.

The railway route from Cork to Killarney is by way of
Mallow, while the main road and bus route (T 29, 54 miles)
is via Macroom, up to which point it ascends the valley
of the Lee. Be careful to leave Cork by Western Road,
so as to drive along the famous three-mile 'Cork Straight,'
which extends from Victoria Cross to Carrigrohane Station
and is used for international motor races. The Lee scenery
is at its best between Inniscarra (with a hydro-electric
station) and Carrigadrohid (castle on a rock in midstream).
Macroom ('sloping field') has a great square keep which
was once owned by, and was perhaps the birthplace of,
Admiral Sir William Penn, father of the Quaker founder
of Pennsylvania. The road thence to Killarney commands
very fine river and mountain views, attaining a height of
958 feet where it crosses the Derrynasaggart Mountains
and enters Co. Kerry.

The route followed in this chapter, however, is a great
detour enabling you to see as much as possible of the
wonderful scenery of the south-west coast, with its great
sea loughs, peninsulas, and mountains, and the mildest
climate in the British Isles. The district in question is
served by bus services: Cork–Kinsale, Cork–Bandon–
Bantry–Glengarriff, and Cork–Bandon–Clonakilty–Rosscarbery–Skibbereen. West Cork and Kerry have many
factories set up since the war by German and other continental industrialists.

The tortuous coastal road which you should take (L 42
to Skibbereen, 61 miles) leaves Cork by the South Gate
Bridge, Evergreen Street (left), and Douglas Road South,
in which you should be careful to turn left. As far as

Kinsale (18 miles; bus service available) the road, concrete for some miles, winds and undulates through pretty country. After gradually climbing to 498 feet, it drops down, with a deep glen on the left, to Fivemilebridge over the Owenboy River. Beyond Belgooly, where a direct road from Carrigaline comes in on the left, it hugs the shore of Oyster Haven and then crosses its two arms —a particularly beautiful bit.

A place of great historic interest, *Kinsale* is a singularly picturesque little port, engaged in the herring, mackerel, and scallop fisheries. The town is a maze of narrow streets and passages, and the women of this part of Co. Cork still wear (especially on Sunday mornings) black hooded cloaks of fine wool, which are handed down as heirlooms. Kinsale lies in a lovely site on the estuary of the Bandon River, for the best view of which you should climb Compass Hill. The De Courcys have been Barons of Kingsale since 1181, and are the premier barons of Ireland, with the privilege of keeping their hats on in the presence of the Sovereign. A Spanish force landed here in 1601 and held out for ten weeks until forced to surrender to Mountjoy and Carew. James II landed here in 1689, and hence he sailed again for France after the defeat at the Boyne. The church of St. Multose at Kinsale dates from the second half of the twelfth century and has a curious tower, an old font, and a set of stocks. Three of the *Lusitania* victims, including an unknown woman, are buried in the graveyard. Charles Fort dates from 1677; the Old Fort on the opposite bank of the estuary is now in ruins.

Two miles above Kinsale you cross the Bandon River by a bridge 300 yards long and have a long ascent and descent to Ballinspittle. Here a road on the left diverges, via the tiny resort of Garrettstown Strand, to the Old Head of Kinsale (4 miles), an elongated promontory with a lighthouse, commanding a grand view of the coast in both directions. This is the first landfall made by east-ward-bound liners, and off this point the Cunard liner *Lusitania* was torpedoed by a German submarine at 2 p.m. on 7th May 1915, with the loss of 1,198 lives.

Beyond Ballinspittle L 42 descends to skirt Courtmac-sherry Bay, where it becomes very narrow and twisting, but with splendid marine views. To find your way through this labyrinth of rough by-roads a large-scale map is necessary, supplemented by the information of passers-by. If you miss the right road you will probably pass through Kilbrittain, in a lovely glen, with a picturesque old bridge and a modern castle. At Harbour View there is a sharp 1-in-10 rise. Timoleague, 23 miles from Kinsale, derives its name (House of St. Molaga) from a sixth-century monastery founded by the saint of that name. Here, in the fourteenth century, Donal Mac-Carthy, Chief of Carbery (as this district is called), established an important Franciscan friary, of which the roofless church, on the bank of the Argideen River, with its slender tower and south arcade, survives. A road runs thence to Courtmacsherry, a small fishing village and summer resort.

The next town, 6 rather bumpy miles from Timoleague, is Clonakilty (i.e. Clan O'Keelty), a biggish place which was founded by the 'Great' Earl of Cork in 1614 at the head of Clonakilty Bay. Woodfield Farm, near the village called The Pike, 3 miles away, was the birthplace in 1890 of Michael Collins, who was shot by irregulars in ambush at Bealnabla, near Bandon, in 1922, while motoring with a strong escort from Skibbereen to Cork. Four miles along the Bandon road from Clonakilty is Ballinascarty, whence Henry Ford's grandfather and father emigrated to the States in the famine year. Antiquarians should digress north from Clonakilty, via Enniskeen, to see the Round Tower at Kinneagh (13 miles), 68 feet high and unique in that the lowest 18 feet are hexagonal.

The ensuing countryside (Clonakilty to Skibbereen, 20 miles) is rather bleak, with gradients of 1 in 10 or 11. An alternative road to Rosscarbery takes in Galley Head with its powerful lighthouse and ruined castle of Dundeady. There are pretty views—e.g. a glimpse of the seashore, with Galley Head and its lighthouse—on approaching Rosscarbery (ross = wood), at the head of the like-named bay. In the sixth century St. Fachnan (Fachtna) established a monastery here which became the seat of the bishopric of Ross, the cathedral of which (now Protestant) was rebuilt in 1612, the spire being added in 1808. Its choir screen (like Cloyne's) is an unusual feature for Ireland. There are monuments to the Lords Carbery.

Between Rosscarbery and Skibbereen L 42 keeps inland, via Leap, a picturesque village with a view of Glandore Harbour from the hill above. It is preferable, however, to take the stony road nearer the coast, by way of Glandore, a sheltered spot of great attractiveness, with a nice-looking hotel. The bridge over the harbour leads to the quaint village of Unionhall. Dean Swift, who stayed at Rock Cottage there in 1723, wrote a poem in praise of 'Carberiae Rupes.' From the lower road between Unionhall and Skibbereen a side-road leads to Castletownshend, on the still more beautiful inlet of Castle Haven.

Skibbereen ('little boat harbour'), market town for a bleak but not poverty-stricken district, lies at the head of the Ilen estuary and is a centre for excursions. The pro-cathedral of the Roman Catholic Bishop of Ross is a Grecian structure of 1826. Drishane House, to the south of Skibbereen, was the residence of the late Dr. E. Œ. Somerville, author, with her cousin Martin Ross (Miss Violet Martin of Ross), of the famous *Experiences of an Irish R.M.*, *In Mr. Knox's Country*, etc. But none of their settings has any actual foundation in geography— 'Skebawn' is not Skibbereen, and 'Shreelane' is the name of a bare and rocky hill. Four miles south-west of Skibbereen is Lough Hyne, a sea inlet with a very narrow entrance and a ruined tower on an islet.

A road runs from Skibbereen down the Ilen estuary to Baltimore, 8 miles south-west, a small fishing port founded 1608, with a school that trains for the fishing industry. The castle, now a ruin, belonged to the O'Driscolls, famous sea-rovers. The Algerine corsairs raided the place in 1631 and carried off a hundred persons into slavery, as related in Thomas Davis's ballad *The Sack of Baltimore*— 'The summer sun is falling soft on Carbery's hundred isles.' With these Baltimore Bay and the adjoining Roaringwater Bay are studded, and the chief of them are Sherkin Island and Clear Island, served by motor-boat from Baltimore. Clear Island has a Gaelic-speaking population, fine cliffs, and, at Cape Clear, the southernmost point of Ireland. Some 3½ miles farther out is the Fastnet Rock, Europe's Land's End, with its famous lighthouse.

The direct road from Skibbereen to Bantry (18 miles), over the moors, cuts across the base of the first two of the five peninsulas that form the geographical feature of south-western Ireland—a classic example of a 'ria' coast-line of drowned valleys, due to the sinking of the land. The peninsulas are worth exploring. To do so, you take the excellent road (L 48, 15 miles) to Skull, which touches Roaringwater Bay, with striking scenery, at Ballydehob. As you approach Skull you pass the ruins of an enormous workhouse built during the potato famine. *Skull* (for-merly Schull), meaning 'stony place,' in a wild district, with abandoned copper mines, is the last place with hotel accommodation in this direction. It lies on a small bay, at the foot of Mount Gabriel (1,339 feet). Ardentenant Castle here belonged to the O'Mahonys.

The road goes on via Toormore and Goleen, with fine seascapes, to Crookhaven (12 miles), which faces east, possesses a lobster fishery, and enjoys a reputation as the safest yacht harbour on the south coast. To reach *Mizen Head*, the southmost point on the mainland, return to Goleen and take the road (6 miles) round Barley Cove. The top of the headland, 765 feet above the tumultuous sea, commands grand views of the other two capes in which the West Carbery peninsula terminates, viz. Brow Head, to the east, and Three Castle Head, to the north, the latter named after its three ruined castles of the O'Mahonys.

Return to Toormore (12 miles; thence to Bantry, L 56, 14 miles) and take the road to the left, leaving Mount Gabriel to the east. Beyond the ruins of Kilcanger Church we run parallel to the south shore of Dunmanus Bay, the turquoise-coloured fiord separating the Mizen Head and Sheep's Head peninsulas. The scenery is of an open, rocky type, with views of the Seefin hills across the bay. Dunbeacon Castle, yet another Mahony ruin, is passed (left) on the way to Durrus ('black wood'), at the head of the bay. On reaching the main road (T 65) turn left for Bantry.

Or from Durrus you can make a wonderful but somewhat adventurous 30-mile trip round the peninsula that ends in Sheep's Head, otherwise Muntervary. On the way back turn left at Kilcronane and cross the shoulder of Seefin (1,136 feet), a terrific up-and-down, but with marvellous views from the top, both of the Mizen Head peninsula to the south and of the Slieve Miskish and Caha mountains to the north, across Bantry Bay.

Bantry Bay, 21 miles long and mostly about 4 miles wide, provides safe anchorage for the largest ships. Twice, in 1689 and again in 1796, the French attempted a landing here. On the latter occasion 32 ships with 14,000 men under General Hoche set sail, but owing to bad weather only 16 ships (without Hoche) reached the rendezvous, and these soon departed. *Bantry* is a pleasant little agricultural and fishing town at the head of the bay, with a large market-place. Tim Healy, the first Governor-General of the Irish Free State, was born here, a son of the Clerk of the Bantry Union. Bantry House has beautiful grounds and interesting art collections, open to the public for a small fee. On Whiddy Island, opposite the town, is Reennabanny Castle, a ruined stronghold of the O'Sullivans. Three redoubts here are relics of the British naval station.

The Bantry–Glengarriff–Kenmare–Killarney road (T 65, 50 miles), sometimes known as the 'Prince of Wales's Route,' is the most popular touring ground in Ireland. As far as Glengarriff (11 miles) the road winds round the head of Bantry Bay, passing Ballylicky House and crossing Snave Bridge, beyond which it commands a famous view of Glengarriff Harbour, backed by the Caha Mountains. The Macroom road comes in at Ballylicky, and before or after seeing Glengarriff you simply must drive along it for 12 miles (passing the falls of the Ouvane River and the ruins of Carrigeness Castle) and cross the grand Pass of Keamaneigh ('pass of the deer,' 662 feet), to see one of the most romantic and most colourful scenes in Ireland. This, the tarn of *Gougane Barra* ('St. Finnbarr's hollow'; on a side-road to the left), source of the River Lee, is girt on three sides with steep mountains, from which silver streams descend into a sheet of water that resembles black marble. On an islet opposite the hotels (good places to stay at, out of the season) is the chapel of St. Finnbarr, goal of a once popular pilgrimage on 24th September.

Glengarriff or Glengariff ('rugged glen'), on an island-studded inlet of Bantry Bay, is one of Ireland's most fascinating beauty-spots, a veritable paradise. Its scenery is strangely reminiscent of the landscapes in early Italian art: sometimes almost Japanese in effect. Sheltered by wooded mountains on all sides except the south, it boasts the mildest climate in the British Isles and attracts winter (especially Christmas) visitors besides shoals of summer tourists. Thackeray's words are famous: 'Were such a bay laying upon English shores it would be a world's wonder. Perhaps if it were on the Mediterranean or Baltic, English travellers would flock to it in hundreds.' Palms, bamboos, fuchsias, arbutus, and other sub-tropical plants flourish here, and woods of oak, holly, hazel, yew, and rhododendrons grow right down to the water's edge. Every stone is extravagantly patterned; ivy and dainty mosses and ferns grow on every wall and tree-trunk. Higher up the most striking features of the landscape are the strange glacier-scratched outcrops of rock rising from the heather and bracken. The numerous hotels of Glengarriff are of good repute, and bathing, boating, freshwater and sea fishing, and rough shooting are available.

Walks and water excursions of consummate loveliness are innumerable. From the bridge on the Castletown Bere road you have a view of the broken-down Cromwell's Bridge. There are views of the harbour from the grounds of Lord Bantry's Lodge, north-west of the village. But perhaps the gem of Glengarriff is Garinish, or Garnish, which is also known as Ilnaculin Island, with its exquisite Italian gardens and loggias (admission 2s. 6d., boat fee by arrangement). Tons of soil were brought from the mainland to cover the barren rock. Shaw wrote most of *St. Joan* when staying at the Eccles Hotel. The most repaying climbs among the encircling mountains are Cobduff (1,244 feet), to the east, and the Sugarloaf (1,887 feet), to the south-west, three and six hours there and back respectively. North of the latter, among the precipices of the Caha Mountains, is a crowd of tiny tarns, alleged to be 365 in number.

The road from Glengarriff to Kenmare (T 65) is a tortuous and magnificent mountain drive of 18 miles, with breath-taking views. The road is splendidly engineered and can be climbed in top gear either way and free-wheeled down. At the top of a long ascent to 983 feet, with Killane Mountain (1,716 feet) on the left and Turner's Rock (1,393 feet) on the right, we pass through a tunnel into Co. Kerry. Every visitor to Glengarriff should get at least as far as this point. On either side (especially on the ascent) there is a profusion of wildly beautiful prospects. Three short tunnels are passed through on the way down, the beautiful cataracts of the River Sheen are seen, and finally the road crosses the Kenmare River by a two-span concrete cantilever bridge, 410 feet long, completed in 1936 to take the place of a suspension bridge that was the first of its type in Ireland (1838).

An alternative road from Glengarriff to Kenmare (both should be driven over if at all possible) is around Peninsula No. 3, that comprising the barony of Bere (pronounced 'Bear')—53 miles, by L 61 to Castletownbere, then L 62, a switchback route, narrow and winding, with gradients up to 1 in 10. Good surface for some miles, then rather rough. The landscapes of rocky outcrops, torrents, and mountains—Caha Mountains and, father west, the less elevated Slieve Miskish—are highly picturesque, and there are grand views across Bantry Bay and, on the latter half of the drive, of the great fiord called Kenmare River. Adrigole village is situated on a delightful harbour at the foot of Hungry Hill (2,251 feet), the highest in the peninsula. When in spate its stream forms a grand cascade as it dashes down over a rocky ledge 700 feet high.

The road from Adrigole over the mountains to Lauragh (a short cut to Kenmare) should be ascended at least as far as the Healy Pass, for the sake of the exquisite views therefrom. The road over the pass was constructed in

1931–5, at the instigation of Tim Healy, the Governor-General. There are countless hairpin bends on the Adrigole side. The top of the pass is marked by a white stone Calvary group.

Castletown Bere, once a copper-mining centre, has hotel accommodation. A natural roadstead separates it from Bere Island, which was retained by the British Government as a naval base when the Irish Free State was created, but was transferred to the Eire Government in 1938. A by-road goes on towards the end of the peninsula—Dursey Head, on Dursey Island, with grand cliffs—passing Dunboy Castle, once the stronghold of The O'Sullivan Bere. The story of its heroic resistance to Sir George Carew in 1602, after the battle of Kinsale, is told in Froude's *The Two Chiefs of Dunboy*.

The main road turns north at Castletown Bere to cross a gap in the Slieve Miskish and descends to Eyeries and Ballycrovane Harbour, on the shore of which stands a pillar stone with an Ogham inscription (page 47), the tallest (17½ feet) in the British Isles. The next inlets of Kenmare Harbour skirted by the road are Ardgroom Harbour (where Co. Kerry is entered) and Kilmakilloge Harbour. At the head of the latter, near Lauragh, lies Derreen, a wooded demesne. The side-road that leads thence across the mountains by way of the Healy Pass (cf. above) to Adrigole passes above Glanmore Lough, a lovely islet-dotted tarn. Farther on L 62 skirts Lough Cloonee and then runs close to the upper reach of the Kenmare River, passing Dinish Island and commanding a fine view of MacGillycuddy's Reeks. T 65 is joined on this side of the new bridge.

Kenmare, a featureless little town, but interesting on market-day (Wednesday), lies at the head of the Kenmare River, a lovely sea-lough 30 miles long, near the point where it is joined by the Roughty River, which is reputed to be the best unpreserved salmon river in Ireland. Sir William Petty, who superintended the redistribution of Irish lands and was destined to become the ancestor of the Marquises of Lansdowne, founded the town in 1670, with seventy-five soldier colonists, on land granted by the English Government. A fishery and ironworks were established, and the colony, expelled by the Irish in 1688, was refounded under William III. Kenmare now makes tweed, and the Convent of Poor Clares runs a lace industry. The town has good bathing, and is an excellent centre for angling and for excursions by land and water (Grand Atlantic Tour, see page 118).

The old road from Kenmare to Killarney (27 miles), like the bus route, is by way of Kilgarvan and the valley of the Flesk. Very much finer is the newer road via Moll's Gap (T 65, 21 miles), a remarkable piece of engineering, with an excellent surface. It climbs the valley of the Finnihy, with a splendid prospect of the Caha Mountains at your back. On the left rise Letter South (1,186 feet) and Boughil (2,065 feet); on the right, Peakeen (1,825 feet) and Derrygarriff (1,617 feet). At the rocky, narrow Moll's Gap the road is 864 feet above sea-level. Mac-Gillycuddy's Reeks then come into view on the other side of the valley of the Owenreagh River, far below.

Beyond Looscaunagh Lough, which lies at the foot of Foardal (1,308 feet) and Looscaunagh Hill (1,280 feet), you *must* stop to enjoy that 'ultimate beauty,' the world-famous 'Ladies' View' of the Vale of Killarney. The three lakes are framed in a sea of verdure, in strong contrast to the bareness of the uplands—in winter a symphony in gold and brown. The road winds its way down past the Upper, Middle, and Lower Lakes in succession, with the Purple Mountain (2,739 feet) and Shehy Mountain (1,827 feet) on the left, and Cromaglan Mountain (1,226 feet) and Torc Mountain (1,764 feet) on the right. You then pass, just below Galway's Bridge, the Derry-cunnihy Cascade, which is worth a few minutes' stop. Above Torc Cottage, by the Middle Lake, is the Torc Waterfall of the Owengarriff River, with a splendid view of the lake from the top.

Killarney ('Church of the Sloe') is the high spot of Ireland's scenic beauty and a place of world-wide renown. Its combination of mountain, lake, and river scenery with luxuriance of vegetation is incomparable, and Scott ('The grandest sight I have ever seen'), Wordsworth, Tennyson, and Thackeray are among those who swell the chorus of praise. To the west of the lakes, separated from Purple Mountain (2,739 feet), Shehy (1,827 feet), and Tomies (2,415 feet) by the Gap of Dunloe, rises Ireland's greatest mountain range, MacGillycuddy's Reeks, culminating in Carrantual (3,414 feet), while to the south-east, behind Torc Mountain, is the Mangerton range (Mangerton Mountain, 2,756 feet; Stoompa, 2,281 feet). The Upper, or MacCarthy More's, Lake, embedded in red sandstone mountains, is the smallest (430 acres) but the most beautiful of the three lakes. A broad stream called the Long Range, 2½ miles long, connects it with the Middle, or Muckross, Lake (680 acres, with eight islets), which in its turn drains into the Lower Lake, or Lough Leane (5,000 acres and more than thirty islands). The Middle and Lower Lakes are set in limestone and slate. The River Flesk flows into the Lower Lake, and the River Laune drains it into Dingle Bay. The eastern banks of all three lakes, including the Muckross estate and abbey, are now a national park.

One of the chief attractions of the Killarney district is the beauty of its lanes and the exuberance of its vegetation. Cedars of Lebanon, fuchsias, the Kerry arbutus, London Pride, and many ferns (including the royal fern and the rare Killarney fern) thrive in this sheltered situation. Keep a look out, too, for the spotted slug of Kerry, which is found nowhere else in the British Isles.

Killarney town itself, situated not far from the north-east bank of the Lower Lake, is of little interest and is heavily commercialized for the tourist traffic. Many of the shops are devoted to the sale of lace and wood-carvings, and the place is infested in the high season with vendors of souvenirs, would-be guides, etc. The simplest way to see Killarney's sights, for visitors in a hurry at least, is to resign oneself to the inevitable and join the official tours. The Roman Catholic cathedral, built from Augustus Welby Pugin's masterly designs in 1846, is considered to be the best Catholic church in Ireland. Killarney House was burnt down in 1913, but the demesne is open to the public and is worth visiting for the sake of the lovely view from the terrace.

A road, 1¾ miles long, leads from the town direct to Ross

Castle, which is situated at the neck of Ross Island, a peninsula projecting into the Lower Lake. The castle was once the chief fortress of The O'Donoghue and was defended by Lord Muskerry against Cromwell in 1652. It consists of outworks with round corner-towers and of a fourteenth-century keep ascended by a winding staircase and commanding a grand view. A boat should without fail be hired here for the visit to Innisfallen, the largest island in the lake and generally considered the gem of Killarney, with its splendid rowans and hollies. Macaulay declared it was 'not a reflex of heaven, but a bit of heaven itself.' On it are the remains of a monastery founded in the seventh century by St. Finian Lobhar (the leper).

Close to the Kenmare road, about 2½ miles from the centre of the town, is *Muckross Abbey*, in the lovely demesne of Muckross House (no motor-cars admitted). Refounded as a Franciscan friary by Donal MacCarthy in 1440, the monastery was not finally extinguished till 1652. Members of the MacCarthy, MacGillycuddy, O'Donoghue, and O'Sullivan families (including Owen Roe, the poet) are buried here. The features of the ruins are the square tower and east window of the church, and the tiny but beautiful cloisters, with round arches on two sides and pointed on the other two, and an old yew-tree, 60 feet tall, growing in the centre. On the narrow strip of land between the Lower and Middle Lakes the jarvey points out various spots imaginatively connected with the murder of the 'Colleen Bawn' (page 142). You cross Brickeen Bridge ('brickeen' = small trout) to Dinish Island, and then cross the Meeting of the Waters, an exquisite spot, to gain the main road (over 4 miles from the entrance to the demesne).

For the visit to Aghadoe, take the Tralee road north-wards, keep left by the old road, and turn left. The church of Aghadoe ('Field of the Two Yews'), now in ruins, was founded by St. Finian and has a Romanesque doorway, while the choir is a thirteenth-century addition. Adjacent are the stump of a Round Tower, 12 feet high, and a Round Castle of the ninth (?) century, with walls six feet thick. But far and away the chief attraction of

Aghadoe is its tremendous view of the Lower Lake in its mountain setting.

A fine day is essential for the next excursion, the classic one from Killarney—a 20-mile round, including the drive to Kate Kearney's Cottage, the walk or ride through the Gap of Dunloe, and a boat trip on the three lakes (inclusive charge about 40s. each, including the hire of a pony through the Gap). Boats are not easily obtainable out of the tourist season. It is almost essential to join an official tour, because, though motorists can drive as far as Arbutus Cottage and walk through the Gap to Lord Brandon's Cottage, they are not likely to find a boat there unless previously ordered, and in any case they would, of course, have to get back to Arbutus Cottage in order to recover their car. You take the Killorglin road and after 6½ miles turn left to cross the River Laune at its efflux from the Lower Lake. On the right is Dunloe Castle, the modernized fastness of The O'Sullivan, dating from 1215.

Turn left again for the *Gap of Dunloe,* an amazingly wild and boulder-strewn gorge through the heart of the mountains—Tomies and Purple Mountain on the left, MacGillycuddy's Reeks on the right. Cars park at Kate Kearney's Cottage or (out of the season) at Arbutus Cottage, which is the limit for wheels, more than a mile farther on. Ponies may be hired for the four-mile ride through the Gap. The would-be pedestrian is beset by 'guides,' pony-drivers, photographers, and musicians of all kinds, who offer to arouse echoes from the cliffs for a suitable fee. The sombre Coosaun Lough (on the left) and the Black, Cushvally, and Auger Loughs (right) are passed. St. Patrick is supposed to have drowned Ireland's last snake in the Black Lough. There is another Black Lough above Arbutus Cottage. The head of the Gap, a good hour's walk from Kate Kearney's Cottage, is 795 feet above sea-level. On the right rises Drishana (1,490 feet), and the Gentleman's Rock and the Balanced Rock are passed on the left. The view of the Upper Lake from a point farther on is superb. On the right is the Black Valley and its loughs.

On the descent you keep to the left, pass Lord Brandon's

E

Cottage, and arrive at the bank of the Upper Lake, where you embark on the return journey. The boatman entertains his passengers with legends about various points of interest. You pass through the Long Range, noting the arbutuses and royal ferns on its banks, while the boatman's bugle shows off the echo from the Eagle's Nest Rock (1,100 feet), towering above the stream. The swift current carries the boat under the Old Weir Bridge and through the Meeting of the Waters (a particularly lovely spot) into the Middle Lake, whence, passing under the Brickeen Bridge, you gain the Lower Lake and the landing place near Ross Castle.

The best hill to climb near Killarney is Mangerton Mountain, the ascent of which is easy, but will occupy about two and a half hours. Take the road to the left beyond Muckross, keep left, and after about a mile take the bridle-path to the right. High up on the mountainside you come to the Devil's Punch Bowl, a crater-tarn reputed to be 700 feet deep. Below, to the east, lies a deep glen with three sombre tarns. The view from the top (2,756 feet) is the finest in the Killarney area, and on a clear day you can make out MacGillycuddy's Reeks, the Slieve Mish, the Shannon, the Galtee Mountains, the Caha Mountains, and Kenmare River.

MacGillycuddy's Reeks (pronounced Máclicuddy), Ireland's greatest mountain range, are a shapeless mass of sandstone, with four peaks of over 3,000 feet, of which Carrantual, or Carrantuohill (3,414 feet), is the highest mountain in Ireland. The Reeks (i.e. rocks) were once the fastness of the MacGillycuddy clan, the chief of which is still known as The MacGillycuddy of the Reeks. The ascent of Carrantual takes a long day, and a guide is advisable. The usual route is by a bridle-track diverging from the Gap of Dunloe and the Gaddagh valley. The view from the top is disappointing, and the expedition is hardly one that can be recommended to the average tourist. The very picturesque drive, however, skirting the north side of the Reeks, via Beaufort Bridge, Kilgobnet, and Lough Acoose to the lonely Glencar Hotel (22 miles), is well worth doing for its own sake.

The 'Grand Atlantic Tour,' or 'Ring of Kerry,' accomplished by motor-coaches from Killarney in the season, usually in the reverse direction to that described below, is a round of 110 miles encircling the Iveragh peninsula, the fourth great peninsula of the south-west, between the Kenmare River and Dingle Bay. Its mountain spine extends west from MacGillycuddy's Reeks and includes many peaks of over 2,000 feet (the highest, Coomacarrea, 2,541 feet). The bus route from Killarney is via Farranfore to Killorglin, Cahirciveen, and Valentia Harbour.

The tour begins with the drive to Kenmare by Moll's Gap, as described on page 114 (well worth repeating in the reverse direction for its own sake). Outside Kenmare you turn right by T 66 along the north shore of the Kenmare River, passing (left) the O'Sullivan castle of Dunkerron and the O'Mahony castle of Dromore. On the right rises Knockanaskill (1,170 feet), and there are fine views of the Caha Mountains across the Kenmare River. After a long, dull stretch, with views hidden by a wall, you cross the mouth of the wooded valley of the Blackwater, with Knocknagullion (1,360 feet) on the right, and enjoy a splendid stretch of 'corniche' road. Then Fadda Lough, to the right, with its extraordinary bank of smooth, rounded, terraced rock. Opposite is Rossmore Island. Beyond the hamlet of Tahilla, on Congar Harbour, are the entrances to the Parknasilla Hotel and Derryquin Castle, facing Rossdohan Island.

Parknasilla, 14 miles from Kenmare, consists mainly of a first-class railway hotel, formerly the mansion of Dr. Graves, Bishop of Limerick (d. 1899), with lovely grounds. The winter climate is of the mildest, and subtropical plants flourish here. The bathing is excellent, and the boating among the innumerable islands of the inlet is incomparable. Perhaps the finest water excursion is to the exquisite island of Garinish (permission necessary), with its elaborate plantations, which are now, however, overgrown.

Sneem lies in a basin at the head of the inlet, with a magnificent circle of mountains rising in all directions. The road (T 66 still) then runs inland for a while, passing through a gap in the hills, but approaches the shore again at Glanlough. Next comes a splendid run through a wilderness of rocks, with the sea close at hand. From Castlecove a by-road on the right, recently remade, ascends into the mountains, to *Staigue Fort* or Póna na Stéige, about 2½ miles. This ranks as the finest pre-historic stone fortress in Ireland (outside the Aran Islands). Almost circular, with a diameter of 114 feet, it is composed of an unmortared wall of excellent craftsmanship, still keeping its original height of 18 feet on the north side and with two small chambers and several elaborate stair-ways in its thickness (5–13½ feet). The only entrance doorway is on the south side.

The colouring of Cove Harbour is particularly attractive. At White Strand and elsewhere along this coast there are alluring sands. Scariff and Deenish are conspicuous islands at the mouth of the Kenmare River. From Caherdaniel a side-road on the left leads to beautiful Derrynane, famous as the home of the 'Liberator,' Daniel O'Connell.

On Abbey Island there are the remains of a primitive 'abbey.' The road, splendidly engineered, then climbs high up on the mountainside to Coomakista Gap (683 feet), whence you obtain magnificent views in both directions. On the equally grand four-mile descent to Waterville—you can free-wheel all the way down—a group of menhirs is passed on the right. You catch a glimpse of the Skelligs, beyond Bolus Head.

Waterville, 24 miles from Parknasilla, is situated on a narrow neck of land between the wide Ballinskelligs Bay and the freshwater Lough Currane, and has been described as a 'sportsman's paradise,' with shooting, fishing, golf, and bathing. It is certainly a most attractive-looking place for a holiday. The Butler Arms and the Southern Lake Hotel are highly commended, and their terms are moderate.

Lough Currane, 17 miles in circuit, is famous for its free sea-trout fishing. On Church Island, one of its innumerable islets, are the primitive house of St. Finan, circular outside and rectangular inside, and the ruins of a Romanesque church.

Favourite excursions are to the headlands that enclose
Ballinskelligs Bay, Hog's Head on the south and Bolus
Head on the north, the latter rising to a height of 1,330
feet and commanding grand views.

The main road (T 66, 10 miles) cuts across the neck of
a wide peninsula direct to Cahirciveen, while the coast
road (23 miles), diverging on the other side of Inny Bridge,
and, very rough and lonely, passes Ballinskelligs, skirts
St. Finan's Bay, scales a terrific zigzag hill, and drops
down to Portmagee, opposite Valentia Island (ferry). In
calm weather a motor-boat should be hired here for the
most interesting thirteen-mile trip to the *Skelligs* (i.e.
rocks), breeding-places of gannets and shearwaters. Great
Skellig, or Skellig Michael, is a slaty cone of 705 feet with
a lighthouse. A stone stairway of 600 steps mounts to
a group of early monastic ruins within an enclosure wall,
at a height of 540 feet. These surpass everything of the
kind in Ireland and comprise six beehive cells, two holy
wells, two drystone oratories, and a church of later date.
In days of old Skellig Michael was a famous place of
pilgrimage.

Cahirciveen (pronounced 'Care-see-veen'), i.e. 'Fortress
of Sabina,' is a market town on the Valentia River, at the
foot of Bentee (1,245 feet). As you approach it, you have
a splendid view of Valentia Island and River. On the
opposite bank of the inlet are Ballycarbery Castle, once
a MacCarthy stronghold, and a stone fort 75 feet in
diameter, with a wall 14 feet thick.

From Valentia Harbour, at the mouth of the inlet,
two miles from Cahirciveen by road, a motor-ferry plies
to Knightstown, the chief place on *Valentia Island*. The
ferry accommodates motor-cars, and there are jaunting
cars for hire on the island. The island, which is seven miles
long by two miles wide, is said to have been given its name
(often spelled Valencia) by Spanish merchants; actually it
is a corruption of Beal Inishe. Knightstown was named
after the owner of the island, the Knight of Kerry, of
the Fitzgerald family. Among the island's attractions
are a mild climate—fuchsias and arum lilies are rampant
here—bathing and golfing, the cliffs of Fogher and Bray
Head, and the view from Deokaun (888 feet). The first

Atlantic cable was laid by the *Great Eastern* in 1866, after many failures, from Valentia Island to Newfoundland, and the Western Union cables now come to land here.

The fine road from Cahirciveen to Killorglin (T 66, 26 miles) passes Carhan House, a mile out of town, the birthplace of O'Connell but now a ruin. It then surmounts a gap in the mountains—Knocknadober (2,267 feet) on the left, Mullaghmarakill (2,182 feet), Been Hill (2,199 feet), and Drung Hill (2,104 feet) on the right—and follows the south shore of Dingle Bay for a while, half-way up the hillside, with entrancing views across the bay of the Dingle mountains and the Blasket Islands, and of the remarkable line of sand dunes at the head of the bay. On the right an exquisitely beautiful line of mountains, ending in Seefin (1,621 feet), comes into sight.

Glenbeigh is a delightful spot, with two excellent hotels, fishing, golfing, and bathing, pretty walks in the glen of the Behy, and a magnificent view from Windy Gap. Beyond Caragh Bridge a road diverges right for the beautiful Lough Caragh. At Killorglin, an uninviting little market town, those who are not returning to Killarney (T 67, 14 miles) should keep left and connect up with the following tour at Milltown.

TOUR V: KILLARNEY TO LIMERICK

DINGLE—THE BLASKETS—GALLERUS—BRANDON MOUNTAIN—
TRALEE — ARDFERT — BALLYBUNION — ADARE — LIMERICK
—SHANNON SCHEME—KILLALOE—LOUGH DERG—CLONFERT
—BIRR—ROSCREA—HOLYCROSS ABBEY—CASHEL—CAHIR—
MITCHELSTOWN CAVES—KILMALLOCK.

Total distance by road: about 400 miles.

THE direct road, 69 miles (followed by the railway and bus routes, except that they digress westward to serve Tralee), is by T 29 to Farranfore, L 103 to Castleisland, and T 28 via Abbeyfeale, Newcastle West, and Adare, 4 miles beyond which T 11 is joined.

The tourist's route, however, is by the coast and the south shore of the Shannon estuary, including a visit to Corcaguiny, or the Dingle Promontory, which is the northernmost of the five great peninsulas of south-west Ireland and has first-class scenic and archaeological attractions. The first section is from Killarney to Dingle, 42 miles—by railway via Tralee, but the light railway from Tralee to Dingle has been superseded by a bus service. Bearing right from the Killorglin road after 3¼ miles, you join T 66 at Milltown and turn right. In the grounds of the Elizabethan Kilcolman Abbey at Milltown are the ruins of Killagh Priory, an Augustinian foundation of the thirteenth century. Castlemaine, a picturesque little place, has lost its trade through the silting up of the River Maine.

Here you turn left by L 103 and soon skirt the north side of Castlemaine Harbour, as the shallow innermost portion of Dingle Bay is called. On the north are the grand Slieve Mish ('Mountains of Phantoms'), culminating in Baurtregaum (2,796 feet). Inch is a sheltered place with an hotel and a famous strand. It is situated at the neck of the sandy spit, 3 miles in length, which gives it its name. The road then hugs the shore of Dingle Bay, with a view of

MacGillycuddy's Reeks across the water; it turns inland to join T 68 at Annascaul, which is noted for its prehistoric forts. Croaghskearda (2,001 feet) is the most prominent peak of the mountain range on the right of the road, which now describes a rather complicated corkscrew climb.

Dingle ('fortress'), the most westerly town in Europe, is situated on a landlocked inlet and once traded with Spain, though its harbour is now chiefly devoted to fishing. Bathing, boating, and golf are available. The nearest of the mountains that rise in the background is Ballysitteragh (2,050 feet). Dingle is the centre of the Gaeltacht (Gaelic-speaking district) of Kerry, which is much frequented by civil servants and others who come here to learn the language at summer schools. The Dingle district is almost unrivalled for its combination of lovely scenery with a plethora of prehistoric and early Christian antiquities. Most of these are to be seen in the following two rounds by rough roads from Dingle, about 50 miles' driving in all. A large-scale map is desirable.

Menhirs known as the Gates of Glory are passed on the way west to Ventry, between which and Slea Head is a unique collection of over four hundred 'clochans,' or bee-hive huts. These are mostly grouped near Fahan, which must have been the site of a great prehistoric settlement. At Fahan, too, is the cliff castle of Dunbeg, with a stone wall 25 feet thick at one place. Slea Head, and Mount Eagle above it (1,695 feet), command fine views of the Iveragh peninsula and the Blaskets, but Dunmore Head, farther north, is the westernmost point of the Irish mainland.

From Dunquin a boat may be hired for an expedition to the rocky *Blasket Islands*. The lighthouse on Tearaght is the most westerly habitation in the British Isles, the westernmost fragments of soil being the Foze Rocks.

There are now less than a hundred people in Blasket, living in two dozen stone houses, of which a few are still thatched, the most are roofed with boards and tarred canvas. Little mortar shows in the chinks between the flat stones. An old box serves as a chimney-pot—there are no sparks from peat. . . . Floors are of driftwood and ships' hatches, well sprinkled daily with fine sand from the White Strand. When a man desires a house for himself he builds it from native rock and driftwood wherever he pleases on the unenclosed land (no rent, rates, or taxes are paid by Blasket people—they said because the new Government cherished them for their good Irish!), which is free to all, and without troubling his head about minimum cubic capacities, sanitation, water, and suchlike. The result is picturesque but not everywhere pleasant underfoot. One must turn one's eyes to the sky, the sea, the mountain, and the fields in Blasket, for the village itself is a wilderness of nettles and weeds, with hens scratching in dung and midden heaps, and cows and donkeys browsing here and there, both in and out of doorways. Such conditions and the wild lonely winters are driving out the young people with ambition. They tell you in Blasket that in twenty years more there will not be a house occupied in the island. There has been scarcely one marriage or birth for a decade now.

R. M. LOCKLEY in *The Countryman*, January 1938.

The last inhabitants of Great Blasket, however, were removed in 1953.

The road goes on from Dunquin to Ballyferriter, near Smerwick Harbour, where a Spanish force landed in 1579 and built the Fort del Oro. In the following year, however, the fort was stormed by Lord Grey and the garrison put to the sword. Curraghs used by the intrepid local fishermen (made of tarred canvas over a frame of laths) are to be seen hereabouts. The neighbouring cliffs of Sybil Head are magnificent. From Ballyferriter a road leads direct back to Ventry; or you can cut across country by a farm road to Ballynana (accent on last syllable), for Gallerus.

Taking the road north-west from Milltown, the western suburb of Dingle, you cross a gap in the hills, the view from which, of Smerwick Harbour with the Three Sisters on the left and Ballydavid Head on the right, is one of exquisite loveliness. Just beyond the top of the gap a road leads half left to Ballynana, in the fields beyond which is seen the famous primitive *Oratory of Gallerus*, not far from the south-east corner of Smerwick Harbour. Dating from the seventh century, this is the best preserved example of its kind in existence. It is built with consummate skill of drystone masonry, in the shape of an upturned boat; the base is rectangular (22 by 18½ feet), while the

* E

roof is formed on the corbel principle, by the gradual approximation of the side walls. Both the doorway, which narrows towards the top, and the sole window, semicircular and with deep splays, are the work of master craftsmen. At Kilmalkedar (accent on 'kee'), a little farther on, the ruined church is a good example of Hiberno-Romanesque of the twelfth century, with decorated arches and a row of columns in either wall of the nave, while the churchyard contains a cross, a sundial, and Ogham and other incised stones, curious cairn tombs, etc. Turning right at the wayside school, beyond the Catholic church, you pass Feohanagh on your devious and bumpy way to Ballynahow (alias Tiduff), and follow the turf-cutters' road as far as you can beyond that hamlet to the best starting-point for the three hours' climb to the top of *Brandon Mountain* (3,127 feet). This, the highest mountain in Ireland outside MacGillycuddy's Reeks, is the more striking as it rises almost immediately from the sea. It is associated with St. Brendan (483–576), who, according to the legend, sailed hence in a curragh and discovered America. The mountain top, which commands a most impressive view, used to be the goal of a pilgrimage. The cliffs of Brandon Head are over 1,200 feet high. If you cannot spare the time for Brandon, at least climb Beennamman (1,238 feet) for a grand view of the iron-bound coast, with the white surf of the Atlantic rollers breaking against the cliffs, all misty with spray. You can return direct from Ballynahow to Dingle by quite a decent road.

The main road from Dingle to Tralee is T 68, with grand views of the Slieve Mish, but it is very little longer (30 miles) and much more exciting to take the steep road over the mountains by way of the spectacular Connor Pass (1,300 feet), whence there are magnificent views in all directions. It descends along the side of the cliffs and then runs between Beenoskee (2,713 feet) and Brandon Bay and by-passes Castlegregory, which is a nice little bathing resort with good sands and a comfortable hotel or two. To the north of it stretches the sandy headland terminating in Rough Point, at the entrance to Tralee Bay. Off the point are the Seven Hogs, or Magharee

Islands. The road then skirts the shore of Tralee Bay, with the lovely Slieve Mish (the south side of which was seen in the earlier part of this tour) rising on the right. The approach to Tralee is along the remains of a ship canal.

Tralee, the busy capital of Kerry, lies on the River Lee, near its influx into Tralee Bay, with which the town is connected by a ship canal. There is a bus service to Fenit, the foreport. Tralee has had a stormy history and has lost all its old buildings. The shops are good, and the central part of the town wears a distinguished air. Tralee was the chief residence of the Fitzgerald Earls of Desmond, the last of whom was slain in the mountains near here in 1583 by Ormonde's men.

The touring route from Tralee to Limerick is via Bally-bunion, 81 miles in all, mostly by L 105. The scenery is tame and bleak in comparison with what has just been seen. *Ardfert*, pronounced 'Ard-fairt' and meaning 'hill of the grave,' was the seat of a bishopric founded by St. Brendan but now merged in that of Limerick. The ruins of the thirteenth-century cathedral, a grand, fortress-like structure with curious battlements, are approached by steps in the wall at the south-east corner of the neglected graveyard. Near this is an Ogham stone, and the church-yard contains a great many ponderous vaults and two ruined churches. The cathedral has a Romanesque west door and arcading, while the choir is lighted by lancet windows, including a magnificent triplet at the east end. In the grounds of Ardfert Abbey are the considerable ruins of a Franciscan friary founded in 1253 by Thomas Fitzmaurice. Sir Roger Casement was landed on Ardfert sands by a German submarine on Good Friday, 1916, but was promptly arrested.

Ballyheigue, where you bear right, is close to Kerry Head, on the south side of the mouth of the Shannon. Just short of Ballyduff a rough lane leads to the Round Tower of Rattoo, which is seen rising among the trees on the right. In a pretty setting, it is 92 feet high and 48 feet in girth, and perfect except that the cap is a restoration. Farther on you cross the Cashen River.

Bear left at Ballyconry—the mountain on the right is

Knockamore (880 feet)—for *Ballybunion* ('town of the
saplings'), a popular and pleasantly unsophisticated little
seaside resort, with fine cliffs and caves, the battered fragment of a castle, miles of splendid sands, first-class golf,
and plenty of amusements in summer. The Castle, the
Central, and the West End are the chief hotels.

The only mono-rail track in the British Isles (on the
Lartigue system) was constructed between Ballybunion
and Listowel in 1888, but regrettably, in the opinion of
railway enthusiasts, it was dismantled in 1925.

There is some remarkable cliff scenery in Doon Bay,
which our road passes a mile farther on. Near Beale you
get noble views of the mouth of the Shannon, which
redeems an otherwise monotonous countryside. (The
Shannon is the greatest river in the British Isles, 214
miles long, though its source is only 20 miles from the
sea.) Ballylongford lies at the head of a creek, at the
mouth of which (west side) is Carrigafoyle Castle, once
the property of the O'Connors of Kerry; there is an excellent view of the Shannon estuary from the top of its
tower. Opposite is Scattery Island with its Round Tower
and other ruins (see page 142).

Lord Kitchener was born in 1850 at Gunsborough Lodge,
4 miles from Ballylongford, on the way to Listowel, but
spent his early years at Ballygoghlan, on the top of a
wooded hill two miles south of the Tarbert–Glin road. In
1857 the family moved to Crotta House, 10 miles from
Listowel on the Tralee road.

At Tarbert you join the splendid main road (T 68), leave
Kerry for Co. Limerick, and for twelve very scenic miles
run close to the south shore of the Shannon estuary, which
here is from one to two miles broad. On this side of Glin,
a picturesque Shannon resort, you pass Glin Castle, which
has been held by the Knights of Glin (FitzGerald family)
for over seven hundred years. Beyond Loghill comes
Mount Trenchard, former seat of Lord Monteagle, one of
whose ancestors is commemorated by a great cross on
the hill.

Foynes, with Foynes Island opposite, was a seaplane
base in the Second World War and the jumping off place
for the British, French, and American transatlantic

aircraft. Looking back beyond Foynes, you have a striking view of an old ruined church and its graveyards on the skyline of the hill above Foynes.

On an island in the River Deel, at Askeaton, are the gaunt and broken remains of Desmond Castle, the last home of the last Earl of Desmond (page 127). (Desmond = South Munster.) The beautiful cloisters of the Franciscan friary on the east bank date from 1420. The feature of the road thence to Limerick is the extraordinary number of ruined castles and peel towers, erected for the security of the Shannon estuary. But it is very much preferable to take the second turning on the right beyond Askeaton and follow a by-road through a pretty country-side of quite an English aspect in order to see Adare.

Adare ('ford of the oaks'), on the high road from Killarney to Limerick, is a model village, quite un-Irish in its spick-and-spanness, and a creation of the Earls of Dunraven, whose Irish seat is Adare Manor. The Catholic church represents the church of a Trinitarian friary founded in 1230 and known as the White Abbey. Apply at the Dunraven Arms, one of Ireland's most famous hotels, much frequented by hunting and fishing folk (black ties in the evening), for a permit (1s.) to visit the lovely and exceedingly trim demesne of Adare Manor, the entrance to which is opposite. Here, beyond a private bridge over the River Maigue, is the old castle of the O'Donovans, rebuilt by the second Earl of Kildare (d. 1328), with a moated keep and other buildings (all labelled) within a battlemented wall. Adjacent are the ivied ruins of the parish church, and farther upstream are the extensive ruins of a Franciscan friary, founded in 1464 by the seventh earl, with Fitzgerald tombs in carved niches, pretty chapels, tiny cloisters with a tall yew in the centre, and various domestic buildings (all labelled). The beauty of the setting is unforgettable, though the golf links strike a rather inharmonious note. Near the picturesque old four-teen-arch (public) bridge is the Protestant church, a relic of an Augustinian friary (1315). On the exterior of the south aisle (formerly the Lady Chapel) is a Tudor rose, said to be the only example of its kind in Ireland. The font is believed to be an Italian work of early Christian days. Adjoining the cloisters is the mausoleum of the Dunravens (Wyndham-Quin family). The old refectory is now used as a school.

From Adare you drive direct to Limerick (10 miles) by T 28, soon joining T 11.

Limerick ('bare spot'), the third largest city of Eire, with a population of 51,000, is a busy seaport on the south bank of the Shannon, just above the estuary. It is an animated town, with a trade in bacon, butter, and condensed milk, tobacco factories, etc., and is noted for its lace (fine guipure lace made at the Convent of the Good Shepherd). There are plenty of good hotels in Limerick since the opening of Shannon Airport (page 141). The city is divided into three districts—English Town, the dirty old walled quarter on the north side, within the curve of the Abbey River; Irish Town, in the centre of the city; and Newtown Pery, which was laid out in chessboard pattern by Edmond Sexton Pery (d. 1806), M.P. for Limerick and ancestor of the Earls of Limerick.

A Danish foundation, Limerick became, under Brian Boru, the capital of the kings of Munster and the centre of the O'Brien power. In the course of the Civil War it was captured by the Irish in 1641, but in 1651 Hugh O'Neill, after holding out for six months against Ireton (who died of the plague here), had to surrender it to Parliament. The famous siege of Limerick, however, was that of 1690–1, when it was the last refuge of the Irish Royalists. The Earl of Tyrconnel successfully repulsed William III's initial assault, and after his death Patrick Sarsfield, Limerick's hero, sallied forth to surprise and destroy the siege train. It was not till 3rd October 1691 that Sarsfield capitulated to General Ginkel, on honourable terms that were subsequently violated, with the result that 11,000 Irish soldiers enlisted in the French service—the beginning of the 'Flight of the Wild Geese.'

Everybody wants to know why 'limericks' are so called. According to the *Concise Oxford Dictionary*, they are said to be from the chorus 'Will you come up to Limerick?' sung after extempore verses contributed each by a member of the party.

The main (and most presentable) thoroughfare of

Limerick is O'Connell Street, with its fine rows of Georgian houses and a statue of the Liberator at the south end. Patrick Street and Rutland Street continue it to the north, leaving the Customs House (dating from 1769) on the left. Thence Mathew Bridge crosses the Abbey River to English Town.

The cathedral of St. Mary, founded *c.* 1172 by Domhnall O'Brien, King of Munster, possibly on the site of his palace, is a building of various periods, with double aisles, a slim west tower (view from the top), and battlements of the Irish type. There is a Romanesque west doorway, and fine lancets at either end of the church. The interior is notable for the twenty-four fifteenth-century misericords on the choir-stalls (unique in Ireland), each carved out of a single piece of oak, with quaint subjects, and for the splendid series of monuments (all labelled and described), including those of the Earls of Limerick in the chapel at the west end of the south aisle. In the choir, on the left of the altar, is the tomb-slab of the founder (d. 1194), below a Jacobean monument (1678) to his descendant Donough O'Brien, Earl of Thomond.

Bow Lane, by the side of the cathedral, leads to the County Court, City Court, and (disused) Gaol, handsome eighteenth-century buildings. Nicholas Street leads from the cathedral to King John's Castle, on the river bank, a splendid example of Norman military architecture, with massive walls and drum-towers and a fine gateway in the middle of the picturesque river front, which still bears marks of bombardment and is well seen from Thomond Bridge. (Thomond was the ancient principality of North Munster.) At the farther end of the bridge is the famous stone on which the repudiated treaty of 1691 was signed.

Return to the cathedral and take Athlunkard Street on the left to see the unsightly remains of O'Brien's Castle, a fortified house. Then return and follow Mary Street (left) past Whittamore's Castle (on the right), a much better example of the same, and Barrington's Hospital (1829). From Ball's Bridge over the Abbey River the street straight on leads to St. John's Hospital and St. John's Catholic Cathedral (1860).

Kate O'Brien, the Limerick novelist, was born at Boru

House, a red-brick villa on the outskirts of the town, and three of her novels are set in 'Mellick,' the Shannon valley, the 'Bearnagh hills' of Clare, and the 'Vale of Honey' (Golden Vein).   The Limerick of the sixties and seventies of last century is dealt with in *Without My Cloak*, the Limerick of 1880 in *The Ante-Room*, and the Limerick of 1937 in *Pray for the Wanderer*.   In the first of these is a memorable description of the Old Town, with 'its broken monasteries and looms and wine-vats, its decaying panelled parlour, its walls broken in siege, its humpy old bridges linking canalled and rivered islands—all, all of the past, their purpose and glory done and only the grey beauty of patience left in them to face the unclean end.   But what a beauty . . . like the beauty of an old woman at prayer.'

To see the famous Shannon Scheme, leave the city by Athlunkard Street, and after crossing the Abbey River, the Shannon, and the canal, turn left for Ardnacrusha, 3½ miles from Limerick.   The Shannon hydro-electric development was carried out by the Irish Government in 1925–9, with the help of the firm of Siemens-Schuckert, and was the first step in providing a national electricity supply system.   Twelve other new power stations are under construction or planned to meet the demand for electricity for domestic and industrial use.

The three Shannon lakes, Loughs Derg, Ree, and Allen, provide the water storage for the Ardnacrusha station, and the main control at O'Brien's Bridge comprises a weir with three sluice gates built across the old river bed and the adjoining intake to the head-race canal.   This canal, 7½ miles long, conveys the water required for the turbines to a 100-foot head at Ardnacrusha, where it is used at the rate of 100 tons a second through each of the 20-foot wide penstock pipes.   The power station, which may be visited any day, contains three turbo-generators of 38,600 h.p. each and one of 40,000 h.p.   Current generated at 10,500 volts is stepped up to 38,000 and 110,000 volts for transmission over the grid to Dublin and other parts of the country. The oil switches are at a distance from the main building, the most fascinating part of which is the control room.

A tail-race over a mile long, excavated completely

through rock, carries the water back to the Shannon. Barges are lifted from the tail-race to the head-race through a navigation lock. A salmon ladder is provided at the O'Brien's Bridge weir, and a fish pass of the lift type will be constructed at the Ardnacrusha power station.

Before proceeding with your exploration of the west coast, it will be as well at this juncture to amplify your acquaintance with southern Ireland by the following 200-mile circular tour inland from Limerick, which covers excellent roads all the way.

From Ardnacrusha make for Killaloe by way of Cloonlara and O'Brien's Bridge. If you drive from Limerick to Killaloe direct, you should take the road via Castleconnell, a decayed but delightful Georgian spa, noted for its salmon-fishing.

Killaloe ('Church of St. Dalua,' who died A.D. 622; pronounced 'Killaloo'), 14 miles from Limerick, is a small town beautifully situated at the south end of Lough Derg, between the Arra Mountains on the east (1,517 feet) and the Slieve Bernagh on the west (1,746 feet). The Shannon is here spanned by a narrow thirteen-arch bridge near its efflux from the lough. St. Flannan's Cathedral, now Protestant, was built in 1170–1200 by Domhnall O'Brien (the founder of Limerick Cathedral), and is lighted wholly by lancets. The south-west doorway, as seen from inside, is a gem of Hiberno-Romanesque sculpture, with its four orders decorated with chevrons, lozenges, foliage, grotesque animals, and human heads. In front of it is the only stone in existence with a bilingual inscription in Runes and Oghams (a full description hangs on the wall). Note also the old cross (immured) and the font. In the churchyard is St. Flannan's Oratory, a primitive structure with a steep stone roof and a doorway with quaint capitals. St. Lua's Oratory, by the Catholic church, has been moved from its original site on an island in the Shannon.

Lough Derg is the largest of the string of lakes formed by the Shannon, being 23 miles long and 2–3 miles broad. The road on the west, or Clare, side gives at first a perfect idea of its exquisite beauty; later on you have only distant glimpses. A mile from Killaloe the green mound of

Kincora, where Brian Boru had his palace, is passed on
the right. Scarriff ('rough place'), near the head of
a lovely bay, and Mountshannon are passed on the way
to Portumna (34 miles; L 12 to Tuamgraney, which has a
tenth-century church, then T 41). From either place a
boat trip may be made to Holy Island or Iniscaltra, on
which there are remains of a monastery founded by St.
Caimin in the seventh century—St. Caimin's Church,
with its unique triangular window, St. Brigid's and St.
Mary's Churches, and a Round Tower 80 feet in height,
with its cap missing, but visible from the main road.
T 41 enters Co. Galway at Cannagh. Portumna, a smart
little town, is at the north end of Lough Derg. Portumna
Castle was rebuilt on a different site after a fire in
1826.

From Portumna you should pick your way through excellent country lanes, north-east, via Eyrecourt, to *Clonfert*
(16 miles), which is close to the Grand Canal and the
Shannon. Its name means 'Meadow of the Grave,' i.e. of
St. Brendan. The tiny Protestant cathedral here, built of
a lovely grey limestone, represents the final effort of native
Irish architecture, dating from 1166, six years before the
arrival of the Anglo-Normans. Its west doorway, of six
orders (the seventh is a later addition), shows the utmost
variety of motifs and ranks among the greatest achieve-
ments of Romanesque art in Europe. The pediment above
it encloses an arcade with carved heads and diaper work
of portrait heads and foliage. The key of the church is
kept at Clonfert House (ask at the shop opposite). The
twin east windows, deeply splayed, are chaste in design
and of perfect proportions, the jointing of the masonry
being of unsurpassable finish. Note also the strange little
reliefs on the chancel arch, the vaulting under the tower,
and the old font and tomb-slabs at the west end.

Co. Offaly is entered as the Shannon is crossed at
Banagher (two old bridge-towers), where Anthony Trollope
spent ten years as post office surveyor (1841–51), and began
his novel-writing, unsuccessfully at first. You then come
in 15 miles, after enjoying a view of the Shannon valley,
to *Birr* ('a spring'), in Co. Offaly. Known from its
central position in Ireland as 'Umbilicus Hiberniae,' Birr

is a regularly built town in the dignified Georgian style. Once the seat of the O'Carrolls, it was granted in 1620 to the Parsons family, whence its former secondary name of Parsonstown. Birr Castle was the home of the third Earl of Rosse, the great astronomer, who is honoured by a statue in St. John's Square. In the castle park are the remains of his telescope, which in its time (1845) was the largest in the world. The statue of the Duke of Cumberland has been removed from the tall column in the market square. Birr has a modern Catholic cathedral.

Then south, by T 32 (bus or train if desired), to *Roscrea*, in Co. Offaly again, 12 miles. Nothing calls for comment on the way—in fact, as far as Cashel the country is rather dull. At Roscrea (turn left in the centre of this charming town) the castle, a square keep with earlier walls and round tower, belonged to the Ormonde family. Lower down, to the left, are the very fine remains of an Augustinian priory, which was originally founded by St. Cronan in the seventh century. The west end of the priory church, now forming the entrance to the churchyard, shows an effective arcade decorated with chevrons and a doorway with a tall pediment. Close by, on the right, is an old cross with the Crucifixion. The Round Tower, opposite, lacks its cap. Mount St. Joseph Abbey, west of the town, is a modern Cistercian foundation.

On south by T 9 to Thurles, 20 miles (the railway route is via Ballybrophy), with mountains rising to the west. Templemore, with its twin churches, is passed on the way. Here the Knights Templars had a castle and a church, the remains of which are in the grounds of the modern abbey. To the west is the Devilsbit Mountain (1,577 feet), connected in legend with the Rock of Cashel (page 136). Thurles, a fishing, hunting, and racing centre, has a castle guarding the bridge over the Suir and the cathedral of the Catholic Archbishop of Cashel. The latter, in the Italian Romanesque mode, is lavishly decorated with marble and has a tuneful peal of bells.

The next step is to go south again by T 9 for Holycross and Cashel (13 miles). There are buses as far as Holycross, 4 miles, where the grand ruins of the Cistercian

Abbey of Holy Cross occupy a charming site on the bank of the River Suir. The abbey, with buildings now mostly dating from the fifteenth century, was founded in 1167 by Domhnall O'Brien, King of Munster, for the Relic of the True Cross given by Pope Paschal II in 1110 to Donough O'Brien and now preserved in the Ursuline Convent at Blackrock, Cork. The caretaker lives at the first shop over the bridge. The really magnificent features of the ruins are the incredible freshness of the limestone masonry and carvings, the groined roofs, and the tracery of the windows, particularly the east and west six-light windows, and the south transept window, all original but a little clumsy in design. The nave has rounded arches on the north side and pointed on the south. In the south transept is a remarkable structure with an elaborately groined roof, between the two east chapels; this was perhaps the sanctuary of the Cross, or it may just have been a mortuary chapel. The north transept still shows traces of wall paintings. The choir has odd bits of stone carving in the Celtic mode. On the right of the altar is the so-called Tomb of the Good Woman's Son (probably sedilia), with the royal arms of England and those of Ormonde and Desmond. The tower of the church may be ascended. (The great building seen to the north-east is the Thurles beet-sugar factory.) The lovely cloisters survive in part, besides extensive domestic buildings.

Cashel ('stone fort') was once the capital of the Kings of Munster. It is the seat of a Protestant bishopric (which was an archbishopric before 1839) and gives its name to a Catholic archbishopric, now seated at Thurles. The Rock of Cashel, a mass of limestone, is a conspicuous landmark rising 300 feet above the plain and sheer on the north side. Legend relates how the devil bit a piece out of the mountains to the north and dropped it here, but as a matter of fact its presence is due to glacial action. Here, in the 'City of the Kings,' the fastness of Brian Boru, Henry II was recognized in 1172 as Lord Paramount of Ireland, and Edward Bruce held Parliament in 1315. The two-acre area on top of the Rock is crowned with the ruins of the cathedral. The first church was built by St. Declan, disciple of St. Patrick, and the latter is said to have here uttered his famous comparison of the Trinity to a shamrock leaf.

The present cathedral, built in the thirteenth century, was burned in 1495 by the Earl of Kildare, who excused himself to Henry VII by saying that he thought the archbishop was in it. When the archbishop declared that all Ireland could not rule this man, the king retorted: 'Then he shall rule all Ireland.' Repaired, the cathedral was unroofed again in 1749 by Archbishop Price, who was too lazy to climb the hill up to it. (At his instigation a new cathedral, begun in 1763, was built in the town.) The defensive character of the building is very marked: the west end, which formed the residence of the archbishop, is simply a fortress, and there is a series of passages within the transept walls. Attached to the north transept is a perfect example of a Round Tower, 80 feet high by 51 feet in girth, dating from the tenth century. Inside the cathedral note the shortness of the nave and the length of the choir, the sixteenth-century tombs in the nave, the carvings in the north transept, the magnificent vault of the crossing, the long lancet windows of the choir, with small windows of unique pattern above, and the archbishops' floor-slabs in the choir. The central tower should be climbed (126 steps) for the view of the Golden Vein (or Vale), i.e. the rich plain of Tipperary, bounded on the south side by the Galty or Galtee Mountains, the highest peak of which is Galtymore (3,015 feet). From the roof you can see, in the fields, the ruins of Hore Abbey, a Cistercian house founded in 1272, and those of a Dominican friary (1243) in the town.

The gem of Cashel is Cormac's Chapel, more than a century older than the cathedral, which enfolds it obliquely between its choir and south transept. Founded by Cormac MacCarthaigh, King of Desmond and Bishop of Cashel, about the year 1124, i.e. fifty years before the coming of the Anglo-Normans, this exquisite chapel, constructed of red sandstone, is the brightest jewel of Hiberno–Romanesque architecture. With blind arcading inside and out, transeptal towers, and sculptured doorways (particularly the exterior of the north door), it combines Byzantine decoration with the high stone roof, barrel vaulting, and overcrofts of the early Celtic churches. The chancel arch and the altar recess are decorative features of the interior. The tomb at the west end (originally outside the north door), with Celtic interlaced work, is believed to be the founder's. The Cross of Cashel, on the south side of the cathedral, bears a representation of the Crucifixion (with the figure of Christ dressed) and a figure of St. Patrick; on the ancient druidical (?) stone that serves it as a base the Kings of Munster used to be crowned. Beyond it is the Hall of the Vicars Choral, dating in its present state from the seventeenth century.

It was my good fortune a few months after I had seen the Acropolis to visit a ruin in Ireland which, to my great surprise, bore many curious resemblances to it—I mean the Rock of Cashel. There is at Cashel the great cathedral—in loftiness and grandeur the parthenon of the place; there is the smaller and more beautiful Cormac's Chapel, the holiest of all, like the Erechtheum of Athens. Again the great sanctuary upon the Rock of Cashel was surrounded by a cluster of other abbeys about its base, which were founded there by pious men on account of the greatness and holiness of the archiepiscopal seat. The prospect from the Irish sanctuary has, indeed, endless contrasts to that from the Pagan stronghold, but they are suggestive contrasts, and such as are not without a certain harmony. The plans around both are framed by mountains, of which the Irish are probably the more picturesque; and if the light upon the Greek hills is the fairest, the native colour of the Irish is infinitely more rich; so again, the soil of Attica is light and sandy, whereas the golden vale of Tipperary is amongst the richest in the world.

DR. MAHAFFY, *Rambles in Greece.*

Still following T 9 southwards, we come after 11 miles to *Cahir*, which is pronounced 'Care' and means 'fortified town,' or cathair. It is a bright and clean little place on the beautiful River Suir, at the intersection of the Dublin–Cork and Limerick–Waterford main roads. The magnificent castle, rebuilt in the fifteenth or sixteenth century, is the finest specimen of late medieval military architecture in Ireland, and is remarkably well preserved. In effective contrast at the other end of the bridge is a big modern flour-mill. There are abbey ruins in the lovely **Cahir Park**, to which the public is admitted. For sparkling cleanliness, comfort, and good cooking the Cahir House Hotel has few equals, and its interior is a museum piece of Victorianism.

To visit the *Mitchelstown Caves*, which lie in the limestone trough between the Galty and Knockmealdown Mountains, and are the finest in Ireland, you take the splendid, dead-straight Cork road (T 6) for 8 miles of lovely scenery, and turn right at the A.A. signpost ('Caves, 2 miles'). At Burncourt you turn right and beyond a bridge pick up the guide (fee 2s. each visitor) at a farmhouse on the left (with a board marked 'The Caves'). There are 'Old' or 'Desmond Caves' and 'New Caves,' and the latter (discovered in 1833), with their 1½ miles of underground passages, are those usually shown. Electric torches are useful. The visit is a very strenuous scramble over rocks which after heavy rain are very muddy and slippery. The chief caves are the House of Commons, House of Lords (the largest), Kingston Gallery (the finest), and O'Leary's. There are innumerable stalactites and stalagmites, columns created by their union, and other formations of strange beauty. A rare spider, *Porrhomma myops*, is found in the caves.

You regain the main road by keeping straight on past the caves, and soon approach Mitchelstown, 8 miles, in Co. Cork, which prides itself on one of the largest creameries and cheese factories in Europe. Turn right on this side of it and go north-west by a 20-mile road (rough in patches) over the Ballyhoura Mountains, with glorious views. You re-enter Co. Limerick at Knockanevin and reach a height of 719 feet above Kilfinane, where you turn left on gaining the main street, and fork right farther on. *Kilmallock*, once the stronghold of the all-powerful Earls of Desmond, is a squalid little town that still shows signs of its pristine greatness—sections of town wall, two town gates, and two specimens of the ancient stone mansion, battlemented for defence and with carved doorways and window-frames. Turn right at the cross, then take a lane on the left, to see the ruined church of SS. Peter and Paul. to which the stump of a Round Tower is attached. The Dominican friary, on the other side of the little River Loobagh, was founded in 1291 by Gilbert Fitzgerald; its remains are of great beauty, particularly the five-lancet east window and the tracery of the south transept window.

Return to Limerick (21 miles) by L 8 and T 57, passing Bruff and (right) the pretty Lough Gur, on the banks of which there are castles, crannogs, dolmens, circles, and raths. These have been extensively excavated, and the region has become almost a 'summer school' of Irish archaeology.

TOUR VI: LIMERICK TO GALWAY

ENNIS — KILKEE — LAHINCH — CLIFFS OF MOHER — LISDOON-
VARNA — KILMACDUAGH — GALWAY — ARAN ISLANDS —
LOUGH CORRIB — CONG — JOYCE'S COUNTRY — TUAM —
KILCONNELL — ATHENRY.

Total distance by road: about 350 miles.

THE first part of the route is devoted to Co. Clare, the only part of the province of Munster that lies north of the Shannon. It is largely barren and rocky soil, except in the vicinity of the Shannon, but has splendid coast scenery. Leaving Limerick by Sarsfield Bridge, the gateway to Clare, you follow T 11 as far as Ennis, 23 miles (train or bus available). Glimpses of the Shannon and Fergus estuaries are obtained now and then, e.g. from Bunratty Castle, once a residence of the O'Brien Earls of Thomond and now splendidly restored, with period furnishings, and shown to visitors daily. Then, left, diverges the road to the Shannon Airport at Rineanna, 15 miles from Limerick, between the estuaries. This, the westernmost airport in Europe, opened in 1945, is the jumping-off point for the transatlantic air liners to the United States and Canada, with connections for London, Paris, Brussels, etc. The Shannon Free Airport Development Co. is here creating an industrial estate, based on air transport.

Beyond Newmarket-on-Fergus the entrance to Dromoland Castle is passed on the right; this was the seat of Lord Inchiquin, of the O'Brien family, and is now a first-class hotel. William Smith O'Brien, leader of the Young Ireland Party, was born there in 1803.

The next road on the right, narrow and at first bumpy, leads to Quin (3 miles; turn right at the T), in the Macnamara country, with one of the best-preserved Franciscan friaries in Ireland, founded in 1402 within the precincts of a Norman castle. Inquire for the key at the post office. Macnamaras are buried in the church. The cloisters and domestic buildings are almost intact save for their roofs, as, though the monastery was officially dissolved in 1651, it was actually occupied by friars till 1820. As you approach Ennis, crossing the River Fergus, Clare Abbey, an Augustinian priory of 1194, with a tower, is seen on the left.

Ennis ('river meadow') is the busy county town, with narrow streets and an old-fashioned air. There are good hotels (Old Ground Hotel, etc.), a Catholic cathedral, a fine Court House (1852), and a tall column in memory of O'Connell, who was M.P. for Clare from 1828 to 1831. Ennis prison has been converted into a boot factory. At the end of Church Street are the ruins (kept locked) of a Franciscan friary founded by Donogh O'Brien, King of Thomond, in 1242, with an unusual grouping of lancets as its east window. The monuments include the MacMahon, or 'royal,' tomb, with its spirited fifteenth-century reliefs of the Passion.

Next, south-west by T 41 to Kilrush and Kilkee (35 miles, with a bus service from Limerick), to visit the long, tapering peninsula on the north side of the Shannon estuary. (Or, if in a hurry, you will not be missing a great deal if you go straight to Lahinch, 19 miles: by T 70 to Ennistymon, then T 69.) The countryside is bare and boggy, and it is better and only 5 miles longer to follow the by-roads on the west side of the Fergus estuary and the north side of the Shannon, via Kildysart, Labasheeda ('bed of silk'), Knock, and Killimer. Ellen Hanley, the beautiful and famous 'Colleen Bawn,' who was drowned in the Shannon by her jealous husband in 1819, is buried in Killimer churchyard. Kilrush, on the Shannon estuary, is a market town with a small harbour. Thence an interesting trip may be made to Scattery Island, where St. Senan (d. 554) founded a monastery, with the ruins of six early churches and the highest perfect Round Tower in Ireland (120 feet); its doorway is at ground level. There is also a sixteenth-century castle on the island.

With a 1-in-12 climb out of Kilrush, you go by way of Moyasta, on the landlocked Poulnasherry Bay, to *Kilkee*, on Moore Bay, facing the open Atlantic. This is one of the few pukka seaside resorts on the west coast, with an abundance of hotels and facilities for golf, tennis, dancing, and the rest. The bathing is considered the best in Ireland: the surf-bathing is wonderful, but part of the strand is sheltered by the Duggerna Rocks. A feature of Kilkee is the 'pollock holes,' natural swimming-pools among the rocks. There is superb coast scenery in both directions, with cliffs and caves, chasms, natural bridges, and stack rocks, the 'Puffing Hole' and the 'Lovers' Leap.'

It is a 17-mile drive (with bus service) from Kilkee to Loop Head, with its tall lighthouse, at the end of the peninsula. On a clear day the view from the point is immense, extending from MacGillycuddy's Reeks on the south to the Aran Islands, Slyne Head, and the Twelve Pins of Connemara on the north.

The road leading northwards from Kilkee to Lahinch, T 69, 28 miles, runs for the most part at some distance from the coast. Near Doonbeg, on a little bay, there are sandhills as high as 100 feet; Doonmore is an old castle of the O'Briens. From Quilty a boat may be hired for a trip to Mutton Island. Many of the Armada ships were lost in the wide and dangerous Mal Bay in September 1588, and as many as 1,200 corpses were washed ashore at Spanish Point.

Lahinch, on Liscannor Bay, is a family seaside resort with several good hotels, and is renowned for the golf links laid out on the sand dunes. Ennistymon, $2\frac{1}{2}$ miles inland, is worth a flying visit to see the cascade of the River Inagh, just below the bridge.

The coast road from Lahinch to Galway (61 miles, L 54 as far as Ballyvaughan) is one of the finest marine drives in Ireland. You cross a sandy inlet to reach Liscannor, a picturesque fishing village with curraghs, beyond which there is a long 1-in-10 ascent (keep straight on past the O'Brien Column) to the top of the famous *Cliffs of Moher*, which extend for five miles northwards from Hag's Head and impress not so much by their height (668 feet at the highest point) as by their stupendous sheerness. They are composed of layers of grit and shales of the Carboniferous period, and are the haunt of countless sea fowl. The best viewpoint is O'Brien's Tower, which, like the road itself, was built in 1835 by Cornelius O'Brien, a public-spirited local landowner. A steep descent brings you to Doolin Bay, whence roads on the right (buses) lead to *Lisdoonvarna*, 4 miles inland, which is about Ireland's only spa, much frequented by local patients, especially priests. It is a neat little town, built around a wooded ravine in an otherwise treeless district. The waters are of three kinds, containing sulphur, iodine, and magnesia respectively, and are recommended for rheumatism and gland troubles.

The road passes the ancient O'Brien castle of Ballynalackan, in a fine site, then runs between the sea and Slieve Elva (1,109 feet). In the latter is the Cave of Pollnagollum, which has been explored for 7 miles. At Black Head, bleak and bare, with a tiny lighthouse, it turns to skirt the south shore of Galway Bay (here 7 miles across) to Ballyvaughan. This sterile corner of Clare, the barony of Burren, resembles a vast quarry in its composition of limestone terraces, devoid even of peat and with vegetation growing only in the interstices between the boulders and flags. Yet even in this unpromising Sahara cows seem to pick up some sort of a living. No region is more esteemed by botanists, for gentians, saxifrages, and maidenhair beautify the naked rocks in spring and this is the sole locality in the British Isles for certain sub-alpine plants. Note the beautiful little wayside well-house on this side of Ballyvaughan.

The east end of Galway Bay is broken up into countless inlets and islets. At Ballyvaughan the first-class T 69 is joined. Leaving the road to New Quay on the left, keep straight on by a rough road past Lough Luirk (not seen) and turn sharp left so as to pass near Corcomroe Abbey, an offshoot of Furness Abbey, founded for Cistercians by Domhnall O'Brien in 1182, with a small tower and a five-lancet east window. Conchobhar O'Brien, King of Thomond (d. 1267), was buried here. There is a steep, rough, winding descent (low gear advisable), to rejoin the main road. At Corranroo you leave Co. Clare for Co. Galway. Kinvarra is a small port with oyster beds. T 69 goes on to join the main road from Ennis at Kilcolgan, but it is better to diverge right at Kinvarra through a stony wilderness, turning left beyond Killinny and right at Tirneevin, so as to visit *Kilmacduagh*, the Round Tower of which serves as a landmark. A monastery and bishopric were founded here in the seventh century by St. Colman MacDuagh. Among the ruined buildings are the cathedral, rebuilt in the fifteenth century but retaining the original west door (inside there are O'Shaughnessy tombs), one of the finest of the Round Towers, 112 feet high, with the upper part restored and leaning two feet from the perpendicular, and the church and other buildings of an Augustinian friary.

Turn left beyond the ruins and follow the excellent by-road to Gort ('field'), 3 miles north-east of Kilmacduagh, on the main Ennis-Galway road. Near Gort, on the Galway road, was Coole Park (pulled down), where Lady Gregory entertained the leaders of the Irish literary Renaissance. Yeats lived at Ballylea Castle (now a Yeats museum), close by. Going north from Gort to Galway by T 11, through a bare and bleak district, you join T 4 at Oranmore, near an arm of Galway Bay, with a castle built by Ulick de Burgh, Marquis of Clanricarde, Charles I's chief supporter in western Ireland.

Galway ('foreign place'), a town of 22,000 inhabitants, is the capital of the beautiful but barren province of Connaught (or Connacht). Some visitors think Galway 'the drowsiest, the most magical, the most Irish' of Irish cities, with its quaint, narrow streets, its dilapidated, foreign-looking houses, and its numerous watercourses. Others will be disappointed. Sweeping alterations are being carried out, and present-day Galway is a strange medley of medieval squalor and modern progress. One of its factories makes felt hats for all Eire.

The city is built on the east bank of the short River Corrib, which unites Lough Corrib with Galway Bay. This stream is the sole access to 1,200 square miles of lakes, and in the season shoals of salmon going upstream can be seen from the Galway bridges—a truly remarkable sight.

The Galway district was conquered from the O'Connors about 1230 by Richard de Burgh (founder of the Burke family). It was he who introduced the 'Tribes of Galway,' fourteen patriotic English families (Blake, Browne, Ffrench, Martin, Lynch, Bodkin, Kirwan, Joyce, D'Arcy, Skerrett, etc.) who kept themselves aloof from the Irish for centuries and dominated most of Connaught until the coming of the Parliamentary army in 1652.

Galway was once a considerable seaport, but its overseas trade, which was mostly with Spain, has sadly decayed.

In the centre of the town is the spacious Eyre Square, with the station, the leading hotels, and a quaint statue of Padraig O Conaire, the poet, while Shop Street is, as one would expect, the chief shopping street. In the latter is St. Nicholas's (locked), founded in 1320 and the largest and one of the best parish churches in Eire. The west doorway, the queer pyramidal steeple, and Mayor FitzStephen's tomb are noteworthy features. Christopher Columbus, according to local legend, attended mass here on a visit to Galway before setting out on his momentous voyage. It is a known fact that there was a Galwayman in Columbus's crew, and Columbus may have visited Galway on his early voyage (1476) to the northern seas.

On the north side of the church, in Market Street, is the famous Lynch Stone, a tablet commemorating the unflinching justice of James Lynch Fitzstephen, Mayor of Galway in 1493, who condemned his own son to death for murder and, unable to find an executioner, hanged him from a window in his own house. 'Lynch law' nowadays means something different. The Lynch mansion (restored and occupied by the Munster & Leinster Bank), at the corner of Shop Street and Abbeygate Street, dates from about the year 1600 and bears a coat of arms with the lynx crest; in Abbeygate Street and Market Street are the ruins of other mansions.

The upper bridge leads to Newcastle Road on the west bank of the river and to University College, founded in 1849 and now, with 850 students, part of the National University. It has played a leading part in the revival of Gaelic.

If you keep straight on down Shop Street you will come to the famous Claddagh (i.e. 'beach') or fishermen's quarter on the west side of the river mouth. Another disillusionment awaits you here, for the highly picturesque collection of whitewashed and thatched cabins built in haphazard fashion, and facing in all directions, have been almost entirely supplanted by tidy but ugly rows of modern council houses. Moreover, the old customs and costumes of the fisherfolk, the election of a 'king' and their festival on St. John's Day, are all things of the past. The Galway shops sell reproductions of 'Claddagh rings,' with a crowned heart between two hands, which used to be handed down as family heirlooms. To the west of the Claddagh lies Salthill, Galway's marine suburb and seaside resort, with good hotels and good golf.

Of the many excursions to be made from Galway undoubtedly the most fascinating is that to the *Aran Islands*, made famous by Synge's play *Riders to the Sea* (1904) and Robert Flaherty's film *Man of Aran* (1934). Synge visited the islands annually from 1898 to 1902 and wrote an account of them in 1907. They lie across the mouth of Galway Bay and are three in number—Inishmore, or Aranmore, 9 miles long by 1½ miles broad, Inishmaan, the middle island, 3 miles long, and the smaller Inishere, or east island. A steamer plies once or twice weekly from Galway in four hours to Kilronan (28 miles) the principal village, on Killeany Bay, Inishmore, where simple inn or lodging accommodation is obtainable. The islands consist of bare and windswept terraces of limestone slabs, with ferns and rock plants growing in the crevices, and divided up into small holdings by drystone walls. There is no soil except what is created by the laborious cartage of sand and seaweed, while dripping wells form the sole water supply. Yet the islands are more densely populated than any other non-urban part of Ireland. The inhabitants, numbering over 2,000, preserve their primitive culture, and students come here in summer to learn Gaelic from them. The older peasants wear 'bawneens' or 'bainins' (sleeved waistcoats of white homespun flannel) and rawhide moccasins ('broga ur leathair,' known as 'pampooties'). The women's petticoats are red. This is alleged to be the only genuine national peasant costume in all western Europe. In their curraghs of tarred canvas the fishermen are wonderfully fearless sailors.

The islands are crowded with prehistoric and early Christian antiquities—forts and cashels, dallans (pillar stones), bullans (cup-marked stones), clochans (beehive huts), a score of early churches, holy wells, and the rest. The inhabitants were converted in the fifth century by St. Enda (Eany), who is said to have established no fewer than ten convents here. Going east from Kilronan, you soon come to Killeany, above which, beyond the stump of a Round Tower, is St. Bennen's Church, or Teampull Beanáin (i.e. Benignus), a very good example of its kind, built of very large slabs, with its axis running north and south; it has very high-pitched gables, and only one window. Near Eararna, farther on, are the remains of St. Enda's Church, and at the extremity of the island is another Round Tower. The Black Fort (Dubh Cathair), on the south coast, over against Killeany, is a cliff castle, or promontory fort, with great stone walls more than 200 feet long.

The road going west from Kilronan passes St. Kieran's Church, right, and St. Sorney's, left. Above Oghil, to the left, is Dun Eochaill, a circular fort. From the point where the road reaches the shore a side-track leads to Kilmurvy and MacDuagh's Church (cf. page 144), in excellent preservation, with splayed windows and a round-headed east window of later date. At the nearest point of the south coast to this is Dun Aengus (or Aonghusa), on the edge of a 300-foot cliff and considered by some to be the finest prehistoric monument in Europe. One-half of it has been carried away by the encroachment of the sea. It covers 11 acres and is defended by triple ramparts of drystone masonry. Outside the middle wall the approach is guarded by chevaux-de-frise of pointed stones. What need had barren islands of such great forts? The road goes on to Onaght, near which are Dun Eoghanacht and the 'Seven Churches.'

On Inishmaan are Cill Cananech and Dun Conor, which is esteemed by some as the finest fort in Ireland, while Inishere has St. Kevin's Church, the Fort of the Women, and the O'Brien castle of Firmina.

The best way to see *Lough Corrib* is by motor-boat, but there is no regular service. Thirty miles long from Galway to Cong, shallow, and dotted with islets (which are said, as usual, to number 365), the lake is the largest in Eire, being some 70 square miles in area. Its banks are studded with ruined castles and monasteries, and westwards there are views of the stony heights of Connemara and Joyce's Country. Lough Corrib and its northern neighbour, Lough Mask, afford some of the best trout fishing in Ireland, and the east bank of Corrib is noted for its wild flowers.

On the motor drive from Galway to Cong (27 miles) only distant views of Lough Corrib are obtained, as the road runs some way from its east bank. Taking the Castlebar road, you soon come to a dead straight stretch of six miles in the course of which the River Clare is crossed. About a mile and a half beyond Headford the road crosses the Black River, which separates the counties of Galway and Mayo. Here, to the left, on the Galway bank, are the comely and fairly complete remains of the Franciscan friary of Ross Errilly, founded in 1351 and not finally abandoned till 1765. The west doorway, east window, and round-headed arches (a rarity at such a late date) of the church, and the small but almost perfect cloisters, are the most noteworthy features.

For Cong you turn left at Cross, leaving to the right the great plain of Southern Moytura, scene in the misty past of the first great defeat of the Firbolg ('bagmen'), or aboriginal Irish, by the invading host of Tuatha Dé Danaan (People of the Goddess Danu), seven years before the final rout of Northern Moytura. *Cong*, with several hotels, gets its name ('neck of land') from its situation between Lough Corrib and Lough Mask (the latter 10 miles long and 4 miles wide). In the village street is a four-teenth-century cross commemorating two of the abbots. Ashford Castle, in Victorian Gothic, once the seat of the Earl of Iveagh, is now a palatial hotel. In the demesne (celebrated for its pheasants and woodcock) stand the beautiful late-Romanesque and Transitional remains of Cong Abbey, founded in 1128 by Turlough O'Conor for Augustinian canons. His son Roderic, last native king of Ireland, retired hither in 1183, and here he died and was buried in 1198. The north doorway, east window, and cloisters deserve special notice.

The stream that connects the two loughs runs under-ground for most of its course, and is accessible through various caves, such as the Horse's Discovery and the Pigeon Hole (guide desirable). The canal between the loughs, constructed in the 1840's as a relief work during the famine, failed to hold water owing to the porous nature of the carboniferous limestone.

Cong is a convenient starting-point for a circular drive

F

(46 miles) through *Joyce's Country*, the mountainous home of the Galway 'tribe' of that name, immigrants from Wales in the thirteenth century. The beauty of its heathery grouse moors is beyond praise. Go west by L 101, the Leenane road, along the north shore of Lough Corrib, with the square-topped Benlevy (1,370 feet) rising conspicuously on the right. Cornamona and Claggan are passed; near the latter, on an islet in the Maam arm of Lough Corrib, and opposite Mount Leckavrea (1,307 feet), is Hen's Castle, built by the sons of Roderic O'Conor (page 149). According to the legend, The O'Flahertie was presented by a witch with the castle and a wonderful hen, which would lay enough eggs to sustain the whole garrison in time of siege. O'Flahertie, however, put the hen in the pot and was soon starved out.

Beyond Maam Bridge, an enchanting spot (maam = mountain pass), you ascend the valley of Joyce's River. At Griggins turn right by a narrow mountain road that presently drops down in very steep zigzags to Lough Nafooey, at the foot of the Partry Mountains (Knocklaur, 2,039 feet, Benwee, 2,239 feet, and Maumtrasna, 2,207 feet). You next skirt an arm of Lough Mask, cross a bridge over its mouth, and pass the angling resort of Clonbur on the way back to Cong.

From Cong go north to Ballinrobe (7 miles), choosing the road nearest the lake. This passes close to Loughmask House, the home of Captain Charles Cunningham Boycott (1832–97), land agent for Lord Erne's estates in Co. Mayo, whose treatment by the tenantry in 1879–80 furnished the English language with a new word. About 2½ miles north of Ballinrobe is Moore Hall (burnt in the 'troubles'), the birthplace and early home of George Moore, whose ashes were scattered on an island in the lough.

From Ballinrobe you can either go straight back to Galway (31 miles) or make a detour through a flat countryside (agricultural land or bog) to include three interesting places—Tuam, Kilconnell, and Athenry (78 miles). *Tuam* (20 miles) is reached by T 40 to Kilmaine, then L 4. It is the ecclesiastical capital of Connacht, being the seat of a Catholic archbishopric and of a Protestant bishopric (which was an archbishopric before 1834). The see was originally founded by St. Jarlath (d. 540), and the Cathedral of St. Mary, in High Street, was built *c.* 1152 by Turlough O'Conor, King of Connacht. (The sexton's house faces the west front.) The plan of the cathedral is at first rather difficult of comprehension. Of the original cathedral the sanctuary, i.e. the central portion of the present building, 15 feet square, is a relic. One of the glories of Hiberno-Romanesque architecture is its chancel arch, in six orders, every voussoir elaborately carved with nebules, diamond frets, and chevrons, and its capitals decorated with interlacing and grotesque heads. Above it is an old arcade, and behind it three round-headed windows with delicate ornamentation. In the thirteenth century the old nave was pulled down, and a rectangular, fortress-like church, in red sandstone, was erected to the east of the sanctuary, which thus became the west porch. This east church is now used as the synod hall, and contains twenty-eight Renaissance stalls and candelabra (all brought from an Italian monastery) and eighteenth-century glass in its Decorated windows. In 1861 the present nave was erected from the early Irish Gothic designs of Sir Thomas Deane. The Catholic cathedral, more attractive than most, is a dignified neo-Gothic structure in Bishop Street, with a pleasant setting. Tuam itself, once the centre of the O'Conor power, still has many thatched houses, and Gaelic is largely spoken here. The High Cross in the market-place (once broken into three pieces) is 14 feet high, with the Crucifixion on one side and the figure of an archbishop on the other; the inscriptions commemorate Archbishop O'Hoisin and Turlough O'Conor.

From Tuam you make for Kilconnell, to the south-east, a pleasant but unexciting drive of 26 miles, through an open, stone-wall country. The route to be taken (roughish in the latter part) is via Barnaderg, Horseleap cross-roads, and Glentane, diverging to the right from the Ballinasloe road beyond Trust. *Kilconnell's* claim to notice is that it possesses the finest and best-preserved example of an old Franciscan friary in Ireland. Founded by Liam O'Kelly in 1414, this has a graceful tower, fine window tracery, tombs of the leading families of Galway, and delightful, foreign-looking little cloisters. The small High Cross in the village street dates from 1632.

It is a quick run back to Galway (32 miles) by T 4, via Athenry and Oranmore. *Athenry* (pronounced 'rye,' not 'ree'), i.e. Ath an riogh, 'ford of the kings,' has lost its importance since the days when it was the headquarters of the Anglo-Norman lords, De Burgh and Bermingham. Of its ancient defences sections of town wall, with a gate tower, and a castle with a square keep (1238) are survivals. The chief feature of the Dominican friary is the tracery of the east window (1324), while the choir and tower of the Franciscan friary (1464) now form part of the parish church.

Before taking final leave of Galway, you might well run out on the Tuam road to see Claregalway, with its De Burgh castle and the charming remains of a Franciscan friary.

TOUR VII: GALWAY TO SLIGO

CONNEMARA—CLIFDEN—KYLEMORE PASS—KILLARY HARBOUR
—CROAGH PATRICK—WESTPORT—CLARE ISLAND—MALLA-
RANNY — ACHILL ISLAND — CROAGHAUN — BELMULLET
—KILLALA—SLIGO—LOUGH GILL—GLENCAR LOUGH.

Total distance by road: about 400 miles.

You are now free to devote your whole attention to one
of Ireland's loveliest regions, *Connemara*, the name given
vaguely to the great peninsula between Galway Bay and
Clew Bay and more accurately to the westernmost portion,
around Clifden. Connemara's austere beauty can be
matched only in Greece. A grey-green land of granite
mountains, moors, and bogs, of a thousand loughs and
streams, of bays, sea inlets, and sandy beaches, of picturesque cottages set among rocks, with their thatched
roofs weighted down with stones—no traveller can fail
to be impressed with its subtle colouring and alluring
loveliness of form. In spite of its barrenness, Connemara,
which has been described with some exaggeration as a land
without railways, shops, cars, or telegraphs, is over-
populated with Gaelic-speaking crofters, whose lot is a
hard, but not necessarily an unhappy, one. Many of the
women wear charmingly patterned brown shawls, but the
men's 'bawneens' (see page 147) and red petticoats worn by
the women are now, alas! seldom seen. One curious
custom was to dress small boys in skirts so as to deceive
the fairies.

Between Galway and Clifden there is a choice of roads,
both extremely attractive, and both to be traversed if
possible, even though it means covering the same ground
twice over. The coastal route, L 100 to Screeb, then
L 102, is 80 miles of narrow, winding, and undulating
road, 30 miles longer than the main road, though a considerable saving can be made by taking two short cuts.
There are bus services from Galway to Lettermore and to

Carna. As far as Screeb the road serves the desolate coastal districts of Iar Connacht (i.e. West Connaught), with beautiful cliff scenery and views of Galway Bay and the Arans. At Spiddal there is a college for instruction in Gaelic. From Costelloe a by-road leads to Lettermore and Gorumna islands. At Inver Bridge, beyond Screeb and Screeb Bridge, a short cut to Cashel diverges on the right. The coast road leads via Carna, an angling resort with an hotel, as is Cashel, at the foot of an isolated hill (1,024 feet).

Beyond Toombeola Bridge the roughish road to the right leads direct to Clifden through a maze of small loughs in a district devoid of habitations, while the much more interesting and better-made sea road, to the left (known as the 'Brandy and Soda Road' from its intoxicating air), passes the lobster fishers' village and anglers' resort of Roundstone, a picturesque place with a small harbour. There is a splendid view (including the Twelve Bens and, it is said, 300 loughs) from the isolated hill above it, Urrisbeg (987 feet). Mediterranean heath grows on Urrisbeg's western flank. Farther on the road skirts the lovely Mannin Bay. On the bog of Derrygimlach, 1 mile north-east of Ballyconnealy, John Alcock and Arthur Whitten Brown landed on 15th June 1919, on the completion of the first direct flight across the Atlantic, in 16 hours 12 minutes. Cairn and memorial. On this side of Clifden the road crosses an arm of Ardbear Bay.

The main road from Galway to Clifden (49 miles, T 71), a delightful run through mountain and lake scenery, is served by buses. The railway that once followed it closely is now dismantled. An inordinate number of small loughs keep the road company all the way. For the first part of the journey it winds and undulates (the worst bends are being straightened out) between Lough Corrib and the rock-bound uplands of Iar Connacht, the country of the O'Flahertys, who were such a scourge to the 'tribes' of Galway that over the west gate of that city was the inscription: 'From the fury of the O'Flahertys Good Lord deliver us.' Their principal stronghold was Aughnanure Castle, which you pass on the right between

Killarone Eighter and Oughterard (pronounced 'Ookter-ard'). Its tower and great hall date from the sixteenth century. Oughterard ('high surface'), on the River Owenriff, with Egan's Lake Hotel, is a noted centre of angling and boating in Lough Corrib, the chief excursion being to the isle of Inchagoill, with ruins of two old churches, one primitive, the other Romanesque.

Beyond Oughterard you emerge on the open moorland, with the mountains in full view. On the right of Maam Cross rise Mount Leckavrea and the grand Corcogemore Mountains (2,102 feet), and farther on you have a view of the Maamturk Mountains (2,193 feet) up the side-valley on the right. Recess, by Lough Glendalough or Garroman, with its weird modern church, is a classic beauty-spot and angling resort. Lissoughter (1,314 feet), above it, is worth climbing for its famous view of the surrounding mountains and lakes.

The road then passes between Derryclare Lough (right), on the bank of which Connemara marble (a variegated greenstone) is quarried, and Ballynahinch Lough (left), on the opposite bank of which is Ballynahinch Castle, now a luxurious hotel, with some of the best fishing in Ireland. It was once the home of the Martins (including 'Humanity' Martin, duellist and founder of the R.S.P.C.A.) and was owned after 1926 by 'Ranji' (the Jam Sahib of Nawanagar). To the north rise the Twelve Bens (or 'Pins'), the Beanna Beola, Connemara's pride, conical quartzite peaks covered with heaths and lichens, and unrivalled for boldness and variety of outline. The central and highest of them is Benbaun (2,393 feet), while the easiest to climb is Ben-lettery (1,904 feet), nearest to Ballynahinch Lough. From its summit you get a splendid view of this remarkable district.

Clifden, the capital of Connemara, is a small, clean, stone-built town of one broad street, and an excellent holiday centre, with ample hotel accommodation. It lies at the head of Ardbear Bay and its lobster fishery is important. Clifden Castle was built by the D'Arcys in 1815. A good view of the indented coast-line, the mountains, and the lough-dotted levels is obtained from the

top of Gortumnagh Hill (387 feet), beyond the castle.
The drive to Roundstone by the 'Brandy and Soda Road'
(page 154) and back by the direct road should on no
account be omitted by those arriving at Clifden by the
main road.

The road from Clifden to Leenane (T 71, 22 miles), up hill
and down dale as far as Letterfrack, is another extremely
grand run through wild mountain scenery, with views of
the Twelve Bens to the east. This has many claims to be
considered the finest stretch of main road in Eire. Leaving
by the Westport road, you pass the head of Streamstown
Bay, then, beyond a magnificent view-point, that of
Ballynakill Harbour (with a stone quay, beyond which
rises the isolated Renvyle Hill (1,172 feet)). Letterfrack
('speckled hillside'), a delightful village at the head of the
harbour, is overlooked by Diamond Hill (1,460 feet), the
view from the top of which is incomparable. A side-road
(6 miles) on the left leads to the coast and to the Renvyle
House Hotel, which offers, besides some of the finest
scenery in Connemara, excellent bathing, fishing, shooting,
and boating (e.g. to the open-sea islands of Inishark,
Inishbofin, Inishturk, etc.).

Beyond Letterfrack the road is fringed for miles with
fuchsia hedges, a glorious sight in late summer. The next
thrill is the drive up the valley of the Dawros River to the
Kylemore Pass, which takes the highest rank for its exquisite scenery. Kylemore Castle, on the other bank of
the Pollacappal Lough, has been rebuilt since a fire in 1958.
It was a 'fairy palace' in the Elizabethan style, built about
1880 by Mitchell Henry, the wealthy Manchester merchant
and Irish politician, who spent large sums hereabouts on
the reclamation of bogland.

The road hugs the north bank of Kylemore Lough, with
a retrospective view of the Twelve Bens. You enter an
upland basin, which is surrounded on all sides by gloriously
coloured mountains, and has been compared to 'a Homeric
dream-country.' Next comes Lough Fee, on the left, and
then down to *Killary Harbour*, loveliest of Connemara sea
loughs and said to be the only true fiord in Ireland. Ten
miles in length, with a great depth of water between its
steep mountainsides, it often held a British fleet in security.

The south bank of the lough is followed for three miles to the Leenane Hotel, with good shooting and fishing and much frequented by honeymoon couples. The mountains on the north side of the lough are Bengorm (2,303 feet), opposite the hotel, and, farther west, Benlugmore (2,618 feet), Benbury (2,610 feet), and Mweelrea or Muilrea ('bald king,' 2,688 feet). The last-named is best scaled from Rossroe, on the north bank of the fiord, and commands a magnificent view of the coast from Slyne Head to Achill. The mountain east of Leenane is the Devil's Mother (2,131 feet), an outlier of the Partry Mountains.

Co. Mayo, largely limestone, is entered at the head of Killary Harbour, where the main road to Westport (T 71, 20 miles) keeps straight on up the Erriff valley. The tourist's route, however, is by Louisburgh (L 100, 34 miles), the first part of which is another grand mountain drive and a worthy sequel to that just traversed. Especially careful driving is necessary for some time, as the road is narrow (especially at the bridges), with many bends and occasionally a 1-in-10 gradient. Rounding the head of the fiord at Aasleagh, you follow its north bank as far as Bundorragha, and then turn north through the defile between Bengorm (right) and Benlugmore (left). At the head of the tiny Fin Lough is the famous beauty-spot called Delphi, a fishing lodge amid mountain scenery of the most sublime description. The road, now wider— it was constructed in 1896 by the Congested Districts Board—hugs for nearly two miles the east bank of the Doo ('black') Lough, which is followed immediately by Glencullin Lough, near the head of the pass (234 feet above sea level).

The descent through the vast and melancholy brown moorlands of Murrisk is gradual. Beyond the fishing village of Louisburgh the road is first class, and you soon reach the southern shore of Clew Bay (15 miles long by 6 miles wide), which is girdled on all sides by lofty mountains— a harmony in greys and blues. At its mouth lies Clare Island and its eastern and north-eastern shores are broken up into a maze of islets (365!) and inlets.

On the right of the road towers *Croagh Patrick* (2,510 feet), Ireland's holiest mountain, known as the Reek, i.e.

*F

rock, and for fourteen hundred years a great object of pilgrimage. The great day is Garland Sunday, the last in July. The easiest route up it ($1\frac{1}{2}$-2 hours) is from Leckanvy Church or from Croaghpatrick House, near Murrisk Abbey, 2 miles farther, a 14th-century house of Augustinians, founded by the O'Malleys. There is a little oratory and a statue of the saint on the summit, which commands a superb view of the Connemara mountains to the south and away northwards over Achill to Slieve League in Donegal. It was from this mountain that St. Patrick banished snakes and toads from Ireland (other absentees from its list of fauna are polecats, weasels, and moles). Each time the saint rang his bell he threw it over the precipice, accompanied by a swarm of venomous beasts. Every time angels brought the bell back to him, until the vermin-exterminating process was completed. St. Patrick, the apostle and national saint of Ireland, was a Briton of Roman citizenship, perhaps a native of Dumbarton or of St. David's in Pembrokeshire. He was captured in his youth by Irish raiders and lived many years as a slave in Ireland. Having escaped, he returned as bishop in 432. He died in 461 and is supposed to be buried at Downpatrick.

Westport, with wide streets ('a little bit of Latin Europe'), was laid out by James Wyatt *c.* 1780 for the Marquis of Sligo, whose high-walled demesne (open to the public) separates it from Westport Bay, an arm of Clew Bay. The house was built by Richard Cassels and altered by Wyatt. Derelict warehouses on the quay are a mute reminder of vanished overseas trade. Westport is noted for sea-angling. The Mall is a wide avenue of limes with Georgian houses and a stream running down the centre, and the Octagon has been called the best-designed public square in Ireland. The Protestant church was built in 1880 and is worth a glance. George Birmingham (Canon Hannay) was rector here for twenty-one years, and here all his earlier West of Ireland stories were written. The scenery described in them is that of Co. Mayo, both mainland and islands off the coast. His play *General John Regan* also is sited in Westport.

A motor-boat excursion should be made from Westport Quay to *Clare Island*, one of the most romantic of Ireland's isles, at the mouth of Clew Bay. It is four miles long and has about 500 inhabitants, who live by fishing and kelp burning and by farming the small holdings established in 1895 by the Congested Districts Board. Knockmore (1,520 feet), the highest hill, has fine sea cliffs on the north-west side. At the east end is the castle of Grace O'Malley ('Granuaile'), the famous sea queen of the west, who paid a visit to Queen Elizabeth in London and treated with her on equal terms. One of her quaint habits was to keep her ships tied up to a hawser which passed through a hole in the wall and was fastened to her bed.

Castlebar ('castle of Barry'), county town of Mayo, with an elegant Mall, and a great angling centre, is 11 miles inland from Westport, but is hardly worth a detour. The 'Castlebar Races' were the rout of General Lake's garrison by the French invaders of 1798.

The next goal is Achill Island, served by bus from Westport. T 71 goes on northwards from Westport to Newport (8 miles), at the north-east corner of Clew Bay, with both sea and freshwater angling. The entrance to the townlet, with its two bridges over the Newport River and the handsome Catholic church above, is very striking. The excellent road thence to Mallaranny (T 71, 11 miles) —the railway is shut down—crosses the efflux of Lough Furnace by Burrishoole Bridge, on the left of which stands Carrigahooley Castle, scene of the famous incident when Grace O'Malley slammed the gates in the face of her second husband, Sir Richard Burke, at the end of their year's companionate marriage. The road then leads along the north shore of Clew Bay, with splendid occasional views across it of Croagh Patrick and the Murrisk mountains, and Cushcamcarragh (2,343 feet) rising to the north. Rossturk Castle is passed on the left.

Mulrany, or Mallaranny ('ferny hill-top'), a picturesque village situated on the neck of the Curraun peninsula and dominated by the Claggan Mountain (1,256 feet), has a first-class railway hotel with wooded grounds running down to the sea's edge. The view across the bay is heavenly. Fuchsia hedges and the prevalence of the

Mediterranean heath (which flowers in early spring) testify to the softness of the air. The curious stony beach is worth inspecting. There is a splendid drive round the Curraun peninsula.

For Achill Island, one of Ireland's favourite touring grounds, you leave the main road and follow L 141 round the north side of the Curraun peninsula to Achill Sound (9 miles), the former railway terminus. Thence the road crosses the sound, which is half a mile wide, by a new bridge opened in 1950. There is a fine display of rhododendrons at the exit of the village.

Achill Island (pronounced 'Ackle'; 'eagle island'), L-shaped, is about 15 miles long and 12 miles wide, with an area of 56 square miles. Everything here is on a grand scale, mountains, heathery moorlands, and bogs, and its cliffs are unrivalled save perhaps in Donegal. The 5,000 inhabitants keep a few cattle, pigs, and poultry and cultivate patches of oats and potatoes, eking out a livelihood by the tourist traffic, by harvesting in Scotland and England, and by subsidies from American relatives. There is good sea-angling (and a shark-fishing industry), the hotels are cheap, and an ideal holiday may be spent here by those with simple tastes. Quartz amethysts are offered for sale.

Dugort, or Doogort ('black field'), on the north coast, 9 miles from Achill Bridge by a side-road, is a regular bathing resort with a fine strand and plenty of accommodation. The 'Settlement,' i.e. the visitors' quarter, was founded in 1834 by the Rev. E. Nangle, a Protestant clergyman who made a determined but of course futile effort to convert the islanders. Above Dugort towers the mighty cone of Slievemore (2,204 feet), which rises directly from the sea. It is partly composed of quartz and mica, and at its foot are Seal Caves, much visited by boat.

Keel, 3 miles away on the south coast, with the Achill Head Hotel, is the terminus of the main road and bus route. Its glorious stretch of sands, three miles long, is terminated on the east by the Cathedral Rocks at the foot of Menawn (1,530 feet), whose cliffs are 800 feet sheer. Going westwards from Keel, you come to the clean and tidy village of Dooagh.

A very steep and rough road (cars should be left at the gateway half-way up the hill, which is the entrance to Corrymore House, built by Captain Boycott, page 150) goes on to the entrancing strand of Keem, with its marvellous colouring. Above looms the dark and weirdly shaped mountain of *Croaghaun* (2,192 feet), which fills up the north-west corner of the island. The panorama of sea, mountains, and islands from the summit is unforgettable. The sea cliffs on the north side are nearly 2,000 feet high (keep away from the edge). The west end of the island is the sinister knife-edge of Achill Head. Farther north-east is Saddle Head.

Motorists should round off their visit to Achill by a trip along the 'Atlantic Drive' (rather a rough passage) around Menawn and past the primitive village of Dooega.

Recrossing Achill Bridge, they must then make their way back to Mallaranny in order to rejoin T 71, which undulates northwards (rough in parts) through the wildest bog country in all Ireland, passing only the hamlet of Ballycroy on the way to Bangor Erris (20 miles). On the left, at some distance, is Blacksod Bay; on the right, a grand mountain range—Cushcamcarragh (2,343 feet), Glennamong (2,067 feet), Nephin Beg (2,065 feet), Slieve Car (2,369 feet), and, above Bangor, the delightfully named Knocklettercuss (1,208 feet). To visit Belmullet (12 miles) and the Mullet peninsula turn left at Bangor by T 58, leaving Carrowmore Lough on the right and descending the pleasant vale of Glencastle.

Belmullet is Ireland's remotest townlet, with two snug little inns. It is situated on the narrow neck of land (only a quarter of a mile wide) that connects the Mullet peninsula with the mainland. A canal has been cut here to connect the landlocked Blacksod Bay with Broad Haven. It was in Blacksod Bay that *La Rata*, the largest ship in the Spanish Armada, under Don Alonso de Leyva, went down in 1588. The chief attraction of the Mullet is its grand coast-line, particularly in the neighbourhood of Erris Head, the northern extremity. The Inishkea

Islands, near the south end of the peninsula, used to have a whale fishery, but they were abandoned by the inhabitants in 1931.

The main road and bus route from Belmullet to Ballina (T 58, 39 miles) is via Bangor and Crossmolina, but L 133, via Ballycastle, is more interesting and only 9 miles longer. Diverging left from T 58 beyond Atticonaun, it traverses the lonely bogs and moors of the barony of Erris, with hardly a human habitation in sight and no inn this side of Belderrig.   Carrowmore Lough is passed, and then, at Glenamoy, a rough road diverges on the left for Portacloy (9 miles), on a tiny bay enclosed by high cliffs.   To the west of it rises Benwee Head (829 feet), with awe-inspiring cliffs and views of Donegal, Mullet, and Achill.   A mile and a half out to sea are the Stags of Broadhaven, seven remarkable rock pinnacles some 300 feet in height. Porturlin, east of Portacloy, is another picturesque little harbour, reached by a branch road.

Beyond Glenamoy L 133 leaves Cregganbeg (1,117 feet) to the left and Benmore (1,155 feet) and Maumakeogh (1,247 feet) to the right.   From Belderrig, which has a small inn, walkers can explore the surpassingly beautiful coast westwards to Benwee Head, which some consider to be the finest in the British Isles—a constant succession of stupendous cliffs and bays, natural arches and stack rocks, the haunt of myriads of sea birds.

Beyond Belderrig L 133 strikes the coast again, and you enjoy grand marine views on the way to Ballycastle. There is a sharp descent at Glenlossera Lodge.   Ballycastle, where civilization is regained, is a small village on the Ballinglen River, close to Bunatrahir Bay, and is connected with Ballina by a bus service.   There is fine cliff scenery at Downpatrick Head, 5 miles north (road to within a mile), off which is the singular rock of Doonbristy. At Palmerstown the River Clonaghmore is spanned by a handsome bridge.

The village of *Killala*, formerly a railway terminus, is an ancient place, founded by St. Patrick himself.   Its bishopric has been absorbed in the see of Tuam; and the cathedral, with its prominent spire, beside which is a restored Round Tower 84 feet high, was rebuilt in 1671–80.

In the graveyard is a souterrain of great antiquity. At Kilcummin, on the north-west side of Killala Bay, a French force of 1,100 men under General Humbert landed on 22nd August 1798 to assist the Irish rebels, but a month later, after a few successes (e.g. the 'Castlebar Races'), they were driven out of Killala with great loss by General Trench, the survivors being taken off.

Better than the main road from Killala to Ballina is the by-road nearer the estuary of the Moy, which passes Moyne Abbey (1460) and Rosserk Friary (1400), both notable for their well-preserved cloisters. Ballina (accent on last syllable), a railway terminus, is a lively market town with two bridges over the Moy (a good salmon and trout river). The modern Catholic cathedral, with good glass in its east window, is adjoined by the ruins of an Augustinian friary (1427). An excellent thirty-mile drive may be taken around Lough Conn (excellent trout, pike, and perch fishing): passing Castle Gore, you keep left at Crossmolina and leave the bold cone of Nephin (2,646 feet) on the right; at Pontoon, with its anglers' hotels, you cross the channel connecting Loughs Conn and Cullin.

The main road from Ballina to Sligo (38 miles; T 40) runs direct to Dromore West, but it is preferable to take the coast road thus far (L 150, 6 miles longer), which is also the bus route. This soon enters Co. Sligo, commands pretty views of Killala Bay, and passes through Inniscrone (or Enniscrone), a flourishing seaside resort, and Easky, with ruined castles of the O'Dowds. Beyond Dromore West (again there is an alternative coast road) you have views across Sligo Bay to the Dartry Mountains, and in the distance on the right rise the granite Slieve Gamph or Ox Mountains, which increase in height from west to east and culminate in Knockalongy (1,778 feet). Near Beltra you approach Ballysodare Bay, which dries out at low tide. Ballysodare ('Town of the Cataract of Dara') lies at the mouth of the Owenmore River, which here forms a fine cascade, with a famous salmon fishery and fish-ladders. By the river are the remains of a monastery founded by St. Fechin in the seventh century. The road thence to Sligo (T 3) affords views of Lough Gill and its background of limestone mountains.

Sligo ('shelly river'), with a population of 13,000, is the capital of the like-named county and the principal town in the north-west of Ireland. The lay-out of its streets is rather confusing. The town lies mainly on the south bank of the Garavogue River, which drains Lough Gill into an arm of Sligo Bay, and its situation between sea and mountains is delightful. Its sea-borne trade is of some consequence, and it is the chief emporium for the homespuns of Galway and Donegal. The castle of Maurice Fitzgerald, Chief Justice of Ireland, has completely disappeared, but his foundation, Sligo Abbey, survives—a Dominican friary of 1154. It was burnt in 1414, and again in 1641 by Sir Frederick Hamilton. If it is locked, apply at the adjoining cottage. Noteworthy points among the ruins are the tracery of the four-light east window, the row of lancets in the choir, the high altar, the groined roof beneath the tower, and the monument of O'Conor Sligo (1623), while the three-sided cloister is a perfect gem, with beautiful, very low arches and pillars, and a reader's pulpit. The Catholic cathedral is in an Italian-Romanesque style (1869–74).

Sligo has a good railway hotel (Great Southern) and is the centre for splendid excursions. There are motor-boat tours on *Lough Gill*, 3 miles away, which many consider to be as beautiful as Killarney. Five miles long by 1½ miles wide, the lake is encircled by a 25-mile road, but, being mostly enclosed by wooded demesnes (private), is coy in displaying its charms, at least at the Sligo end. Anyhow it is a lovely drive, with views of the lake from the fine road on its south-west shore. On the west bank of the Garavogue River is Cairns Hill, with two cairns, two stone forts, and a stone circle; and in the beautiful demesne of Hazelwood House, on the opposite bank, is the prehistoric Deerpark Monument, an unusual example of the 'horned cairn' type, with side chambers entered by trilithons (one intact) from the central chamber. Church Island, in the middle of the lake, has the remains of a primitive church and is a favourite spot for picnics; and Innisfree is the 'Lake Isle' of the best-known poem of W. B. Yeats, who in his youth used to stay at his uncle's house in Sligo:

I will arise and go now, and go to Innisfree,
And a small cabin build there, of clay and wattles made:
Nine bean-rows will I have there, a hive for the honey-bee,
And live alone in the bee-loud glade.

Near the other end of the lake is Dromahair (11 miles from Sligo), with the seventeenth-century Old Hall on the site of Breffni Castle, by the River Bonet. It was thence that Dervorgilla, wife of Tiernan O'Rourke and Ireland's 'Helen of Troy,' eloped with Dermot MacMurrogh in 1152. The latter appealed to Henry II for help against the vengeance of the Irish chieftains, thereby affording a pretext for the Norman invasion. Dromahair also has the remains of Creevelea Abbey (situated on the other side of the river), a Franciscan friary with a number of interesting tombs. On the way back to Sligo by the north bank, you should take the 'Lough Gill Loop' (A.A. sign), from which you enjoy one of the finest views of the lake.

Buses from Sligo to the rising seaside resort of Strandhill (5 miles), on Sligo Bay, with a view of the great sand-dunes that mark this part of the coast. Above it rises the isolated hill of Knocknarea (1,078 feet), with its impressive cliffs and screes. The cairn on the summit is supposed to be the tomb or memorial of the legendary Maeve, Queen of Connacht (Queen Mab); it is estimated to weigh 40,000 tons. It was Queen Maeve who made the famous raid to carry off the brown bull of Cooley, and had her army held up by the single-handed Cuchulain. The panoramic view from the top of Knocknarea is superb, extending from the Donegal mountains to Croagh Patrick. A road encircles the hill, passing, on the south-west side, near a 'wondrously romantic' glen or wooded chasm, a mile long and 30 feet wide. At the cross-roads turn left for Sligo, passing, at the first road junction, the low hill of Carrowmore (219 feet), the Irish Carnac, with the largest group of megalithic antiquities in the British Isles—cairns, sepulchral chambers, dolmens, and stone circles. It is thought to be the burial place of those slain in the battle of Northern Moytura, i.e. the final defeat of the Firbolg by the Tuatha Dé Danaan (cf. page 149), who then held Ireland until the Celtic invasion two hundred years later.

Rosses Point, 5 miles north-west of Sligo by bus, is another seaside resort, with bracing air, charming views, good hotels, and the first-class links of the County Sligo Golf Club.

There is another worthwhile drive southwards from Sligo to T 3, past Lough Arrow and over the Curlew Mountain (822 feet) to Boyle (26 miles), in Co. Roscommon. Here are important ruins of a Cistercian abbey founded in 1161 by Maurice O'Duffy, with both round and pointed arches in the nave and interesting sculptural details. In the vicinity is Lough Key, praised by Arthur Young as 'one of the most delicious scenes I ever beheld.'

Finally, the circuit of *Glencar Lough*, north-east of Sligo, is another delightful run (20 miles). As you leave the town, note the splendid new surgical and mental hospitals, built with sweepstake profits. North of it tower the Dartry Mountains, shaped rather like Derbyshire 'scars,' with Truskmore (2,113 feet) and King's Mountain (1,527 feet) at the west end of the range. On the south side are the equally impressive cliffs of Lugnafaughery (1,472 feet) and other hills. At the farther end of the lake are three waterfalls. The encircling road runs high above the lake on the south side, and at lake level on the north. Hereabouts hedges take the place of the eternal stone walls. There are barytes workings on the north side of the lough. On leaving the lough you can make straight for Bundoran by a road diverging on the right.

TOUR VIII: SLIGO TO LONDONDERRY

BUNDORAN—BALLYSHANNON—LOUGH ERNE—ENNISKILLEN—
UPPER LOUGH ERNE—LOUGH DERG—DONEGAL—SLIEVE
LEAGUE — GLENCOLUMBKILLE — ARDARA — GWEEDORE —
ERRIGAL—LOUGH VEAGH—HORN HEAD—ROSAPENNA—MIL-
FORD — PORTSALON — LOUGH SWILLY — LETTERKENNY —
INISHOWEN—GRIANAN OF AILEACH—MALIN HEAD—MOVILLE

Total distance by road: about 400 miles.

THE direct road from Sligo to Londonderry (T 18, 84 miles) is via Donegal town, Stranorlar, and Raphoe. But properly to see the granite mountains and glens, the cliffs and bays of *Donegal* (pronounced 'Dùn-ne-gawl'), which by common consent is the most ravishingly beautiful county in Ireland, the following coastal drive, unbeatable of its kind, is recommended. Motorists must drive with great caution, as steep gradients, awkward corners, and rough stretches of road are numerous. Though it is one of the counties in the province of Ulster and stretches farther north than any other part of Ireland, Donegal belongs politically not to 'Northern Ireland' but to Eire, with which it is connected by a single road and no railway. The most salient characteristic of the county's geography is that it is strongly folded from north-east to south-west. Donegal comprises the ancient earldom of Tyrconnel and a little bit more. Its south-west corner is Gaelic-speaking, and its tweeds, made of local wool, washed, carded, spun, dyed, and woven on the hand-loom by the peasants in their cottages, are famous for their beauty and durability.

Leaving Sligo by Markievicz Road and Duck Street, then bearing left, you follow the Ballyshannon road (T 18, 26 miles—good bus service to Bundoran), which first passes through Drumcliffe, on a branch of Sligo Bay. On the right are the Dartry Mountains—King's Mountain

(1,527 feet) and Ben Bulben (1,722 feet), the latter curiously impressive with its long flat back and a happy hunting ground for botanists and geologists. Drumcliffe has the stump of a Round Tower (opposite the church), 40 feet in height (a relic of St. Columba's monastery), and, in the churchyard, an elaborately carved High Cross, 13 feet tall, and the grave of W. B. Yeats—'Cast a cold eye on life, on death. Horseman pass by.' Hereabouts was fought the Battle of the Books. St. Columba borrowed a psalter from St. Finian of Movilla Abbey (at Newtownards, Co. Down) and made a copy of it. St. Finian claimed the copy, and on the dispute being referred to Tara, King Dermot decided that 'the calf goes with the cow.' St. Columba refused to accept the award, and his supporters beat the men of Meath. Shortly afterwards, however, St. Columba, stricken with pangs of conscience, left for Iona to convert the Scottish heathen.

Grange, the next place of importance—Ben Bulben seen from this side is a real 'table mountain'—is the starting-point for an expedition to Inishmurray (4 miles), a small, now uninhabited island in the wide mouth of Donegal Bay, which has 'neither rates nor rats.' Within a wonderful example of a prehistoric cashel, 175 by 135 feet, with walls of drystone masonry, 10 feet high and 7–15 feet thick, are the very complete remains of an early Celtic monastery, founded by St. Molaise in the sixth century—churches, beehive cells, bullans, holy wells, and the rest. There was a curious local belief that if a man's body was interred in the women's burial-place, it would be miraculously removed during the night to the men's burial-place (and vice versa). Of the four grave slabs with early Gaelic inscriptions, one is unique in that it has a Latin addition: 'Hic dormit.'

The road now runs close to the shore of Donegal Bay, the widest and grandest in all Ireland, with great sand-dunes hereabouts. Three of the Armada vessels were wrecked on Dernish, the second of the two islands beyond Grange. Two miles north of Cliffoney is Mullaghmore, a select little seaside resort on a promontory. Classiebawn Castle here, a seat of Earl Mountbatten's, was built by Lord Palmerston in 1842. At Bunduff Bridge the road enters Co. Leitrim's exiguous outlet to the sea, leaving it again for Co. Donegal two miles farther on, at Tullaghan.

Bundoran, entered immediately afterwards, is a notably clean seaside resort in the full tide of prosperity, straggling along the main road for more than a mile, with a view of the Donegal mountains across the bay. It offers plenty of first-class hotel accommodation (Great Northern, etc.), excellent bathing, bracing air, good sandy golf links, trout fishing, and fantastic cliff scenery.

Ballyshannon is a 'little grey homely' town at the mouth of the River Erne. Its name has nothing to do with the River Shannon, but means 'ford of Seanach.' The Falls of Assaroe (seen from the bridge), spoilt by the hydro-electric scheme, have a celebrated salmon leap, and you may be lucky enough to see the salmon packed like sardines, waiting to ascend the river. The little-known strand of Rossnowlagh, 3 miles north, is one of the finest in the country.

Ballyshannon is the most convenient point on our circuit of the Irish coast from which to visit Lough Erne and Enniskillen, although they are inside the frontier of Northern Ireland, a fact which involves a customs examination and formalities with the triptyque.

The road from Ballyshannon to Lough Erne (L 24, 7 miles) follows the south bank of the river, side by side with it, and passes the new power stations and the Cloghore (Eire) and Belleek (Northern Ireland) frontier posts. L 24 becomes A 46.

Belleek ('ford of the flagstone'), in Co. Fermanagh, is just inside the Northern Ireland boundary. It has a beautiful old bridge over the Erne, and is noted for its fine pottery—lustre ware made from Norwegian felspar. There are sluice gates on the river to regulate the height of the lough. Take the road (A 46, to Enniskillen, 24 miles) along the south bank of *Lough Erne*, or Lower Lough Erne, which takes high rank among Ireland's lakes. It measures 20 miles long and as much as 6 miles wide. The south arm is crowded with wooded islets. Hills over 1,000 feet in height rise on the right of the road, which is a fine 'English' road, with some remarkable switchbacks. To the left, on the lakeside (but not easily seen from the

main road), is Tully Castle, dating from the Plantation of
Ulster; its garrison surrendered on honourable terms to
Roderick Maguire in 1641 but were promptly slaughtered
and their castle burnt. Then comes the isle of Inishmac-
saint ('isle of the plain of sorrel'), with the ruins of a small
church of the eleventh or twelfth century and a cross,
10 feet high, unadorned but of interesting form, seventh
or eighth century. On the outskirts of Enniskillen is the
Portora Royal School, a public school founded by Charles I
in 1626, with buildings dating back to 1777. Oscar Wilde
was a pupil. Its new preparatory school is an attractive
building.

Enniskillen ('Cethlenn's island'), the county town of
Fermanagh, is an attractive place, situated on the River
Erne near the upper end of the lough. Few Irish towns
can rival it in beauty of setting. Once the stronghold of
the Maguires, but colonized in 1641 by Sir William Cole,
a Londoner and ancestor of the Earls of Enniskillen, it
has always remained sturdily Protestant, and has given its
name to two Ulster regiments, the Inniskilling Dragoons
and the Royal Inniskilling Fusiliers. Military memorials
abound. Castlecoole, built by James Wyatt, now belongs
to the National Trust, with its 77-acre park (open on
summer afternoons, not Mondays or Thursdays).

There are occasional motor-boat trips from Enniskillen
the whole length of Lough Erne, and more frequent trips
to Devenish (Daimhinis, 'ox isle'), at the south end of the
lough, with ruins of a monastery founded by St. Molaise in
the sixth century. Its Round Tower, quite complete (81⅓
feet in height, 49¾ feet round at the base and 42½ feet under
the cornice), is outstanding for the quality of the mason's
work, its windows of various forms, and the cornice with
sculptured heads below the cap. The tapering is not
gradual throughout, but proceeds from floor to floor. The
tower may be ascended by a modern spiral staircase.
Little remains of the House of St. Molaise (with his stone
coffin) and the Great Church (twelfth century), but higher
up is St. Mary's Abbey (1449), with a tower, one wall of the
choir, and a spiral staircase. There is also a sculptured
cross, 7 feet high, of a type unique in Ireland.

For the visit to Cladagh Glen and its caves, you take

the Swanlinbar road and after 6 miles turn right past the Earl of Enniskillen's demesne of Florence Court. The house, early eighteenth century, now belonging to the National Trust, is open April–September on Tuesdays, Wednesdays, Fridays, and Saturdays, 2–6, also on Sunday afternoons in July–September. The Cladagh Glen is on the left of the road, 3½ miles farther on. Its stream flows through the 'Marble Arch' and, higher up, through an underground channel.

Upper Lough Erne, about 6 miles from Enniskillen, is a most extraordinary maze of channels and islands, and in some people's opinion is better worth seeing even than the lower lough. Though it is at least 10 miles long, there is nowhere an uninterrupted square mile of water. The reason given for this unusual state of things is that the water of the Erne is so charged with carbonic acid that it has progressively disintegrated its limestone banks. It is now possible to make a complete circuit of the lough by car, as the roads into Eire in this direction are open to motor traffic at the frontier. The best way to explore it would be by canoe, but motorists can see quite a lot of its unique beauties by the use of by-roads and a large-scale map, and by crossing the bridge at Ross Ferry.

On the way back from Enniskillen to the west coast, you this time take the road on the north-east bank of Lough Erne (A 35 to Pettigo, 20 miles, with bus service). The scenery on this side, of the English woodland type, is very beautiful, but the road affords only occasional views of the lake and the mountains on the opposite bank. After 3¼ miles you keep straight on at the fork and take the lakeside road (B 82) via Killadeas, and, farther on, choose what the A.A. sign calls the 'hilly, picturesque' road to the left; this commands the best of all views of the lough. Beyond Kesh a new road across the long and narrow Boa Island diverges on the left, enabling the circuit of the lough to be made without entering Eire territory. A 35 reaches the Northern Ireland frontier post at Tullyhomman Bridge, half a mile short of Pettigo, while the Eire customs station is in Pettigo itself. You must stop at both and have your triptyque stamped at the latter. The customs search may be quite a serious affair.

Pettigo ('smithy') has a ruined castle that was once a residence of Meiler Magrath, the Franciscan friar who in 1570 became Protestant Bishop of Clogher. It is the starting-point for the excursion to *Lough Derg*, among bleak moors 5 miles north. The road to it is a cul-de-sac. It owes its fame to 'St. Patrick's Purgatory' on the tiny Station Island, a cave in which the saint spent forty days and nights in prayer and fasting until the devil was driven from this his last stronghold in Ireland. This has been a popular place of pilgrimage since the Middle Ages, in spite of a papal edict in 1497 and various Acts of Parliament. The pilgrimage season lasts from 1st June to 15th August, and the pilgrims stay three days and practise great austerities—one meal a day, at twelve o'clock, of black tea (with sugar) and dry bread, an all-night vigil in the church on the first night, and barefooted 'rounds' to the church, the cross, the 'penitential beds,' etc. Talking and smoking, however, are permitted. Non-pilgrims are admitted to the island only by written permission from the Rev. Prior, and this is never granted after the middle of July. The church, consecrated in 1931, is a 'minor basilica' and has stained-glass windows depicting the Stations of the Cross.

From Pettigo you traverse a wild mountain road (T 35) via the Black Gap, crossing a grand heathery moorland and passing little farmhouses embosomed, strangely enough, in rhododendrons. The Ballyshannon–Donegal road (T 18) is joined at Laghey (pronounced 'La-hee'), which is 12 miles from Pettigo and 3 miles from Donegal.

Donegal town ('fort of the strangers') was the stronghold of the O'Donnell sept in the fifteenth and sixteenth centuries and the chief town of Tyrconnel, their territory. The county town, however, is now Lifford. Donegal is a trim and quiet little place at the mouth of the River Eske, with a handsome Jacobean castle built by Sir Basil Brooke (1610). On the seashore are the remains (choir, south transept, and part of the cloister) of the Franciscan friary founded by Hugh O'Donnell in 1474. Here the historic *Annals of the Four Masters* were compiled in 1632–6 by the three O'Clerys and O'Mulconry, who are commemorated by a handsome obelisk (1937) in the market-place. A five-mile digression may be made from Donegal to see Lough Eske, at the foot of the 'long wavering line' of the Blue Stack, or Croaghgorm, Mountains (2,219 feet).

You now turn west and follow T 72 (T 72a beyond Killybegs) along the northern shore of Donegal Bay to Glencolumbkille, 35 miles of hilly and winding roads (1 in 7 the maximum gradient), with delightful sea and mountain prospects. Buses are available as far as Malin More. You can hardly fail to notice the absence of stone walls in this part of the country. Mountcharles is noted for its hand embroidery; on the left is the wooded demesne of Mount Charles Hall. Inver, at the head of Inver Bay, is passed; then Dunkineely, a fishing resort on the hilly neck of a strange, six-mile-long narrow peninsula ending in St. John's Point.

The really fine scenery now begins. Beyond Mac-Swyne's Bay, with an old castle of the sept of that name, you come to the Round Tower of Bruckless, and then Killybegs ('little churches'), a small fishing port on a sheltered inlet, the prettiest of all this series of bays and used as a submarine base during the First World War. Its entrance is guarded by a lighthouse on a rock. Killybegs is noted for its hand-tufted carpets, and has a fish-curing industry. The buses here turn north for Ardara and Portnoo.

At Killybegs, however, you must keep straight on in order to explore the remote south-western peninsula of Donegal (hotels at Carrick, Glencolumbkille, and in summer at Malin More). Each view is finer than the last. Sometimes the road runs halfway up the mountainside, with charming prospects over Donegal Bay. The mountain scenery is of every variety, ending in bare moorlands. The stony Fintragh Bay, at the foot of Meenboy (1,554 feet) and Crownarad (1,621 feet); Kilcur, an alluring village near the fine scenery and caves of Muckros Head; and Carrick, on the Glen River, with its hotel burnt out in the late 'troubles' but now open again, follow each other in rapid succession.

At Carrick you pause for the ascent of *Slieve League*

(1,972 feet), a mountain rising straight from the sea, with some of the highest cliffs in the British Isles. The most thrilling way of approach is to drive to the base of Carrigan Head (2 miles), where it is advisable to leave the car at the cottages where the good road comes to an end. Beyond that point the road becomes rougher and exceedingly steep, and at the very top there is nowhere to turn. Thence you take to the footpath along the cliffs, past Bunglass Point. It is half an hour's walk from the cottages to the point where the great cliffs of Slieve League come into sight. Between the Eagle's Nest and the summit of the mountain you have a choice between the spectacular One Man's Path, a knife-edge only two feet wide, but quite safe in calm weather, or, if you feel nervous about it, the Old Man's Path, a little lower down on the landward side. The variegated colouring of the cliffs is almost as impressive as their height, and the panoramic views from the summit are superb. If time and weather permit, a boat should be hired at Teelin for a trip along the base of the precipice.

From Carrick the road ascends to 500 feet, then drops down to *Glencolumbkille*, a Gaelic-speaking hamlet in a secluded, melancholy valley, with many relics of the time when this was St. Columba's favourite retreat—the saint's house or oratory, well, chair, and bed (a large flagstone). There are also a dozen standing stones with incised crosses and, on the Ardara road, a well-preserved High Cross. Good walks may be taken, if time permit, north to Glen Head, with a 700-foot cliff, and south-west to Malin More and Malin Beg (with accommodation for holiday makers), beyond which is Trabane Bay, a delightful inlet. A mile offshore is the islet of Rathlin O'Birne, with a lighthouse. The twenty-mile coast walk from Glencolumbkille to Ardara via the Sturrall promontory, Tormore Point, the cliffs of Slievetooey, and the caves of Maghera is extremely grand but very strenuous.

The road from Glencolumbkille to Ardara (16 miles) crosses the rough Glengesh Pass (900 feet), and descends the famous test hill, reputed to be the most dangerous in Ireland, with gradients of 1 in 4 to 1 in 6 and two wicked hairpin bends. Discreet motorists will avoid it by returning to Killybegs, and bearing left beyond it, 12 miles extra. The small town of *Ardara* (accent on last syllable), at the head of Loughrosmore Bay, is a marketing centre for the excellent Donegal homespun tweeds and knitwear, and has a good inn. The Owentocher and Owenea are good salmon rivers. A by-road follows the south shore of Loughrosbeg Bay to the waterfall and caves of Maghera.

The road from Ardara to Gweedore (32 miles) along the west coast of Donegal is a magnificent drive, undulating through a wild countryside of moors, rivers, and many small loughs, with occasional seascapes. Gradients vary from 1 in 8 to 1 in 12. You should take the coast road to Narin and Maas (L 81), passing a dolmen on the right beyond Kilclooney Bridge. At Narin a road goes off on the left to Portnoo (the bus terminus) and Rosbeg, two tiny holiday places with very fair inns and excellent walks in every direction.

T 72, which is joined at Maas, soon crosses the Gwee-barra Bridge, a reinforced concrete structure over the estuary of the Gweebarra, with a view. Careful driving is needed at the remarkable series of bends on either side of the bridge. Then over empty russet moorlands, or wilder-nesses of wonderfully coloured rocks, with grand mountain views. The head of Trawenagh Bay, a landlocked inlet that dries out at low water, is passed.

Dungloe, a small town on its island-studded bay, is an excellent centre for the angler. A side-road leads thence to the north-west to Burtonport, 4 miles away, at the mouth of the bay. A nineteenth-century creation, named after William Burton, fourth Marquis Conyngham, Burton-port has a fishing and herring-curing industry, and granite quarries. The coast-line here is very broken; the largest of the many islands is Aran Island, with a powerful lighthouse.

Between Dungloe and Gweedore lies the curious district known as the Rosses, an astounding tangle of small loughs and huge granite boulders, among which it is easy to lose one's way and dangerous to be benighted off the beaten track. The population is surprisingly large in view of the poverty of the peaty soil.

The direct road (L 130) skirts the lovely Lough Anure, with a large technical school on its bank, passes a waterfall and some enormous rocks near Crolly Station, and crosses the Gweedore River at Crolly Bridge, a particularly pretty spot. Adventurous spirits may prefer to try the old coast road (T 72, 9 miles longer), narrow and intricate, which branches off on this side of Burtonport and passes Lough Waskel (dangerous 1-in-5 descent beyond it), Keadew Strand, Kincasslagh, and Annagry, rejoining the new road at Crolly Bridge. Hydro-electric and peat-fired power station.

Gweedore, an oasis in the wilderness, is the creation of Lord George Hill (d. 1879) and is the terminus of a bus service from Derry.

To climb *Errigal* (2,466 feet), the highest mountain in Donegal, with a shining white cap of quartzite screes, you drive up the valley, past Lough Nacung, to Dunlewy (5 miles), whence the summit can be reached in a couple of hours. The last part of the climb is a 'one man's path,' two feet wide, for 30 yards. The panorama of the coast line is immense, and in clear weather the Scottish isles of Islay and Jura can be made out. The loose screes on the north flank of Errigal should be carefully avoided.

Dunlewy lies at the foot of the 'Poisoned Glen,' where, it is said, the water is unfit to drink owing to the presence of spurge. Walkers should ascend to its head and cross the gap (1,400 feet) in the Derryveagh Mountains, which commands one of Ireland's most classic views. To the south-west rises Slieve Snaght ('snow mountain'; 2,240 feet). On the other side of the gap you can descend to the Doochary–Gartan road, turn left, and leave it almost immediately to descend Glen Veagh to *Lough Veagh* (pronounced 'Vee-ach' and meaning 'ravens'), Donegal's grandest lake, in the middle of a deer forest. Four miles in length, it lies in a trough flanked by steep mountains, wooded with scrub-oak, holly, yew, and juniper. The private road on the south bank passes the modern Glenveagh Castle.

Motorists who are not afraid of rough roads can reach Lough Veagh by continuing up the Dunlewy valley, with a pause at the summit level (828 feet) to admire the view. The mountain on the right (south-east) is Dooish (2,147) feet). Then down to Calabber Bridge, where you turn

right for Lough Veagh. On the way back you can keep
right at Calabber Bridge and cross the mountains by
Muckish Gap (800 feet) to Falcarragh. From the gap the
ascent of Muckish ('pig's back'; 2,197 feet) is a simple
matter, and there is a striking prospect from the summit.

The direct road from Gweedore to Gortahork (L 130,
9 miles) runs inland, but there is an alternative coast
road (T 62, 5 miles longer) via Bunbeg, a quaint little
port in a 'congested district,' and Bloody Foreland, the
north-west point of the Donegal coast, deriving its name
from the red colour of its cliffs. Gortahork, on Ballyness
Bay, which is dry at low tide, has a summer school for
Gaelic-learners.

Gortahork (or Magheroarty) is the usual place from
which to make the ten-mile boat trip to Tory Island, past
Inishbofin, Inishdooey, and Inishbeg. Tory Island (pronounced 'Torry'), the 'isle of towers,' has two ruined
churches and a Round Tower of red granite, 51 feet high
and built like a beehive hut. These are relics of a primitive
abbey which St. Columba is thought to have established
here. The island is barren, and the 300 inhabitants, who
gain their livelihood partly by lobster fishing, pay no rent,
rates, or taxes. H.M.S. *Wasp*, which was sent to collect
the dues in 1884, was wrecked with the loss of all the crew
but six. There is a powerful lighthouse on the north-west
point.

The next section of the road—T 72, 17 miles from Gortahork to Creeslough—runs a mile or more from the coast.
At Falcarragh, in the grounds of Ballyconnell House, there
is a great stone called Cloghaneely, after which the whole
district is named. It is supposed to have served as a
block when a local chief, MacKineely, was beheaded by
Balar, the famous one-eyed 'king' of Tory Island—whence
the red veins in the stone!

Beyond Rinclevan Strand, with its sand dunes, furze,
and rushes, you come to Dunfanaghy, an alluringly bright
little holiday resort on a branch of Sheep Haven, with
excellent sands, three hotels, and a golf-course. A great
attraction is the propinquity of *Horn Head*, 2½ miles away,
with its awesome 800-foot cliffs, sea birds, and strange

rock formations. Splendid view of the neighbouring headlands and islands.

The road skirts the tawny sands of Sheep Haven, where bathing is perfection, to Port-na-Blagh (or Portnablah), on its pretty little bay. Farther on you leave to the left the peninsular demesne of Ards, which is now a Franciscan Capuchin friary. If you take the short cut past Crees-lough (pronounced 'Creess-lĕ') you are confronted by a dangerously steep descent with right-angle turns at intervals. On the shore farther on is seen the keep of Doe Castle, the well-preserved fortress of the MacSwineys, overlooking a delightful inlet.

At Creeslough you turn left from the direct road to Letterkenny (L 76, 16 miles) and take the coast road (T 72, 28 miles). The efflux from Glen Lough is crossed at Lackagh Bridge. At Carrigart a side-road on the left leads to *Rosapenna*, with a large first-class hotel (burnt out in 1962) on the neck of the Rosguill peninsula, the attractions of which include a championship golf-course on the dunes, a sandy bathing beach, and good fishing. Bungalows and smaller hotels have sprung up hereabouts. One of the finest things in all Ireland is the 'Atlantic Drive' round the Rosguill peninsula ('en corniche' between Doagh, or Dooey, and Mevagh), which separates Sheep Haven from Mulroy Bay. A 'unique' view is obtainable from the top of Ganiamore (682 feet). There is a group of churchyard antiquities at Mevagh, on Mulroy Bay.

From Carrigart the road, gold with gorse, clings sinuously for a while to the west shore of Mulroy Bay, a deep and landlocked fiord of far-famed, unforgettable beauty, 12 miles long, with many islands and ramifications among the wild hills—altogether an ideal place for sailing. At the head of the bay you cross the Bunlin River, the glen of which is noted for its beauty. Close to the bridge, which commands a glorious view, are a dolmen and the Bunlin Waterfall (two miles up the glen is another, the Golan Loup). From the winding ascent beyond the bridge you get the best of all views of Mulroy Bay.

Milford, on the hillside above the bay, is a tourist centre with a comfortable hotel and a golf-course. Lough Fern, a mile and a half to the south, is reputed to have the best free fishing in Ireland.

Instead of taking the direct road from Milford to Ramelton (T 72, 4½ miles), a digression should be made to see the Fanad peninsula, anciently the territory of the MacSwineys. The road (L 78) passes the flour mills and runs along the edge of the east shore of Mulroy Bay as far as Kerrykeel, a quaint place at the foot of the Knockalla Mountain, or Devil's Backbone (1,203 feet). You then cross the peninsula obliquely to reach *Portsalon* ('salt fort'), 10 miles from Milford (buses), a delightful spot near the mouth of Lough Swilly, consisting of a neat little harbour, a post office, and a large first-class hotel with golf links on the dunes and perfect bathing. *Lough Swilly* ('lake of shadows') is the noblest of sea inlets, 30 miles long, with excellent sailing and romantic scenery. It was retained by Great Britain as a naval base until 1938, when it was transferred to the Eire Government. Dunree Head, opposite Portsalon, is strongly fortified. The French frigate *Hoche* was captured off the lough in 1798 with Wolfe Tone on board. Tone was taken to Dublin Castle, where, refused a soldier's death, he committed suicide. North of Portsalon there are good cliffs, with the Seven Arches and the Doaghbeg Arch, and the drive over the hills, through scenery that grows ever wilder, to the lighthouse on Fanad Head, where the cliffs are 300 feet high, is a most exhilarating experience.

Instead of returning to Milford you should bear left at the fork when you regain Mulroy Bay and take the really sporting road over the hills (700 feet), very rough in places, with terrific though short pitches and with superb views. This brings you to picturesque Rathmullen (or Rathmullan), a small holiday resort on Lough Swilly. It was hence that Hugh O'Neill, Earl of Tyrone, and Rory O'Donnell, Earl of Tyrconnel, left for France in 1607—the 'Flight of the Earls.' The resulting sequestration of their estates led to the Plantation of Ulster. The ruins at Rathmullen are those of a Carmelite friary founded by the MacSwineys in the fifteenth century. The best viewpoint in this neighbourhood is Crockanaffrin (1,137 feet), which overlooks both Lough Swilly and Mulroy Bay.

Ramelton (accent on second syllable), on the main road, lies on a steep hill by a creek of Lough Swilly (gradient of 1 in 7 or 8). Instead of taking the direct road thence to Letterkenny (T 72, 8 miles), make for the shore of the lough by the charming road to Fort Stewart, which dates from the beginning of the seventeenth century, and go thence to Letterkenny by the road parallel to the shore of the lough. Part of this road is private, but permission to drive through it is granted at the lodge. Beyond the farther gate walk down the grassy track immediately to the left to see the ivy-clad ruins of the Franciscan friary of Killydonnell, a sixteenth-century creation of the O'Donnells.

Letterkenny, the largest town in Donegal, though it consists chiefly of one long street, is conspicuously sited on the hillside ('leitir') above the River Swilly. Its chief building, proudly dominating the town, is the fine Catholic cathedral of St. Eunan, built on Mountcharles sandstone and consecrated in 1901, with interesting carvings (notably on the chancel arch) by local stonemasons.

The shortest route from Letterkenny to Londonderry (21 miles) is by T 59 to a point three-quarters of a mile beyond Pluck, then via Lagan and Ardagh to St. Johnston (Eire customs station), whence you follow the bank of the River Foyle past the Carrigans frontier post (Eire) and the Creevagh boundary post (Northern Ireland), entering Derry by A 40.

But it is much more convenient to visit the Eire peninsula of *Inishowen* before entering Northern Ireland (buses available to Carndonagh, 48 miles. Turn left at Pluck by T 59, and follow it via Manorcunningham, a depressing spot, to a point 1¼ miles beyond Newtowncunningham, where you take T 74, to the left (signpost 'Bridgend'). The road is splendidly engineered, with excellent surface and views of Lough Swilly. At Burt narrow by-roads on the right ascend a hill (803 feet) crowned by the conspicuous *Grianan of Aileach* ('Aileach's summer-house'), one of the most famous concentric forts in Ireland, but maladroitly restored in 1874–8. This stronghold of the O'Neills, kings of Ulster, was destroyed by Brian Boru, Ard Ri (high king) of Ireland, in 1001. Three dilapidated ramparts encircle the cashel, which consists of a circular stone wall 17½ feet high, 15 feet thick, and 240 feet in circumference. There are passages in the thickness of the wall. The view of Loughs Foyle and Swilly is alone worth the digression.

Beyond Burt Church a road diverging across the marshes (a great breeding ground for wild swans) leads to Inch Island. At Bridgend turn sharp left by T 73 (avoiding the customs barriers) for Fahan (pronounced 'Fawn'), on Lough Swilly, opposite Rathmullen, with a lovely view. Note the churchyard cross. Then come the Lisfannon links of the North Western Golf Club, on the sand-dunes, and Buncrana, a small town at the mouth of the Crana River. Here is a castle keep of the O'Dohertys—'you cannot beat a bush in Inishowen without starting an O'Doherty,' a saying that still holds good.

The main road from Buncrana to Clonmany (T 73) ascends the beautiful moorland valley of the Owenboy, with Slieve Snaght ('snow mountain'; 2,019 feet, the highest in the peninsula, rising on the right. Above Mintiagh's Lough is the strange knob of Binmore (1,044 feet). The rough coast road bears right from the Dunree Head road and crosses the Gap of Mamore (860 feet), one of the steepest and most dangerous passes in the British Isles, between the Urris Hills (1,379 feet) on the left and Mamore Hill (1,381 feet) on the right (the latter the better viewpoint). The road thence to Clonmany passes near Dunaff Head (690 feet), at the mouth of Lough Swilly. Beyond Clonmany the main road touches Ballyliffin, near the beautiful sands of Pollan Bay, and then skirts the shallow estuary of Trawbreaga Bay.

Carndonagh makes shirts and is the market and shopping town for the Inishowen peninsula. Note the old cross at the entrance and the modern factory for the distillation of alcohol from potatoes. The road thence to Malin Head (9 miles, with buses) skirts Trawbreaga Bay again, and crosses a quaint old ten-arched bridge at Malin, whence you should follow the A.A. route, passing the good Cross Roads Hotel at Ballygorman, near which there is a radio station. Finally you make for the tower, and leave the car at the foot of the last ascent. *Malin Head*, with fine seascapes and

G

beautifully coloured rocks, is the northernmost point in Ireland. The fine circular drive round the Head should not be missed, passing near Hell's Hole, three-quarters of a mile west of Malin Head. The cliffs at the Head are of no great height, but rise to 800 feet on the way to Glengad Head, 10 miles east by cliff path. About six miles out to sea is Inishtrahull, a deserted islet with a lighthouse.

The next goal is Moville, 20 miles from Malin Head (buses from Carndonagh). The road from Malin onwards is quite a fast one. Return to Malin village and bear left for Culdaff, an attractive village at the head of a creek, whence you have a choice of roads that unite at Moglass Bridge. (The right-hand road is the better one.) The road thence to Moville (fuchsia hedges) crosses a gap in the hills. *Moville* (accent on last syllable) is a pleasant family resort with good sea-angling. It lies near the mouth of Lough Foyle and commands good views of the shipping on that grand estuary, 20 miles long and as much as 8 miles wide. The best look-out is Crockaulin (1,074 feet), behind the town to the north. You should take a run out to Inishowen Head (6 miles; buses available) past Greencastle, which is opposite Magilligan Point and has a ruined castle of Richard de Burgh's and a modern fort, the latter converted into the Fort Hotel, of a most unusual character. Inishowen Head, with its lighthouse, affords a splendid view of the coast of Antrim.

T 73 hugs the west coast of *Lough Foyle* most of the way from Moville to Derry, a pleasant but unexciting run of 20 miles. A good many villas are passed, and long stretches of mud are exposed at low tide. Note the hillside covered with cloudberry canes, as you leave Moville. The highest of the hills on the right are Crockglass (1,309 feet) and Eskaheen (1,377 feet). The Eire customs station is at Muff and is soon followed by the frontier post and the Culmore boundary post for Northern Ireland. The road, now called A 2, passes, on the right, the field in which Amelia Earhart landed after her solo flight across the Atlantic in 1932, and, on the left, Boom Hall, marking the spot where the famous boom was thrown across the Foyle during the siege. The breaking of the boom by Captain

Micaiah Browning in the *Mountjoy* on 28th July 1689
enabled the food ships to enter and put an end to the
blockade. Derry is entered by Strand Road, on the left
of which, if required, is the Northern Ireland customs
station.

TOUR IX: LONDONDERRY TO BELFAST

LONDONDERRY — PORTRUSH — DUNLUCE CASTLE — GIANT'S CAUSEWAY — CARRICK-A-REDE — GLENS OF ANTRIM — FAIR HEAD — RATHLIN ISLAND — CUSHENDUN — CUSHENDALL — GLENARIFF — LARNE — CARRICKFERGUS — BELFAST — ANTRIM—LOUGH NEAGH.

Total distance by road: about 200 miles.

Londonderry is commonly known as Derry ('oak wood'), the 'London' in its name dating from 1608, when the lands of the rebel Sir Cahir O'Docherty were handed over by James I to the 'Society of the Governor and Assistants of London of the Plantation in Ulster.' This society, which still exists under the name of the Honourable the Irish Society of London, was formed from the twelve city companies of London, the lands being divided into twelve parts, which the companies drew by lot. Now the prosperous second city of Ulster, with a population of 54,000, which has long since outgrown the old walled city, Derry lies on the west bank of the Foyle, here a magnificent stream more than 300 yards wide. The only bridge is Craigavon Bridge, erected in 1933 to supersede the narrower Carlisle Bridge. The staple manufacture of Derry is shirt-making, an industry that occupies ten thousand workers in forty different factories. Bacon-curing is another important industry. Derry is the natural gateway to Co. Donegal, from which it is now cut off by the customs barrier.

Derry originated in one of St. Columba's abbeys. The most famous event in its history is its siege and blockade by James II's forces, when it held out successfully against famine and pestilence from 18th April to 12th August 1689.

By far the most interesting sight in Derry is its old city walls, 25 feet high, completed in 1618 and now largely hidden by houses. Wonderfully preserved, they form the most complete set of town walls in the British Isles. The top of the walls has been converted into a public promenade. Steps ascend to it at Shipquay Gate, nearest the river and approached by Shipquay Street, which is said to be the steepest business street in the kingdom. Turning right (northwards) at the top of the steps, you pass a line of old guns. Beyond Castle Gate and Butcher's Gate is the Royal Bastion, with a 90-foot column (1828), which can be ascended, in memory of the Rev. George Walker, Rector of Donaghmore, Co. Tyrone, who was a moving spirit in the defence of the city and fell at the Boyne. He has a Bible in his right hand: the sword in his left hand was blown down in a gale. At the Double Bastion is Roaring Meg, a cannon used in the siege. Bishop's Gate, at the east end of the walls, is a triumphal arch dating from 1789, with classical decorations. In the centre of the south-east wall is the Ferryquay Gate, which the thirteen heroic apprentices slammed in the face of James II's troops, who were being sent by the Viceroy to replace the Protestant garrison. The 'Shutting of the Gates' on 18th December is still commemorated every year by the burning in effigy of Colonel Lundy, the treacherous governor.

The old part of the town within the walls still contains the chief shopping and business streets. In the central square, or Diamond, is a striking War Memorial (bronze figures by Vernon March, 1926). Near Bishop's Gate are the fine courthouse (1813) and the Protestant cathedral of St. Columb, rebuilt on a new site in 1629–33 and an interesting example of Jacobean Gothic. In the vestibule is the bombshell thrown into the city with General Hamilton's offer of terms; the reply was 'No Surrender,' which is still the city's motto. Note the tablet set up in 1633: 'If stones could speake then Londons prayse should sounde who built this church and cittie from the ground.' The Siege Memorial Window (1913), to the right of the entrance, and the interesting relics in the chapter house (entrance to the right of the window) should be seen, also the splendid view from the west tower (191 feet high), which was rebuilt in 1803. The Catholic cathedral of St. Eugene, a

neo-Gothic structure of 1873, is at the top of Great James
Street, a turning off Strand Road.

The first stage of the coastal drive to Belfast is from
Derry to Portrush (railway available). The road (A 2 to
Coleraine, 37 miles) crosses the bridge, turns left, and
keeps fairly close to the south shore of Lough Foyle. As
you approach Limavady, the jagged outline of Benevenagh
is an impressive sight. Limavady ('leap of the dog';
pronounced 'Limmaváddy'), a Plantation town, was
previously the centre of the O'Kanes' territory. Here
the lovely 'Londonderry Air' was picked up in 1851 from
an itinerant musician. Thackeray's 'Peg of Limavaddy,'
with whom he fell eternally in love during the ten minutes
of his stay, was the maid at an inn in Ballyclose Street.
There is good mountain scenery south and east of Limavady, and the valley of the River Roe repays exploration.
At its head stand the Sperrin Mountains, the highest of
which is Sawel (2,240 feet).

A 37 crosses the hills direct to Coleraine (14 miles), with
a long climb to and descent from its summit level at 819
feet—you can free-wheel downhill for miles. The 'wide-
open spaces' character of the hills will be spoiled when
the spruce plantations grow up. A 2, 6 miles longer,
follows the coast and is level as far as Downhill. On the
right of it are the flanks of Benevenagh (1,260 feet),
multicoloured with pines, gorse, and heather, and streaked
with waterfalls. On the left are the levels of the Magilligan
peninsula, stretching away to Magilligan Point at the
mouth of Lough Foyle, east of which are eight miles
of hard silvery sands, sometimes used for speed trials.
The four-mile base line for the trigonometrical survey of
Ireland was measured along the strand with glass rods.
There is a 1-in-10 ascent to Downhill, where the road
touches the coast. Downhill Hall (recently dismantled)
was built by the famous Earl of Bristol who was Bishop of
Derry and a great continental traveller (the many Bristol
Hotels are named after him). His Mussenden Temple
(1783) and a mausoleum survive in the care of the National
Trust. The next side-road leads to Castlerock, at the
mouth of the River Bann, with excellent bathing and golf.

Coleraine ('corner of ferns'), on the Bann, farther

inland, is a Plantation town and seaport, well built and manufacturing various commodities. It is noted also for the salmon fishing.

Thence there is choice of roads to Portrush—either direct by A 29 (7½ miles) or by A 2 (¾ mile longer), the railway and bus route, via Portstewart, the smaller and quieter, but rapidly growing neighbour of Portrush, with equally good bathing and nearly as excellent golf. There is a tiny fishing harbour. The prominent castle-like building on the left side of the bay is a Dominican convent and girls' school. Rock Castle, more westerly and at sea level, was the birthplace of Sir George White, of Ladysmith fame. It is nearly 4 miles from Portstewart to Portrush —bungalows all the way—and as you enter the latter you leave Co. Londonderry for Co. Antrim.

Portrush, largest, most bustling, and best organized of Ulster seaside resorts, with a fair-sized harbour, is famous as the metropolis of Irish golf. The Royal Portrush Golf Club has two courses, one of championship rank. Other amusements are well catered for, and there are some good shops. The town terminates strikingly in Ramore Head, with short stretches of esplanade and views of the rocky coast-line on both sides of the peninsula. There is excellent bathing in both bays and in the natural 'Blue Pool.' The Skerries, a line of rocks offshore, form a natural breakwater for the east bay. The Northern Counties Hotel is possibly the finest in Ireland.

An electric railway, constructed in 1883, the first hydroelectric line in the British Isles, used to run from Portrush to Bushmills and the Giant's Causeway (8 miles), but has been dismantled. The coast road (A 2) passes close to *Dunluce Castle*, the 'mermaid's fort,' or 'strong fort,' of the MacDonnells (Earls of Antrim), who expelled the MacQuillans (or MacUillins) from it in 1558. Dunluce is an extraordinary place, with romantic-looking towers and gables of the late sixteenth century (there is no keep), in one of the grandest sites imaginable, quite impregnable before the invention of artillery. Tickets (6*d.* each) at the cottage opposite. Between the mainland and the basaltic rock on which stands the castle is a gulf 20 feet wide, spanned in ancient times by a drawbridge and nowadays

by a narrow wooden bridge. The buildings on the mainland were probably constructed to take the place of the
kitchens which fell into the sea, with eight servants inside,
one stormy night in 1630.

A side-road on the left leads to Port Ballintrae, a small
seaside resort on a pretty bay, while A 2 crosses the River
Bush at Bushmills, which gives its name to a famous pot-
still whisky.

The second turning on the left beyond Bushmills leads
to the *Giant's Causeway*, one of the world's wonders. Its
like is to be seen only at Fingal's Cave on the Hebridean
isle of Staffa. Molten lava thrown up during a volcanic
eruption has here crystallized into some 40,000 polygonal
(mostly hexagonal or pentagonal) columns of a steel-grey
or greyish-brown basalt and measuring 15–20 inches across.
The bright red bands of volcanic ash in the cliffs represent
quiescent periods between eruptions. The causeway,
which extends into the sea for rather less than half a mile,
was given to the National Trust in 1961 by the Ulster
Land Fund and Sir Antony Macnaghten, Bart., together
with 96 acres of cliff-land. The official guides point out
various special imaginatively named features, such as
the Wishing Well, the Giant's Organ, the Wishing Chair,
Lord Antrim's Parlour, the Lady's Fan, the Mitre, the
Coffin, etc. They also draw your attention to the only
three-sided column and to columns of various sides from
five to nine.

It looks like the beginning of the world, somehow: the sea
looks older than in other places, the hills and rocks strange,
and formed differently from other rocks and hills. . . . The
hill-tops are shattered into a thousand cragged fantastical
shapes. . . . The savage rock-sides are painted of a hundred
colours. Does the sun ever shine here? When the world
was moulded and fashioned out of formless chaos, this must
have been the *bit over*—a remnant of chaos!

THACKERAY, *Irish Sketch-Book*.

Boatmen take their passengers for trips to the
caves, the finest of which are Portnoon Cave, with

exquisite colouring, and Runkerry Cave, measuring 700 feet in length and 60 feet in height.

The exit from the Causeway is by the Giant's Loom, which consists of jointed columns 30 feet high. Every bit as interesting as the Causeway itself is the path that runs eastward along the face of the magnificent cliffs all the way to Dunseverick. The chief points passed on the way are the Organ Pipes; the Chimney Tops, which were fired at by the Armada owing to their resemblance to Dunluce; Portnaspanaigh, where the *Gerona*, a ship of the Armada, was wrecked in 1588, 250 Spaniards being drowned and 5 saved; Pleaskin Head, Benbane Head, and Bengore Head, with superb seascapes; and Portmoon. There is a ruined MacQuillan castle at Dunseverick. The return may be made by the path along the top of the cliffs, about six miles in all.

The Antrim coast road (A 2), 85 miles from Portrush to Belfast, is one of the finest marine drives in Europe and was constructed in the great famine. The cliffs owe much of their striking beauty to the combination of black basalt, dazzling white limestone, and red sandstone. The views extend in clear weather to the coast of Scotland. There is no railway this side of Larne, but there are bus services all the way except between Ballyvoy and Cushendun.

Motorists who have parked their cars at the Giant's Causeway rejoin A 2 beyond Dunseverick, where Rathlin Island comes into view, but beyond Whitepark Bay (a National Trust property of 179 acres) they should quit it again in favour of the coast road (B 15) to Ballycastle via Ballintoy. Off Ballintoy Harbour lies Sheep Island. About a mile farther on a path descends from a farmhouse (small fee) on the left to the *Carrick-a-Rede* ('rock in the roadstead'), a stack rock of basalt which, from 17th March to the end of the salmon fishing season in September, is connected with the cliffs of the mainland by the fishermen's famous swinging bridge of rope and boards. Spanning a chasm 90 feet deep and 60 feet wide, it looks utterly crazy, but is quite safe. At one time there was only a single board and a single hand-rope. The walk thence eastward to Kenbane Head, with its cliff scenery and picturesque ruin, is well worth while.

* G

Ballycastle, 13 miles from Bushmills, is a straggling and attractive place, with the Antrim Arms, a fine strand, sandy golf, tennis, and fishing. It lies at the foot of the lonely Glenshesk (east of Knocklayd, 1,695 feet), the first of the romantically beautiful *Glens of Antrim,* which run inland from the sea and greatly enhance the charms of this glorious coast. The others are Glentaise, Glencorb, Glendun, Glenaan, Glenballyemon, Glenariff, Glencloy, and Glenarm. Moira O'Neill and others have sung their praises. To the east of Ballycastle are the ruins of the Franciscan friary of Bonamargy (*c.* 1475), with the mausoleum of the Earls of Antrim and other MacDonnells.

A great excursion from Ballycastle is to *Fair Head,* 5 miles east, a bold promontory 636 feet in height, one-half of which consists of a precipice of columnar basalt. A road runs along the foot of the cliffs nearly to its base, and another branches off to the left from the Torr Head road. The view from the top of the headland is immense, extending to Islay, the Paps of Jura, and the Mull of Kintyre. You can descend by the Grey Man's Path to view the cliffs from below. The rocks at the base were the landing place of the legendary Deirdre.

Rathlin Island is a five-mile trip from Ballycastle, across a tide-race that can be dangerous in bad weather. Six miles long, it is shaped like 'an Irish stocking,' and it has often served as a stepping-stone between Scotland and Ireland. Near the lighthouse is the cave where Robert Bruce allegedly had his famous adventure with the spider. The inhabitants speak both English and Gaelic. The cliffs rise to a height of 400 feet on the north-west side and are the haunt of countless guillemots, razorbills, shags, and kittiwakes. One of Marconi's earliest successful attempts at radio communication was between Ballycastle and Rathlin.

Between Ballycastle and Cushendun (16 miles) A 2 runs at some distance from the sea over glorious highlands. The coast road diverging at Ballyvoy (the end of the bus route) for Torr Head and Cushendun has most beautiful scenery but is rather rough in parts and exceedingly hilly and tortuous, demanding a powerful car and a skilful driver. Above all, it is for the most part very narrow, and the consequences of meeting another car at one of the more awkward places might be serious. Altogether a worthwhile, thrilling experience. The flowering American currants on this road are a lovely sight in spring.

The main road reaches an altitude of 836 feet before it descends in zigzags to cross Glendun by a handsome viaduct, while an equally tortuous road on the left drops down into *Cushendun* ('at the foot of the brown river'), a lovely seaside village with two cosy hotels, nestling in the hollow at the mouth of the glen. Its natural beauties and freedom from unsightly buildings find much favour with artists, and it is now in the care of the National Trust. The unsophisticated foreshore is a mass of gorse and bracken. Here is the Cairn of Shane O'Neill, the 'proud' Earl of Tyrone, who was murdered by his hosts, the MacDonnells, in 1567. The beautiful sugar-loaf mountain that comes into view between Cushendun and Cushendall is Tievebulliagh (1,346 feet).

A 2 passes the mouth of Glenaan and Glenballyemon on the way to Cushendall, the head of the latter being blocked by Trostan (1,817 feet), the highest hill in the county. *Cushendall* ('at the foot of the blind river') is a rather plain townlet in a pretty situation, overshadowed by the fine ridge of Lurigethan (1,154 feet). It is perhaps the best centre for visiting the Glens of Antrim, and the very least motorists should do is to drive up Glenballyemon and down Glenariff to Red Bay, the latter glen being definitely one of the premier beauty-spots of Ireland. The ruined Layde Church, on the coast road a mile north, contains MacDonnell tombs, and about two miles west is Cloghbrack, a group of stones forming a semicircle, to which the name of Ossian's Grave has been given.

Practically adjoining Cushendall is the village of Waterfoot, situated on Red Bay, which, with its grand amphitheatre of sandstone cliffs, is one of the jewels of the Antrim coast. Moreover, *Glenariff*, the five-mile-long valley extending inland from Red Bay, is the most spectacular of Antrim's glens, and has many lovely waterfalls, such as the Tears of the Mountain, the Horseshoe Fall, and the Fall of the Battlefield, access to which is by a path owned by the railway.

From Cushendall to Larne the road (A 2, 25 miles), the most fascinating section of this magnificent marine drive, is constructed along the foot of the cliffs, mostly on a raised beach. Occasionally tunnels are necessary. The cliffs are broken by countless dells, each with its cascade or waterfall. Beyond Red Bay you round Garron Point, above which stands Garron Tower, which was built in 1848 and is well worth the detour. Knockore (1,179 feet), the hill above it, is a splendid viewpoint. Carnlough, with its little harbour, lies on a crescent-shaped, sandy bay, at the outlet of Glencloy, and is soon succeeded by Glenarm, on a smaller bay, whose good looks are somewhat spoilt by derelict iron mines and limestone quarries. Its lovely, like-named glen is mostly taken up by the park of Glenarm Castle, the seat of the Earl of Antrim (head of the MacDonnells), and is open only to visitors with a permit from the estate office.

Beyond Glenarm the road skirts fine white limestone cliffs, but becomes tamer as the mountains recede from the coast. Out at sea are the Maidens, two rocks that resemble battleships in outline and are said to have been torpedoed by German submarines. It is some miles before the road runs through the modern village of Ballygally, which has good sands and a castle (now an hotel) in the Scots baronial style, built by the Shaws in 1625. The road then rounds Ballygally Head, with its grand pillars of basalt, on this side of which is a sea-girt rock bearing meagre remains of Cairn Castle, once held by the O'Hallorans. Beyond Drain's Bay the road passes through the Blackcave Tunnel, or Dark Arch.

Larne, a busy manufacturing town, has the great B.T.A. turbo-alternator factory and the mail steamer service to Stranraer in Scotland, the shortest sea passage to Ireland. At the entrance to the harbour is a modern copy of a Round Tower. The town is situated at the mouth of the Larne Lough, and is connected by ferry with Island Magee, road access to which is from Whitehead, which you pass farther on. The peninsula on which Larne stands tapers to a promontory called the Curran, at the end of which are a few remains of Olderfleet Castle, the headquarters of the

Scotch family of Bissett, who changed their name to MacQuillan. In 1315, at the invitation of the Ulster chieftains, Edward Bruce landed here with a force of 6,000 men and overran Ireland, only to be eventually defeated and slain at Faughart, near Dundalk, three years later.

The transition from Larne's industrialism to pretty country is blessedly quick. A 2, accompanied by the railway, follows the shore of Larne Lough, past many fine country seats and the attractive village of Glynn, at the foot of Glenoe. Next come the great quarries and works of the British Portland Cement Co. at Magheramorne.

Whitehead, skirted by the main road, is a seaside resort of growing popularity at the mouth of Belfast Lough and at the neck of the Island Magee peninsula. Walk to Black Head past the ruins of Castle Chichester. Island Magee is 7 miles long by 2 miles in width (bus service), and its principal attraction is the Gobbins, basaltic cliffs 250 feet in height, with several caves, and rendered accessible by a most spectacular footway. According to a dubious story, hundreds of the inhabitants were thrown over the cliffs by the Protestant garrison of Carrickfergus in 1642. Near Brown's Bay, at the north end of the 'island,' are a rocking stone and a dolmen.

Beyond Whitehead you round a hairpin bend (the 'Blaw Hole') to reach the shore of Belfast Lough. A side-road towards the sea leads to the ruined church of Kilroot. Here Dean Swift started his clerical career in 1694, attracting his first congregation by trundling stones in a wheelbarrow along the shore. Eden, with its salt mines, is passed.

Carrickfergus, Ulster's chief port before the rise of Belfast, is the 'Rock of Fergus,' legendary founder of the royal house of Scotland, who was shipwrecked and drowned here. It is famous for its grand Norman castle, garrisoned till 1928 and well preserved and recently restored. Its site, on a sea-girt rocky peninsula, made it the key of the whole countryside. Begun between 1180 and 1205, it was built either by the gigantic John de Courcy, conqueror of the Irish kingdom of Ulaidh or Ulidia (i.e. the modern counties of Antrim and Down), or by his successor Hugh de Lacy,

Earl of Ulster. It was taken by King John in 1210 (the castle chapel is named after him); by Edward Bruce in 1316, after a year's siege; by Schomberg for William III in 1689; and by a French naval expedition under Thurot (whose real name was Farrell) in 1760. The castle is shown by the guide for a small fee. A gatehouse with half-moon towers, retaining its portcullis and mechanism (renewed), admits to the lower ward, with a collection of old cannon. In the upper ward stands the square keep, 90 feet high, in the style of the White Tower in London, with five storeys and walls nearly 9 feet thick. It contains a collection of arms and armour, and other quite interesting 'bygones.' You are shown the well, 40 feet deep, and the dungeon whence Con O'Neill of Clandeboye escaped in 1603 with the aid of a rope hidden inside a cheese sent by his wife. On the third floor is 'Fergus's Dining Room,' one of the finest extant examples of a Norman hall (40 feet by 38 feet, and 26 feet high). The roof commands a grand view. On the quay under the western wall of the castle is a much-revered stone marking the spot where William III landed on 14th June 1690.

St. Nicholas's Church is one of the only two Anglo-Norman churches in Ulster, with a north transept (of Elizabethan date) containing several interesting monuments, including that of Arthur, Lord Chichester of Belfast, of which he was the virtual founder (d. 1625), and ancestor of the earls and marquises of Donegall.

The Belfast road, built up all the way, now hugs the shore of Belfast Lough, past Whiteabbey and Whitehouse and Greencastle. On the right towers Cave Hill. You enter the city by York Street and Royal Avenue, with its fine shops.

Belfast, i.e. Beal-feirste, 'ford of the sandbank,' became the capital of Northern Ireland in 1920. It is the second largest city, and the principal seaport and industrial centre, in Ireland, with a population of over 410,000, though in 1757 it consisted of under two thousand thatched houses. With no natural advantages in coal, iron, or timber, and no natural harbour (though its position at the head of Belfast Lough is favourable), its expansion during the Industrial Revolution of the nineteenth century was phenomenally rapid, with the result that the city is badly built and planned. Belfast can boast the biggest shipyard in Europe (Harland & Wolff's), besides the biggest spinning works (York Street Spinning Co.), the biggest tobacco factory (Gallaher's, in York Street), and the biggest rope works. Belfast is supreme in the manufacture of linen and damask (and excels also in cotton goods), the very finest qualities being still woven on handlooms. Its linen owes much to the improved methods introduced by the French Huguenots (notably Louis Crommelin, d. 1727). Belfast was attacked by German aircraft on 15th April and 4th–5th May 1941, and suffered 946 casualties.

Belfast lies at the mouth of the River Lagan, which divides the counties of Antrim and Down, and its splendid harbour and docks, with a water area of 1,525 acres and six miles of quays, were for the most part constructed on mud-flats reclaimed from the lough. Here is the world-famous shipbuilding yard of Harland & Wolff, with the Thompson Graving Dock, 886 feet long, and Short & Harland's aircraft factory.

The City Hall, in the centre of Donegall Square, is Belfast's pride—a great Renaissance palace in Portland stone, which cost half a million pounds. It was built in 1898–1906, and the architect was Sir Brumwell Thomas. The top of the dome is 175 feet above the ground. In front of it are statues of Queen Victoria and eminent citizens; and, on the west side, the War Memorial and Garden of Remembrance. Donegall Place and its continuation, Royal Avenue, are the chief shopping streets in Belfast. At the end of the latter turn right into Donegall Street to see St. Anne's Protestant Cathedral, a great building of the basilican type. Begun in 1898, from the designs of Sir Thomas Drew, whose successors were W. H. Lynn, Dr. MacGregor Chalmers, R. M. Close, and Sir Charles Nicholson, it is still not complete. Lord Carson is buried here.

Return to Donegall Square and from its south-west corner follow Bedford Street and its continuations, Dublin Road and University Road, for about three-quarters of a mile, to the Queen's University of Belfast, which began

life as Queen's College in 1845 and became a separate
university in 1909. In the well-kept Botanic Gardens
beyond it stands the Museum and Art Gallery, among the
treasures of which are a skeleton of a giant Irish deer,
Viking and Celtic ornaments, an exhibit showing the
developments of the linen industry, portraits of Ulster
notabilities (including ten American presidents of Ulster
descent), works by Sir John Lavery (a Belfastian), William
Conor, J. H. Craig, and others of the progressive Ulster
school, views of Old Belfast, etc.

Belfast's utilitarian aspect is compensated for to some
extent by the natural beauty of its environs, a quality in
which no other great city in the British Isles can rival it,
save Glasgow. The best view of the city and its lough is
obtained from Cave Hill (1,182 feet), at the north end of
the range that dominates Belfast on the west. In clear
weather the Ayrshire coast and the Isle of Man can be
descried. The way to it is by bus to Bellevue Park, or
it may be climbed from the road to Antrim, which skirts
its base. On the south side of Bellevue, and conjoint with
it, is Belfast Castle (with restaurant and ballroom), built
for the Marquis of Donegall in 1840 and presented to the
city in 1935, with its lovely 200-acre park, by the Earl of
Shaftesbury. The city's newest park, named after Sir
Thomas and Lady Dixon, has a vast rose garden.

The Parliament House of Northern Ireland is at Stormont, 3½ miles out of Belfast on the Newtownards road
(via Queen's Bridge). Buses run to it from Castle Place.
The austerely classical building was erected in 1928–32
from the designs of Sir Arnold Thornley; it cost a million
and a quarter pounds and was a present from Great
Britain. Stormont Castle, in the Scots baronial style, is
the official residence of the Prime Minister.

Leaving the south-eastern seaside environs of Belfast
to be explored later, on the way to Dublin, you would do
well to interpolate a flying visit to Antrim and Lough
Neagh at this point. The Antrim road (A 6, 17 miles) is
wide, with a concrete surface, but the countryside, beyond
Cave Hill, is agricultural and featureless. The bus and
railway services are good.

Antrim is of little interest in itself, and Antrim Castle,

formerly seat of the Earl of Massereene, is now derelict. It
dates from 1662, was rebuilt in 1816 after a fire, and was
again destroyed by fire (accidentally) in 1922. In the
grounds of The Steeple, three quarters of a mile north-east
of the town, is one of the finest and best-preserved Round
Towers in Ireland. It measures 92½ feet in height and 50
in girth; the cap is a restoration.

Lough Neagh (pronounced 'Nay'), a half-mile west of
Antrim, is easily the largest lake in the British Isles. Its
measurements are: area 155 square miles, circumference
65 miles, length 18 miles, width 11 miles. Islands are
rare. Although ten rivers flow into the lough, there is only
one outlet, the River Bann. Lough Neagh contains large
numbers of 'pollen,' a freshwater herring, in the capture
of which regular fleets of fishing-boats are engaged. The
water of the lake is supposed to have petrifying qualities,
a legend due to the fact that pieces of fossil wood are often
picked up on the shore. The banks are low and fringed
with extensive fens, and it is not easy to get a good view of
the lake (best seen from the road west of Glenavy), but
there are motor-boats that make trips from Antrim in the
summer to Shane's Castle, Lord O'Neill's seat, burnt down
in 1922, and past Aldergrove Aerodrome to Ram's Island,
on which there is a stump of a Round Tower, 43 feet in
height.

TOUR X: BELFAST TO DUBLIN

BANGOR — ARDS PENINSULA — DOWNPATRICK — NEWCASTLE
— MOURNE MOUNTAINS — NEWRY — ARMAGH — CARLING-
FORD — DUNDALK — DROGHEDA — MONASTERBOICE —
MELLIFONT ABBEY — NEWGRANGE TUMULUS — KELLS —
TRIM—TARA.

Total distance by road: about 350 miles.

THE first duty on this the last section of the Irish coastal tour, as you wend a devious way southwards to Dublin, is a visit to the delightful peninsula of Ards—A 2 to Porta-ferry, and back to Newtownards (62 miles in all) by A 20. There are buses all the way, and a railway to Bangor (but none within the peninsula itself).

Cross Queen's Bridge into Co. Down and keep on as far as the rope works, then bear left (signpost) through the suburb of Sydenham and soon gain the south shore of Belfast Lough. Many fine country seats are passed. Holywood has the ruined church of the Franciscan friary of 'Sanctus Boscus,' founded in 1200, and in the main street is the only maypole in Ireland, around which merrymaking still takes place on the eve of May Day. There follow in rapid succession Marino, Cultra (head-quarters of the Royal North of Ireland Yacht Club), and Craigavad (with the excellent links of the Royal Belfast Golf Club).

A 2 bears right and skirts the Clandeboye demesne, while the more direct road to Bangor keeps straight on through the attractive village of Crawfordsburn. From Helen's Bay, a pretty spot near Crawfordsburn, a three-mile avenue leads to Clandeboye, seat of the Marquis of Dufferin and Ava. At the farther end of the park (for admission, apply to the steward) is the celebrated Helen's Tower, erected by the first earl to the memory of his mother, a granddaughter of Richard Brinsley Sheridan. Inscribed on its top storey in letters of gold are the verses addressed by the mother to her son on his coming of age in 1847, and tablets with verses written by Tennyson, Browning, and Kipling are affixed to the tower. Tennyson's are famous:

> Helen's Tower, here I stand,
> Dominant over sea and land.
> Son's love built me, and I hold
> Mother's love in letter'd gold.
> Would my granite girth were strong
> As either love to last so long.
> Love is in and out of time,
> I am mortal stone and lime.

Bangor, i.e. 'beann chor' (peaked hill), once had a great abbey founded in 555 by St. Congall. At one time it had three thousand teachers and students, and it sent forth SS. Columban and Gall to convert Central Europe. Now Bangor, with a population of 24,000, is Ulster's third largest town—'Belfast-by-the-Sea,' a very popular resort with a harbour, two golf courses, and excellent bathing (the favourite spot being the Pickie Pool, in the central bay). The Royal Ulster Yacht Club holds a regatta here in July. The marine drive stretches for five miles, from Strickland's Glen on the west to Ballyholme Bay on the east. The castle, Elizabethan, is the seat of Lord Clanmorris.

Continuing along the coast, you pass through Groomsport, a village at the mouth of Belfast Lough. The three Copeland Islands, with two lighthouses, come into view. Then comes Donaghadee (accent on last syllable), with good golf and bathing. There are some very attractive new houses here, each on its small peninsula. Donaghadee is the nearest port to Great Britain, and at one time (till 1849) there was a packet service to and from Portpatrick, which is only 21 miles away.

You are now following the coast of the *Ards Peninsula*, a fertile and secluded tongue of land, 20 miles long by 4 miles in width, with the Irish Sea on one side and, on the other, Strangford Lough, an inland sea 20 miles long.

> The comely Ards, the pleasant Ards,
>   Dear land of little hills,
> Of bosoming fields, of cresting woods,
>   Of twisting lanes, where spills

The humble wealth of buttercups
　　And meadowsweet and ferns;
Of darkling bogs and long dry moss
　　Where the whin's gold glory burns.

ALEXANDER RIDDELL.

This was the country of the Savages, who were great castle builders. Millisle and Ballyhalter, with the seat of Lord Dunleath, are passed—bungalows and shacks cease hereabouts—and beyond Ballywalbert the Mourne Mountains come into sight. Burial Island, near here, is Ireland's farthest east. A 2 turns inland, returning to the coast for a while between Portavogie and Cloughey Bay. Portaferry is an old-fashioned little clam-fishing port on the half-mile channel between Strangford Lough and the sea. The Danes gave the fiord its name because of the tide-race. Passenger ferry to Strangford town, opposite.

The return journey is made by A 20 along the side of the lough, the opposite bank of which is dotted with islands. At Ardkeen are the ruins of a castle built by William de Savage, companion-in-arms to John de Courcy. Beyond Kircubbin is Greyabbey, named after the ruins of a Cistercian monastery (in a demesne, but visitors admitted). Founded in 1193 by Affreca, wife to John de Courcy, it is one of the most extensive and complete of its kind in Ireland and mainly of the Early English period (1200–50). The chief features are the lancet windows, the beautiful west door, the west wall of the south transept, the remains of the chapter house doorway, the south gable of the refectory, and the staircase leading to the reader's pulpit.

The road then passes the demesne of Mount Stewart, seat of the Marchioness of Londonderry. Its superb gardens (78½ acres), noted for their flowering shrubs and topiary work, belong to the National Trust (open April–September on Wednesday, Saturday, and Sunday afternoons). The Londonderry monument on Scrabo Hill (534 feet), topping the lough, is a landmark.

Newtownards (accent on last syllable), by the head of the lough, is a linen-manufacturing place. The town hall, in the spacious market-place, dates from 1770. In the High Street are the Old Cross, reconstructed in 1666, and the ruins of a Dominican church founded by Walter de Burgh in 1244, with the Londonderry family vault. The Catholic church was built at the expense of the Marchioness of Londonderry (a Protestant).

You next take A 21, past Newtownards airfield, to Comber, noted for its whisky, and thence A 22 to Downpatrick (22 miles), keeping fairly close to the west bank of Strangford Lough. The Mourne Mountains, often of an intense blue, come into view in the distance, straight ahead. The bus route is via Saintfield, close to which are the National Trust gardens of Rowallane, 50 acres of loveliness, with many rare trees and shrubs (April–Oct., on Wed., Sat., Sun. afternoons). Killyleagh was the birthplace in 1660 of Sir Hans Sloane, whose collections were the nucleus of the British Museum. He was the seventh son of Alexander Sloane, who was one of the Scottish 'planters' and Receiver-General for Taxes for Co. Down. Next comes some very pretty scenery in the vicinity of Quoile Bridge.

Downpatrick, the county town of Down and a great hunting centre, is a prosaic-looking place, owing its name and fame to St. Patrick, who both landed and died at Saul, close by, and is supposed to be buried here. Some even claim the bones of SS. Columba and Brigid, too, for the town. The cathedral was rebuilt between 1790 and 1818, on the site of the medieval choir, but it retains the east door, carved capitals, font, and other fragments of the old building destroyed by Lord Grey in 1538. The granite stone inscribed 'Patric' in the churchyard is not considered by any competent authority to cover the grave of St. Patrick. The 'dun' from which the town gets the first part of its name lies north-east, on marshy ground; it is the largest artificial mound in Ireland, measuring 2,100 feet round and 60 feet in height, with three ramparts.

You can go direct from Downpatrick to Clough by A 25 (6 miles, with buses). It is better to go by the coast, though the distance is 30 miles (A 25 to Strangford, then A 2). Strangford, at the neck of the lough, had four Anglo-Norman castles to defend this strategic point. One of these is Audley Castle, in the beautiful grounds of Castleward (National Trust), open daily. The house (1765) is shown on Wednesday and Saturday afternoons in summer. The drive on to Ardglass passes through the pretty scenery described in Filson Young's stories, *The Sands of Pleasure* and *When the Tide Turns*. Ardglass ('green height'), once the leading seaport in Co. Down and still a 'Royal Port,' is now a quaint and most unusual little place, noted for its flourishing herring fishery. It was formerly guarded by seven castles, of which Jordan's Castle, a merchant's fortified residence and storehouse of the sixteenth century, in the form of a four-storeyed peel tower, is still extant. Note the stone dovecote on the battlements. Killough, in the next bay, is a dreamy, old-world village with a harbour, and farther on you pass Tyrella, with a famous strand, caravans, and shanties.

A 2 now describes a detour round Dundrum Inner Bay (which dries out at low tide), passing Clough. The road thence to Newry (A 2, 39 miles), with bus services all the way, is one of the finest marine drives in Ireland. Dundrum, a picturesque fishing village, has a splendid circular and moated castle keep (a rarity in Ireland), 43 feet high and 45 feet in diameter. It was built in Henry III's reign and 'slighted' by Cromwell in 1652. As you approach Newcastle you pass the 'Rabbit Warren,' with the championship links of the Royal County Down Golf Club.

Newcastle, Co. Down, is not only a renowned golfing resort, but a very pleasant watering place, with a long sea front, a small harbour at the south end, excellent bathing, tennis, music, dancing, etc. There are three miles of firm, rock-strewn sands. The town nestles under the shadow of Slieve Donard (2,796 feet), which is the highest of the Mourne Mountains and can be climbed in two hours via the granite quarries near the harbour. The view from the top extends to the Isle of Man and the Scottish coast, and is unrivalled in this part of Ireland. The following demesnes in the Newcastle district are open to visitors: Donard Lodge; Tollymore Park (Government property), at the village of Bryansford, 2½ miles, noted for rare species of wild flowers; Castlewellan Park, 4½ miles to the north-west.

From Newcastle to Newry the road, mostly dotted with farms, cottages, and bungalows, runs high up on the hillside between the sea and the *Mourne Mountains*, of which it commands ever-varying views as they 'sweep down to the sea.' The mountains are as much renowned for the songs and poems that they have inspired as for their bewitching beauty. They are largely composed of granite and of Silurian shales, and produce a most varied flora. From Annalong, a tiny, picturesque fisher-village, you may climb the Chimney Rock (2,152 feet), the Rocky Mountain (1,718 feet), or Slieve Bignian (2,449 feet).

Kilkeel, where buses are changed, was the capital of the ancient kingdom of Mourne. It is now a busy little port and bathing resort, with fine sands and free trout and salmon fishing. There is a good dolmen north of the town. The Kilkeel River flows through the Silent Valley, which has a great reservoir high up in the mountains, supplying Belfast with ten million gallons of water per day; the wall bounding its catchment area is an excellent example of modern drystone masonry. The road from Kilkeel to Hilltown (B 27, 12 miles) bisects the Mourne Mountains; it passes between Slieve Muck (2,198 feet), on the right, and the Eagle Mountain (2,064 feet), on the left, and has gradients of 1 in 7 to 1 in 10. You simply must take this road as far as the point where the view of the central plain opens out in blues, greens, and purples. Hilltown itself is a good centre for the exploration of the Mournes.

A 2, ever beautiful, now leaves the coast for a time and skirts Mourne Park, the stately home of the Earl of Kilmorey, behind which rises Knockchree (1,013 feet). It then hugs the shore of Carlingford Lough, opposite the fine range of the Carlingford Mountains (1,935 feet).

Rostrevor, a peaceful spot of peculiarly Victorian charm, is a cosy little sun-trap, sheltered from north and east winds by lofty wooded hills. Some of its gay modern bungalows have very pretty rock gardens. On the shoulder of Slievemartin (1,595 feet), which should be scaled for the sake of the view, is a famous erratic boulder of granite called Cloughmore and weighing 30 tons. It is supposed to fit into a gap in Slieve Foy and to have been hurled across the lough by Finn MacCoul, the Irish giant, who was aiming at his adversary Benandonner, a Scottish giant. The 'Fairy Glen' of the Kilbroney River is very charming.

The road next passes an obelisk in memory of Major-
General Robert Ross of Bladensburg, a native of Rostrevor, who captured Washington in 1814 and died of
wounds the same year. Warrenpoint, at the head of the
lough, is a clean and attractive, well-laid-out resort with
a Victorian esplanade, wide streets, charming views, and
good golf. A 2 then runs along the east bank of the
picturesque Newry Canal, an eighteenth-century enter-
prise. Narrow Water Castle, on the left, is a square tower
erected by the Duke of Ormonde in 1663.

Newry ('yew-tree') is named after a yew planted by
St. Patrick. It is charmingly situated in a strategic
position between the Mourne Mountains, to the east, and
Camlough Mountain (1,389 feet) and Slieve Gullion (1,893
feet), to the west. Newry no longer deserves Dean Swift's
scathing description: 'High church, low steeple, dirty
streets, proud people.' St. Patrick's (1578), the first
church built for Protestantism in Ireland, and the Catholic
Cathedral are both in the main street. The thatched
Derrymore House, on the Newtown Hamilton road, where
the Act of Union (page 42) was drawn up, belongs to the
National Trust (open April–October on Wednesday,
Thursday, and Saturday afternoons).

At this point you may round off your Northern Ireland
tour by a visit (by bus) to Armagh, the winding road to
which (A 26, 20 miles) traverses pleasant, undulating
country, with wide views towards the end. *Armagh* has
and air of gracious Georgian and Regency repose, suited to
its dignity as the ecclesiastical metropolis, 'the city of red
marble' (i.e. red sandstone), 'Ireland's Canterbury.' Yet
it has had a more chequered history than perhaps any other
town in Ireland, having been five times laid waste with fire
and sword. St. Patrick built his cathedral here, on the
'Height of Macha,' Queen of Ulster, and the monastic
establishment attached to it became a famous centre of
learning. Brian Boru and his son were buried here after
the battle of Clontarf.

The cathedrals of the Catholic and Protestant Metropolitan archbishops occupy neighbouring heights and are
both dedicated to St. Patrick. The Protestant Cathedral, in
a most commanding site, with a lovely view, was last rebuilt

by Lewis Cottingham in 1834, in the thirteenth-century style, and is a dignified structure in sombre sandstone, mainly of interest for its monuments, e.g. Roubiliac's statue of Sir Thomas Molyneux (1733), the recumbent figure of Dean Drelincourt (1722), by Rysbrack, Nollekens's bust of Archbishop Richard Robinson (Lord Rokeby; 1794), Chantrey's monument to Archbishop Stuart (1822), and the memorials of the Earls of Charlemont in the north transept. No trace remains of the tomb of Brian Boru. The crypt dates from the tenth century. The tower may be climbed. The sexton, if required, lives in Vicars' Hill, opposite the west front.

The Catholic Cathedral, with its twin spires, rises at the top of a flight of sixty steps. Begun in 1840 in French Gothic style, it was not consecrated until 1904. Its walls are entirely lined with mosaics and the marble decoration is lavish in the extreme. The adjoining archbishop's palace is likewise a building of somewhat exotic magnificence.

Other interesting institutions in Armagh are the Royal School, which was founded by King Charles I in 1627, and the Observatory, which was built, equipped, and endowed in 1791 by Archbishop Robinson, a great benefactor to the city, for he was the founder also of the archbishop's palace, the public library, and the public slaughter-house. The County Museum, in the Mall, is one of the best of its kind. Navan Fort, two miles to the west of Armagh, is the site of Emania (Eamhain Mhacha, or 'Macha's brooch'), the palace of the Ulster kings from *c.* 300 B.C. to *c.* A.D. 332. It gets its name from a legend that Queen Macha traced out its plan with her brooch. Here Conchobar brought up Deirdre 'of the Sorrows' to be his bride, and here the Knights of the Red Branch, a kind of military order, were founded. The Armagh district, particularly Richhill, grows roses, flax, and the best fruit in Ireland.

Returning to Newry—over the hills via Newtown Hamilton (28 miles), for the sake of variety—you next make for Carlingford and Dundalk, 31 miles. Eire (Co. Louth) is entered, with the usual customs examination and triptyque-stamping formalities, between Upper Fathom and Ferryhill frontier posts, and B 79 becomes T 63. The drive along the west bank of the Newry Canal and

Carlingford Lough, where the mountains approach the shore, is beautiful in the extreme. Omeath, a tidy village, is passed.

Carlingford, a small and charming seaport and now an Eire customs station, is situated at the base of Slieve Foy. It is one of the places where St. Patrick landed in 432. The Anglo-Normans fortified the place with great energy, and an extraordinary number of old buildings survive. King John's Castle, begun by John de Courcy in 1210, resembled Carrickfergus in its general lay-out, though of later date. Note the platform running round the walls with loopholes for archers. Altogether there are said to have been thirty-two castles defending Carlingford (Taaffe's Castle, near the station, is worth exploring), but nearly all of these were fortified houses of Elizabethan date. The Tholsel, or town hall, and the Mint, with quaintly sculptured windows, should be seen, and the ruined church of the Dominican friary founded in 1305 by Richard de Burgh, the great Earl of Ulster and Connaught. Finally, Slieve Foy (1,935 feet), highest of the Carlingford Mountains, should be climbed for its glorious views.

A slight detour eastwards takes you into and out of Greenore, a quiet seaside resort, with good golf. T 63, with views over Dundalk Bay, then passes Ballymascanlan, near which is the important Proleek dolmen, and Faughart, birthplace in 453 of Brigid, Ireland's greatest woman saint, and scene of the defeat and death of Edward Bruce in 1318. He is supposed to have been buried in the old churchyard on the hillside.

Dundalk, commanding the Ulster Gap, derives its name from the Dun of Delga (Castletown Hill, a mile west), the fortress of the mythical Cuchulain. Modern Dundalk, the county town of Louth, lies on an inlet of Dundalk Bay and is a seaport as well as a prosperous market town, with a population of 20,000. The Catholic pro-cathedral is a copy of King's College Chapel, Cambridge. 'Seatown Castle' was the tower of a Franciscan friary church.

From Dundalk you make for Drogheda by railway or by T 1, 22 miles of gently undulating main road. At Castlebellingham, however (with the seat of the Bellingham family), you should take the alternative coastal road (L6, 6 miles longer), which gives you an opportunity of taking a final farewell of the distant Carlingford and Mourne Mountains. Clogher Head, with cliff scenery, and Baltray, a small bathing and golfing resort, are passed.

Drogheda (pronounced 'Draw-ĕ-dă'), the 'bridge at the ford,' lies for the most part on the north bank of the River Boyne, which separates the counties of Louth and Meath. Four miles from the sea, with a good harbour and 17,000 inhabitants, it is a town of pleasant, prosperous aspect, with miscellaneous factories. Here the Parliament of 1494 enacted Poynings' Law, whereby no law passed by the Irish Parliament could come into force until it was approved by the English Privy Council. But to most people the name of Drogheda connotes the blackest stain on Cromwell's fame—the storming of the town on 10th September 1649, and the massacre of two-thirds of the garrison and very many of the inhabitants, without mercy for age or sex, the survivors being sent to the Barbados plantations.

I am persuaded that this is a righteous judgment of God upon these barbarous wretches, who have imbued their hands in so much innocent blood, and that it will tend to prevent the effusion of blood for the future.

The river harbour is spanned by a splendid railway viaduct, 90 feet high. In West Street, the main thoroughfare, are the old Tholsel (now the Hibernian Bank), at the corner of the street leading to the bridge, and the Oliver Plunket Memorial Church, built in memory of St. Oliver Plunket, Archbishop of Armagh, who was executed at Tyburn in 1681 during the Titus Oates plot. The saint's head is preserved in a shrine here. The magnificent East, or St. Lawrence, Gate, in nearly perfect condition, is the only survivor of the ten town gates. The conspicuous Magdalen Steeple in the north part of the town is a relic of the Franciscan friary where the four great chiefs of Northern Ireland paid homage to Richard II in 1395.

Drogheda is the centre for excursions to several places of first-rate interest. Take T1, the main Dundalk and Belfast road, as far as Newtown Monasterboice, 5 miles,

keep straight on when the main road bears right, and make
for the Round Tower of ancient *Monasterboice*, which is
seen in a small churchyard to the left and is reached by
a lane at the top of the hill. The abbey was founded
by St. Buite (Boethius), who is said to have died on the
very day St. Columba was born, A.D. 512. The Round
Tower, with its broken top, is 110 feet high and may be
ascended; it has a fine round-headed doorway with a
pointed window above it. The larger of the two churches
is coeval with the tower (ninth century), while the smaller
church, adjoining the tower, is thirteenth. But the chief
attraction of Monasterboice is its two High Crosses, the
finest in the country. The larger, or West Cross, near
the tower, 27 feet tall, has twenty-two panels carved
with weatherworn biblical subjects, surmounted by a
stone in the shape of a small chapel. Muireadach's
Cross, commemorating the abbot of that name, who
ruled from A.D. 890 to 932, is 15 feet high, also with
twenty-two panels, and is in a much better state of
preservation. The costumes of the ecclesiastics and
soldiers are interesting. Note the damned being
kicked into hell by the devil on the Day of Judgment.
The third cross is fragmentary. It is worth while
ascending the ridge above Monasterboice for the sake
of the noble prospect over the rich plains of Louth and
Meath.

It is a bare three miles from Monasterboice to Mellifont
—keep straight on westwards from the ruins to the Collon-
Drogheda road, keep straight on (left), and take the first
decent road on the right. *Mellifont Abbey* (Latin, 'honey
fountain') was the first Cistercian establishment in
Ireland. St. Malachy O'Morgair, Archbishop of Armagh,
founded it in 1142 on land granted by Donal O'Carrol,
prince of Oriel. The buildings, representing the earliest
example of Gothic architecture in Ireland, are sweetly
situated by the River Mattock. They include the gatehouse; the roofless 'baptistery,' or lavabo, an octagonal
structure, half of which has disappeared; and the chapter
house, or St. Bernard's Chapel (partly restored), with
its lovely vaulted roof. Two archbishops, two bishops,
twenty-five abbots, and three thousand monks are buried

here, and Dervorgilla (page 165) rests beneath the chancel pavement.

The site of the battle of the Boyne, 1st July 1690, one of the decisive struggles in British history, lies amid pretty river scenery a short distance west of Drogheda. (The Boyne curraghs, now extinct, were the oldest type of vessel surviving in the British Isles.) Take the Slane road (T 2, then T 26, bearing left), with a 1-in-10 climb out of Drogheda, as far as Oldbridge, a white iron structure, 3 miles. The obelisk here, marking the spot where William III was slightly wounded in the battle, was destroyed in 1920. James II's Irish army was posted on Donore Hill, on the south side of the river. William's army (a composite professional force of Dutch, Germans, Danes, and Huguenots) coming from the north, descended King William's Glen and the next valley to the east, and crossed the Boyne at four places—the right wing at Slane, to outflank the enemy, the main body under Schomberg at the Oldbridge ford, the left wing at the ford between Yellow Island and Grove Island, and the cavalry lower down. Schomberg was killed at the ford in an Irish cavalry charge (his tomb is in St. Patrick's Cathedral, see page 70). After losing the battle, James II returned to France, leaving the Irish to ruin themselves in his cause.

Between Oldbridge and Slane, on the ridge north of the valley, is the late-Neolithic or Early Bronze Age necropolis of Brugh-na-Boinne, where the pre-Gaelic kings were buried. Its date is conjectured as 2000 B.C. or earlier. There are three great tumuli—Dowth, Newgrange, Knowth —but non-archaeologists may content themselves with Newgrange. For all three you take the first road on the left beyond Oldbridge, crossing the River Mattock near its confluence with the Boyne. The Dowth Tumulus (keys from the caretaker, who lives at the adjoining farmhouse, which is also the Dowth post office; gratuity) consists of a conical cairn (now overgrown with grass), surrounded by a stone kerb. From the central entrance, reached by a deep well with an iron ladder, a passage 27 feet long, with sides and roof of flagstones, leads to a cruciform central chamber containing a stone basin. There are two other series of passages and chambers. The decoration of the stones is crude and shows that Dowth is probably earlier than New-grange.

For the *Newgrange Tumulus*, admittedly the finest monument of its class and one of the most thrilling sights in Ireland, keep straight on and turn left along a lane leading to the river. The caretaker lives at Dowth, in the last cottage on the right (with window-frames painted red, some way back in the fields). The cairn, a hundred thousand tons of loose stones, covers an acre of ground (diameter 240 feet, height 45 feet) and is now overgrown with trees and brushwood. Twelve of the thirty-five stones that formed an outer circle are *in situ*. The base of the cairn is surrounded by a stone kerb serving as the foundation for a drystone wall. The entrance, on the south side, has a stone with interlaced spiral decoration as its threshold. (There are two other similar stones at the back of the tumulus.) The passage, 5–8 feet high and 62 feet long, and so narrow in places that a stout person can hardly squeeze through, is formed of enormous flag-stones and lighted by electricity. It leads to the domed tomb chamber, 20 feet high, the beehive vaulting of which (resembling the Tumulus of Gavrinis in Brittany and the Treasury of Atreus at Mycenae) is formed of horizontally laid stones, each projecting inwards more than the one below it. The three recesses are elaborately carved with coil, spiral, lozenge, and leaf-form patterns. In the recesses are three oval basins (one of non-local stone), which may have held cremated interments. These spiral patterns and basins are paralleled at Malta. Both tumuli were plundered by the Northmen.

For the Knowth Tumulus retrace your wheel tracks, leave the Dowth road on the right, and then turn left. This earthen mound is much larger than Newgrange, being 700 feet across and 50 feet high, but no entrance has been discovered.

Slane is a pretty village on the north bank of the Boyne, 9 miles from Drogheda by the direct road. Four Georgian houses face the cross-roads, and there is a nice little inn, the Conyngham Arms. On the hill above, with a grand view of the Boyne valley, are the ruins of a monastery of primitive date, but rebuilt for the Franciscans in 1512;

and near the parish church by the river is the hermitage of St. Erc, the first Bishop of Slane. Slane Castle is the modern residence of the Marquis Conyngham (ask to be shown the Apostles' Stone). Visitors are admitted to the grounds of Beau Parc, on the opposite side of the river.

T 26 goes on from Slane to Navan (8 miles), shortly before reaching which you pass on the right the Round Tower of Donaghmore, 100 feet high, with a carving of the Crucifixion over the doorway. From Navan (An Uaimh, 'the grotto') you go north-west by T 35, up the valley of the Blackwater, to Kells, 10 miles (bus service available).

On the way you pass Liscartan Castle, with two massive square towers, built by Sir William Talbot in 1633, and Teltown House, likewise on the right. On the Hill of Tailten (292 feet), behind the latter, is the Rath Dubh, or 'black fort,' the site of one of the four ancient royal residences in Ireland, where the Aonach Tailteann, a kind of Irish Olympic Games, were held from time immemorial until the death of Roderic O'Conor, the last native king of Ireland (1198).

Kells, or Ceanannus Mor, the 'great head fort,' an agreeable little town in a pretty district, with some delightful Georgian houses, was an important seat of art and learning in early days, and famous above everything as the place of origin of the Book of Kells, now in Trinity College Library, Dublin. The monastery established here by St. Columba about the middle of the sixth century was ravaged by the Danes in 1019 and by Edward Bruce in 1315, and finally dissolved in 1551. Several interesting relics of early Celtic Christianity are still to be seen here. Most of these are in the churchyard—make for the fine detached steeple (pre-Reformation) of the Protestant church, which was rebuilt at the end of the eighteenth century. At the foot of the tower is a thirteenth-century tomb-slab. The Round Tower, 90 feet high and lacking the conical cap, is of a late type. At the top, haunted by jackdaws, are five (instead of the usual four) windows, inserted, it is thought, to command the five roads that radiated from Kells in olden days. At its base is the largest and oldest of the five Crosses of Kells, nearly 11 feet high and lavishly decorated. There are three more in the churchyard: one, by the church door, dating from the tenth century and lacking its upper portion; another, on the south side of the church, of great interest because it is unfinished (twelfth century); and the round base of a cross near the belfry. St. Columba's House, which is outside the churchyard—apply at the house with the yellow door in the road leading up to it—is an excellent example of primitive Celtic construction, dating from about the year 804. Its high-pitched roof is constructed in the manner of a beehive hut (page 210). The present entrance is modern; the original entrance, well above ground level and very small, was at the west end. The lower storey, once divided into two, is barrel-vaulted. The top floor, now reached by an iron ladder, is divided into three small rooms. The 'Cross of Kells,' in the market-place, 8 feet 9 inches high, has a frieze of cavalrymen and infantrymen; it is the second oldest of the Kells crosses. Some of the rebels were hanged from it in 1798.

Headfort, seat of the Marquis of Headfort, lies north-east of Kells, beyond the Blackwater; the lovely park is famed for its almost unrivalled collection of conifers. The lighthouse tower that dominates the landscape west of Kells was built to provide employment during the potato famine of 1846 by the Lord Headfort of the period.

From Kells you make for Trim, 17 miles south: by a road to Athboy, and thence by L 3 (bus or train). *Trim* ('elder-tree'), the county town of Meath, has many interesting old buildings and very pleasant surroundings. The grand ruins of King John's Castle, founded by Hugh de Lacy in 1173 to guard the English Pale (King John only stayed here), cover two acres. The outer walls are defended by ten drum-towers, a gatehouse, and a barbican, and by a moat into which the Boyne could be turned. The square keep, with two side towers, is 70 feet high and once contained a chapel. Prince Henry (afterwards Henry V) and Humphrey, Duke of Gloucester, were confined here by order of Richard II. The tall, gaunt 'Yellow Steeple,' a relic of St. Mary's Abbey, one of St.

Patrick's foundations, is a thirteenth-century watch-tower, 125 feet in height. The Duke of Wellington (Arthur Wellesley, fourth son of the Earl of Mornington), whose early home was at Dangan Castle, four miles south of Trim, received the first part of his education at Trim. He was M.P. for Trim in 1790–5, and had a house in Dublingate Street, which contains a column erected in his honour in 1817.

Newtown Trim, a mile along the Dublin road, has an old five-arch bridge over the Boyne and an abbey founded in 1206 by Simon Rochfort, Bishop of Meath. The church, with lancet windows, illustrates the Transitional style. At the other end of the bridge, completing the picturesque group, is a ruined castle with a small chapel. Laracor, of which Dean Swift was incumbent from 1700 to 1710, is two miles south of Trim, on the Kilcock road, but it has now no souvenirs to show, for both the church and 'Stella's' house have been rebuilt.

By-roads take you from Trim to Bective and Tara. Leave Trim by the Navan road (T 26) and after four miles take the second turning on the right (signpost 'Kilmessan') beyond the railway, which is closed for passenger traffic. This brings you to Bective Abbey, a daughter house of Mellifont and founded by the King of Meath in 1146. The buildings are strongly defensive in character, with immensely thick walls and a crenellated tower at the corner of the cloisters. The church has disappeared.

Tara is 5 miles east of Bective Abbey: keep straight on to Kilmessan, crossing the railway twice; then left, right, left. *Tara*, Teamhair na Riogh, 'the high place of the kings,' is the site of the most famous of the four royal residences of Ireland. Objects found here date back to about 4000 B.C., but the period of its greatness, when it was the seat of the Ard Ri, or high king, and more or less the national centre, lasted from the time of Cormac MacArt in the third century to that of King Dermot in the sixth, the last assembly being held here A.D. 559. But for non-Irishmen there is not much of interest now to be seen, for Tara's great buildings were of wood and have entirely disappeared in the course of time. The earthworks, still under excavation, alone survive. Yet the view from the

H

top of the hill (512 feet) is alone worth the visit. A great modern statue of St. Patrick somewhat inappropriately presides over the scene. The principal remains are as follows, starting from the north end: (1) The Assembly or Banquet Hall, two parallel mounds, 795 feet long by 90 feet wide. Built by Cormac on the model of a Roman basilica, this was twice as large as Ireland's largest church, St. Patrick's Cathedral, Dublin. (2) Rath or enclosure of the Synods, surrounded by three concentric banks, each with its ditch, and supposed to be the site of synods held by SS. Patrick, Ruadhan, and Adamnan. Roman material has been found here, and the rath is believed to date from the first centuries of our era. (3) Royal Enclosure, or Rath of the Kings, 853 feet in diameter and containing the Mound of the Hostages, Cormac's House, and the Forad. (4) Grave Mound of the Hostages, 75 feet in diameter, covering a stone cairn 8 feet high (Middle Bronze Age, i.e. 2nd millennium B.C.). (5) Cormac's House, with the statue of St. Patrick and the so-called Lia Fail, or Stone of Destiny, on which the kings were crowned (though some think that the genuine stone is in Westminster Abbey). The stone used to signify its acceptance of a new king by uttering a cry. It formerly lay on the Mound of the Hostages and was brought here to mark the graves of some of the 1798 insurgents. (6) Royal Seat, or Forad, dwelling of Cormac's predecessors. (7) Fort of Leary (Laoghaire), where that king, whom St. Patrick failed to convert, was buried. (8) In the plantation west of the Banquet Hall is the Fort of Grainne, Cormac's daughter, who drugged the guests at her wedding with Finn MacCumhaill, her father's general, and eloped with Diarmait, a young lieutenant. Note also, in the churchyard, the so-called Adamnan's Cross, carved with what is believed to be a representation of Cernunnos, the Celtic god of wealth. The quaint little church has a startling modern east window, by Evie Hone.

It is 22 miles from Tara to Dublin by T 35, across the fat pasture lands of Co. Meath. Co. Dublin is entered at Clonee, and Dublin is regained by way of Blanchardstown and the north side of Phoenix Park.

TOUR XI: DUBLIN TO ATHLONE, AND BACK VIA KILDARE

MAYNOOTH — MULLINGAR — ATHLONE — LOUGH REE —
CLONMACNOISE — TULLAMORE — KILDARE — THE CURRAGH
—CLONDALKIN.

Total distance by road: about 200 miles.

THIS tour, the only wholly inland one in this volume, is
calculated to give the visitor an idea of the pastoral plains
or bleak and exposed bog country of central Ireland, in
sharp contrast to the picturesque scenery of the coastal
districts. Ireland is unique in that its chief mountain
ranges are on or near its seaboard. The flatness of the
huge central plateau, which was once thickly forested and
is now to a great extent covered with the resultant peat-
bogs, is such that the railway between Dublin and Galway
(126 miles) has not a single tunnel and scarcely a cutting.
Yet there is nearly always some mountain range in sight.

For Athlone, 78 miles, with a bus (or train) service all
the way, you take the Galway road (T 3, joining T 4 at
Kinnegad), leaving Dublin by the north quays and crossing
the Liffey at Chapelizod ('Isolde's Chapel'). For the first
10 miles the road follows the Liffey valley, one of the
fairest stretches of river scenery in the country. It keeps
near the south bank of the river, past Palmerston, as far
as Lucan, and then crosses the stream again (pretty view
from the bridge) to reach Leixlip, with a modernized castle,
a hydro-electric plant, and the famous salmon leap which
gives its name to the place. A little higher up is a bridge
believed to be the oldest in Ireland.

The road now leaves the Liffey valley and is accompanied
more or less closely by the Royal Canal all the way to
Mullingar. It skirts the vast domain of Carton, the mansion of which was designed or reconstructed by Cassels in

1739. *Maynooth*, 15 miles from Dublin, is celebrated for its great college, founded in 1795, where some 600 students are trained for the secular priesthood. Maynooth Castle, the ancestral stronghold of the Fitzgeralds, earls of Kildare and (from 1766) dukes of Leinster, consists of a massive ivy-clad keep, with several smaller towers and fragments of curtain walls.

About 10 miles farther on is Cloncurry, which has a ruined church and a curious mound with a tree growing on top of it. You then cross the once dreary wastes (now largely reclaimed as pasture) of the Bog of Allen, most famous of the Irish peat-bogs, which cover about one-seventh of the whole area of the country. Another 10 miles bring you to Clonard, which has nothing to show for its ancient fame as the seat of the early Celtic college where SS. Columba and Kieran were instructed.

At Kinnegad diverges an alternative route to Athlone, with better scenery and only a mile longer, via *Mullingar*, which is the county town of Westmeath and the centre of a pretty lake district. The principal lakes are Lough Ennell or Belvedere, 5 miles long, and, to the north, Lough Owel and Lough Derravaragh.

Athlone ('Ford of the Luain'), on the Shannon, is an important centre with a stormy history, the gateway to Ireland west of the Shannon, but not now of great interest in itself, though there is much to see and explore in the surrounding country. On the other side of the bridge are the remains of the castle and the elaborate Catholic church of SS. Peter and Paul, erected in 1931-7 from the designs of E. R. Byrne. At Moydrum, near Athlone, is the principal Eire broadcasting station. About two miles north of the town begins *Lough Ree*, an extraordinary expansion of the Shannon, 16 miles long by as much as 7 miles wide at one point; a motor-boat may be hired at Athlone to take you to Lanesborough at the farther end. The lough is studded with islands, most of which possess ecclesiastical ruins of early date, and on the west bank is Rindown Castle, a most interesting specimen of a medieval fortress.

About 8 miles from Athlone, along the Ballymahon road, is Lissoy, with the old homestead, known as Auburn and now falling into ruin, where Oliver Goldsmith, the second son of the parson ('the village preacher,' 'passing rich on forty pounds a year'), spent his boyhood. He was born *c.* 1728, traditionally at his grandfather's house, Smith Hill, Elphin, Co. Roscommon, and the family lived for a time at Pallas, a townland near Ballymahon, before moving in 1730 to Lissoy, the 'Sweet Auburn' of *The Deserted Village*. The Rectory has gone, but a pleasant hour or so may be spent in an attempt to identify

> The never-failing brook, the busy mill,
> The decent church that topped the neighb'ring hill,

and the rest.

The principal excursion from Athlone, however, is to *Clonmacnoise*, once among the greatest of the old religious centres of Ireland and a focus of Christian culture, but now a lonely group of ruins. It is 13 miles from Athlone by road (diverging right from the Birr road at Ballynahown), wavy at first, then rather rough, but only 9 miles by motor-boat on the Shannon. Clonmacnoise, the 'meadow of the sons of Nos,' is situated in a lovely spot between the red bog and the sluggish river, on one of the curious 'eskers,' or gravelly ridges of glacial formation, that like colossal caterpillars intersect Ireland from east to west. It was founded about the year 548 by the 'gentle, loving, tender-hearted' St. Kieran, the friend of St. Columba and best beloved of all Irish saints, the site being given him by King Dermot. In spite of its chequered history—it was repeatedly devastated by the Norsemen, the Normans, and the English—it became the seat of a great abbey, of European fame for its learning, forming a veritable university, and of a bishopric that survived till 1568. Here, as elsewhere, the Irish preferred to multiply churches instead of enlarging existing ones.

Of the 'Seven Churches'—actually there are eight surviving out of twelve—the chief is the Great Church, or Cathedral, the Teampull MacDermot, built *c.* 904 and rebuilt in the fourteenth century, with the fragmentary west door and the north door as its principal features. The latter, with figures of SS. Patrick, Francis, and Dominic, is one of the most beautiful things in Ireland; incidentally, it has the peculiar property of transmitting the faintest whisper along its hollow mouldings. In the open-air 'arcade' is displayed an unrivalled collection of 188 engraved tombstones, showing that Clonmacnoise was for centuries the favoured burial-place of kings, princes, and abbots. (The caretaker lives in a cottage to the east, beyond Devery's shop.) Dowling's Church was rebuilt in the seventeenth century, and MacClaffey's Church, attached to it on the east, is of the same date. The West Cross, or Cross of the Scriptures, facing the west front of the cathedral and 13 feet high, was made by Abbot Colman for King Flann, founder of the church; its sculptures represent Passion scenes on one side and the foundation of Clonmacnoise on the other. By it is a curiously shaped stone that cures backache! To the north of the cathedral are the remains of St. Kieran's Chapel, and to the east of it the King's Church, with lovely east windows. The Teampull Conor, restored for use as the Protestant parish church, has a round-headed doorway of the twelfth century. The Teampull Finghin, thirteenth century, with chevron decoration on its chancel arch, has MacCarthy's Tower attached to it, a Round Tower of 1124, 56 feet high, unusually perfect and retaining its original cap, but with no bell-openings at the top. O'Rourke's Tower, 62 feet high and 59 feet round, is a watch tower of the tenth century, large enough to hold the whole community in time of danger. It lost its top portion in a thunderstorm, and the eight openings at the top are not original. Of the other High Crosses the best is the South Cross, 12 feet high, showing the Crucifixion on one side and spirals and interlaced work on the other. The shattered ruins to the west of the churchyard are those of De Lacy's castle, and about a quarter of a mile to the east are the remains of the Nuns' Church founded by Dervorgilla in 1167. Its west doorway is in four orders and the chancel arch in three, both showing a mixture of Celtic and Romanesque decoration, with exquisite details deserving the closest attention.

The return journey from Athlone to Dublin should be made via Tullamore and Kildare: best by train to Port-

arlington and thence by bus. The distance by road is
88 miles: T 4 to Moate, T 47 to Tullamore, L 108 to
Monasterevan, T 5 to Dublin. From Clonmacnoise motorists can find their way direct to Clara. From Athlone
they return the way they came as far as Moate (with some
Georgian houses in its wide street), 10 miles, and then bear
right, by a good, winding road through a gently undulating
countryside, for Clara and Tullamore, another 15 miles.
Tullamore is the county town of Offaly, as King's County
is now called. King's County and Queen's County (now
Leix, or Laoighis, pronounced 'Leesh') were named for
Philip and Mary, in whose reign they were 'planted.'
Tullamore is not of much interest, but in the vicinity there
are numerous fortified residences of the early settlers, and
an excursion may be made to Rahan, 6 miles to the west,
where St. Carthach founded an abbey in the sixth century.
Ruins of three Romanesque churches of the twelfth century
are to be seen there, one of which has a remarkable chancel
arch with sculptured heads, besides a beautifully ornamented round window. The Grand Canal, which passes
through Tullamore, is the oldest canal in the British Isles;
it was begun in 1765 to connect Dublin with the Shannon
and, including branches, is 166 miles long, but it was
closed down in 1959. A very efficient passenger service by
means of 'fly-boats' was carried on it till 1850.

Between Tullamore and Portarlington, 17 miles, the
road traverses flat open pastures without stone walls and
largely reclaimed from bog. Here, as so often in Ireland,
the hedgerow timber is ruined by ivy. The only place of
note passed is Geashill, a pretty village with a modern
castle and remains of the old castle of the O'Dempseys,
ancient lords of Offaly. Portarlington derives its name
from the Earl of Arlington, to whom the district was
granted in 1641. It owes its dignified air to a colony of
Huguenots settled here by the Earl of Galway in William
III's reign. Its superb series of Georgian houses, with
doorways of the most diverse types, makes Portarlington
one of the most attractive towns in Ireland for lovers
of eighteenth-century architecture. At Portarlington is
Ireland's first power station for the generation of electricity

from peat, with a conspicuous water-cooling tower. You cross the Mountmellick branch of the Grand Canal four times on the way to Monasterevan (or Monasterevin), 6 miles farther on, where you join the main Limerick–Dublin road. The monastery that gave Monasterevan its name has entirely disappeared.

Kildare, the 'Church of the Oak,' a small town of ancient fame, originated in a convent for monks and nuns founded by St. Brigid in the year 480. The cathedral is practically a reconstruction by G. E. Street (1875–96) of the fine cruciform church begun by Bishop Ralph de Bristol in 1223. The groups of three lancets in each of the four arms of the church has a particularly striking effect, and all the windows are filled with good modern glass. Note the Celtic font, the collection of old tomb-slabs, and especially the quaintly carved stone at the foot of the chancel arch. The Round Tower, 108 feet high by 54 feet in girth, with walls 5 feet thick, has an ornamented doorway 14 feet from the ground and incongruous modern battlements. It can be ascended on application at the verger's house at the entrance to the churchyard. The churchyard is, for once, well kept, and contains a broken wheel-cross and also a fragment of the Fire House, where the nuns, like vestal virgins, used to tend a never-dying flame. Kildare Castle, originally founded by Strongbow, was one of the strongholds of the Fitzgeralds, earls of Kildare, and was finally destroyed in the Cromwellian war.

The National Stud, two miles south of Kildare, breeds, trains, and sells racehorses on the 2,000-acre estate. It was presented in 1916 by Sir Frederick Hall-Walker (afterwards Lord Wavertree) to the British Government, which transferred its establishment in 1944 to Sandley in Wiltshire. Tully House, Lord Wavertree's former residence, possesses a famous Japanese garden, one of the sights of Ireland. A Japanese landscape-gardener, with forty-five assistants, laboured for four years on its construction.

Beyond Kildare the Dublin road (33 miles), fast and straight, crosses the gorse-dotted *Curragh* (marsh or lowland plain), one of the finest expanses of unenclosed grassland in the world and more than eight square miles in area. It provides magnificent pasture for cattle and horses, and there are several training stables here, besides the famous race-course, to the left of the Dublin road. Races, including all the Irish classics, are held from April to October at this, the headquarters of the Irish Turf Club. From 1646 onwards the Curragh has been a permanent camp and training ground, the headquarters of the English military power in Ireland, and it is now the Aldershot plus Salisbury Plain of Eire's regular army.

At Newbridge (Droichead Nua), which makes cutlery, the Liffey is crossed. Naas, pronounced 'Nace' and meaning 'meeting-place,' was the ancient capital of the kings of Leinster, of which the rath, or mound, is now the only vestige. Then come Kill and Rathcoole, beyond which, a mile or so to the left, is Baldonnel Aerodrome, headquarters of the Irish Air Corps. Four miles beyond Rathcoole you see, to the left, the Round Tower of *Clondalkin*, 84 feet high and 47 feet round, built on a solid mass of masonry, with a doorway 15 feet from the ground. You can ascend to the top to see the view from the four windows, which, as usual in the Irish round towers, face the four points of the compass. Dublin is regained by the north quays, or via Crumlin and Harcourt Street.

INDEX

The figures in square brackets are map references